I0806789

Margaret Paton

Margaret Paton

Letters from the South Seas

Edited by

JAMES PATON

with an Introduction by

IAIN H. MURRAY

THE BANNER OF TRUTH TRUST

THE BANNER OF TRUTH TRUST

Head Office
3 Murrayfield Road
Edinburgh, EH12 6EL
UK

North America Office
610 Alexander Spring Road
Carlisle, PA 17015
USA

banneroftruth.org

First published as *Letters and Sketches from the New Hebrides*, 1894

First Banner of Truth edition 2003
Reprinted (re-typeset) 2024

*

ISBN
Print: 978 1 80040 454 0
Epub: 978 1 80040 455 7

*

Typeset in 12/14 pt Adobe Garamond Pro at
The Banner of Truth Trust, Edinburgh

Printed in the USA by
Versa Press, Inc.,
East Peoria, IL

Contents

Introduction vii
A Paton Family Table xv
Preface xvii

1. Bound for the Islands 1
2. First Impressions of the New Hebrides 5
3. Settling Down on Aniwa 25
4. Glimpses of the Aniwans 47
5. Early Mission Days 55
6. The Church of God on Aniwa 65
7. Death and the *Dayspring* 71
8. To the Children of the *Dayspring* 75
9. A Trip to the Colonies 79
10. Family Life and Church Life 93
11. The Shipwreck and the Angel-Child 105
12. Home, Sweet Home, on Aniwa 135
13. The Mission Forces at Work 151
14. The Year of the Hurricane 163
15. The Madness of Mungaw 189
16. Slavers and Friends 233
17. To Her Dear Sister-in-Law 251
18. Days of Sunlight and Shadow 257
19. A Tour Round the Islands in 1889 273

20. To Her Husband 291
21. The Passing of Margaret Whitecross Paton 307

Key to Principal Missionaries Named 315
Index 317

Introduction

THE hidden side of church history has been the part played behind the scenes by Christian women. Occasionally the work of outstanding single women has been better known, but for those married, and whose lives have been of strategic importance in the kingdom of God, it has generally been their husband's names that have come down to posterity. The work of the men was more public, more documented, and thus more available to the writers of history. The wives, without whom eminent men would not have been what they were, were content to remain little known or remembered.

This fact is illustrated in the remarkable story of the evangelization of the islands of the South Pacific. That story surely provides one of the most inspiring chapters in the long history of the church. It began with the thirty missionaries from the London Missionary Society who sailed for Tahiti in 1796. Six were married. They were ill prepared for what they found and few remained when John Williams, 'the apostle of Polynesia,' reached that island in 1817. Thereafter Williams, constantly aided by Christian natives, led an advance of the gospel westwards—first to Raratonga in the Cook Islands; then Samoa in 1830; and at last to the New Hebrides (now Vanuatu) where he was immediately killed by cannibals on 20 November 1839. The islands of the New Hebrides were to prove exceptionally hard. It is said that 'up to 1856, over 50 missionaries, white or coloured, had died or had been murdered by their inhabitants.'[1]

[1] C. H. Robinson, *History of Christian Missions* (Edinburgh: T.&T. Clark, 1915), p. 456.

It was into this situation in the New Hebrides that the Scottish Canadian John Geddie came in 1848, to be joined by John Inglis in 1852, at their base on Aneityum. When he looked back on those first conditions, Inglis wrote: 'It would have been morally impossible on Aneityum for any man to have conceived of such a character, morally and religiously, as that of the man Christ Jesus. To have done so would have been a miracle as great as that of his resurrection.' Yet within ten years, Geddie and Inglis saw the island of Aneityum not only itself transformed but made into a stepping stone for evangelistic outreach to the islands beyond. John G. Paton arrived on the neighbouring island of Tanna in 1858 for a different experience. After four years of hard struggle and suffering, including the loss of his first wife and son, he was forced to leave in 1862. He returned, this time to the island of Aniwa, in 1866.

It was Paton's *Autobiography*, first published in January 1889, which was to become the best known of all the literature from the New Hebrides. Along with a continuation, published in October 1889, it remained in print, in different languages and editions, for much of the last century and is still published today.[2] John Geddie's journal, no less valuable, was not published until 1975, when a limited edition was printed in Australia.[3]

The lives of these men are available in various books, yet who today associates this success of the gospel in the Pacific with Mary Chauner, or Charlotte Leonora MacDonald, or Jessie M'Clymont, or Margaret Whitecross, that is to say, with the women who married Williams, Geddie, Inglis and Paton? 'She never wrote anything for the press,' John Inglis wrote of

[2] *John G. Paton, Missionary to the New Hebrides,* ed. James Paton [1891], (repr., London: Banner of Truth Trust, 1965; new retypeset edition 2024).

[3] *Misi Gete: John Geddie, Pioneer Missionary to the New Hebrides,* ed. R. S. Miller (Launceston: Presbyterian Church of Tasmania, 1975).

his wife. 'She was always kept so busy making history that she had no time to write it … She never thought of herself but as an ordinary woman doing an ordinary woman's work.'[4]

Just the same could have been said of the wives of the other men. But there is a difference in the case of Margaret Whitecross Paton. While she did not write for the press, she often wrote home to family and friends and it was some of these letters, first published in 1894, which are here reprinted.

Margaret Whitecross Paton, described by Dr J. Graham Miller, the chronicler of the Christian history of Vanuatu, as 'a woman of rare gifts and graces,'[5] married John G. Paton during a furlough to Scotland in 1864. 'The dear Lord,' her husband later wrote, 'had brought to me one prepared, all unknown to either of us, by special culture, by godly training, by many gifts and accomplishments, and even by family associations, to share my lot on the New Hebrides.'[6]

The couple, with their year-old son, reached Aniwa, an island measuring seven miles by two, in the summer of 1866, Margaret being the first white woman to land there. 'It was,' said Paton, 'the nearest island to the scene of my former woes and perils, in the hope that God would soon open up my way and enable me to return to blood-stained Tanna.' In the event Aniwa was to remain their home until August

[4] John Inglis, *In the New Hebrides: Reminscences of Missionary Life and Work* (London: T. Nelson, 1887), pp. 284, 287. He adds: 'I never wrote anything for publication which I did not read first to her for her criticism. Many a line and many a sentence she made me score out, and many a one she made me alter.'

[5] J. Graham Miller, *Live: A History of Church Planting in Vanuatu,* vol. 3 (Port Vila, Vanuatu: Presbyterian Church of Vanuatu, 1985), p. 273. This important history forms seven paperback volumes. Volumes 1 and 2 (1978 and 1981) were published by the Presbyterian Church of Australia, and vols 3 to 7 (1990) by the Presbyterian Church of Vanuatu. Available from: The Assembly Clerk, Presbyterian Church of Vanuatu, P.O. Box 150, Vila, Vanuatu, South Pacific.

[6] *John G. Paton, Autobiography,* p. 285. [2024 ed., pp. 287-88.]

1881. Thereafter she was either with family in Australia or, less often, travelling with her husband in Australasia, raising funds for the mission and seeking fresh missionaries. Her last letter in the 1894 edition of this book tells of one such tour in 1889 which included a revisit to Aniwa. In 1892 they left Australia for deputation in the United States and Britain. How long Margaret remained with him on that occasion is unclear. He did not return until the late summer of 1894, whereas she was with one of her sons in the New Hebrides at that date. Another of her sons wrote of 'the loneliness of months and even years' which his mother sometimes experienced in his father's absence.[7] They were reunited in Australia later in 1894, but Paton's hope of resettling in the New Hebrides, and preferably on Tanna, was not then realized. The interests of the mission demanded his continued visitation of the churches in Australia and New Zealand. By then in his seventies, Margaret wrote of him, 'He *runs* like a boy, and seems far more active than some men not half his age.' Her own health was more doubtful, as it would appear from a letter to them from one of the Christians of Aniwa, dated 19 December 1896. It commenced:

> Dr Paton and *Missi* Woman and Minnie and all of you, I rejoice if you are all strong, but cry greatly that *Missi* woman [Mrs Paton] is very sick. It is good that she recovers and gets strong, that Jehovah helps her, and gives her strength and life and every good thing.[8]

After two years of travelling in Australia, with Margaret at the home base in Melbourne, Paton again made a round-the-world journey from August 1899 to July 1901. On his return he was able to hand over to the Victorian Foreign Missions

[7] A. K. Langridge and Frank H. L. Paton, *John G. Paton: Later Years and Farewell* (London: Hodder and Stoughton, 1912), p. 72.

[8] *Ibid.*, p. 138.

Committee a cheque for £13,014. But deputation work was never his first love and, in April 1902, to the joy of husband and wife, the Mission Committee gave them leave to return to Aniwa. From there Margaret wrote the last letter which has been added to this book. They had been there less than a year when Paton wrote of her to friends in Britain in January 1903:

> Since we have been back on Aniwa, Mrs Paton has had serious turns of weakness, and for her sake we go up to Australia some time this month. Were it not for her, I would risk all with Jesus and remain on Aniwa. I have had a severe turn of lumbago, but am better now … I have been able to conduct the afternoon school and all church services daily.[9]

Soon after when they departed 'the whole population gathered to weep, and to wave their goodbyes … To him they looked up as their Father in God. And to Mrs Paton equally, the women clung, as the one white woman who had first dared to live amid the savagery of their heathen days, and who had won their hearts and purified their lives. Though she kept the thought as a secret of her heart, there is little doubt that Mrs Paton knew that day, that this Farewell would be the last.'[10]

They returned to Melbourne where she died on 16 May 1905. The account of her passing has been added to this book from the rare volume, *John G. Paton, Later Years and Farwell.* To mark their love for her, The Presbyterian Women's

[9] *Ibid.,* pp. 189-90. His daughter, then present with her missionary husband, noted, 'My father's health for his age is wonderful. He always seems to take a new lease of life in the New Hebrides.'

[10] *Ibid.,* p. 191. It was not her husband's last visit. After his eightieth birthday he was there again for a visit in 1904 when his son says, 'I caught him lifting forty-pound weight boxes.' He died in Melbourne on 28 January 1907 in his eighty-third year.

Missionary Union raised a Memorial Fund which was sufficient (£1,700) both to build a church as a memorial to her in Vila, New Hebrides, and a hospital at Chinju in Korea.

As her husband wrote of the time of their marriage, Margaret Paton was abundantly gifted for the calling that lay before her. She had the power of a writer, as the reader of these pages will soon see. Not without reason, the editors of *Later Years and Farewell* believed that her letters 'are perhaps as clear and vivid a description of the inner and more personal side of life amongst sunken heathen as has ever been written.' To this gift were added those of a winsome speaker, a musician, and an artist—it was she who designed and painted the flag which flew at the masthead of Mission ships and launches for sixty years. She shared the strong biblical convictions of her husband and was as enthusiastic for the theology of the *Shorter Catechism* as her father had been back in 1828 when he first published his well-known book on it.[11] These convictions she sustained by the practice of serious Christian reading.[12] During her extended periods in Australia 'she was one of the foremost leaders of the Presbyterian Women's Missionary Union, and her literary gifts and wonderful power of organization were always used in the sacred cause of Foreign Missions.'[13]

[11] John Whitecross, *The Shorter Catechism Illustrated from Christian Biography and History* (reprinted with revisions, London: Banner of Truth Trust, 1968).

[12] In his tribute to his wife, John Inglis underlines the importance of her own reading practice by speaking of a question once put by one Christian woman to another on what books she was reading. 'Books!' the woman replied, 'I read no books; the housework and the baby occupy all my time.' To which her friend replied in astonishment: 'Read no books! And what do you think you will become? Your husband is reading daily, and if you read none, will you be a companion to him then years hence? No; do what you like, but you must read.' *In the New Hebrides*, p. 266.

[13] Langridge and Paton, *John G. Paton: Later Years and Farewell*, p. 217.

Yet, next to the support Margaret Paton gave to her husband, her greatest service lay in the nurturing of the children which she gave to the world. The cause of seeking missionaries began in the Patons' own home, and they were honoured by Christ in the calling of four of their children to the work of the gospel, three of them in the New Hebrides (see p. xv). In her son Frank's tribute, given more fully later in these pages, we read:

> Her influence over her children was deep and permanent. There was in her nature a rare combination of saintliness and humanness, that made the Christian life very real and winsome to all with whom she came into touch. Her life was, in her own words, 'a pure white-heart of love for her children.' No wonder they loved her passionately, and with deep reverence sought to follow in her steps.

As publishers of this reprint we are conscious of some sense of connexion with this much-used family. The Rev. Fred Paton, second son of the Patons, was still alive and serving in the New Hebrides in 1941. In May of that year, and not long before his death, he welcomed the Rev. J. Graham Miller and his wife, Flora, on their arrival from New Zealand. As missionaries, the Millers at once took up the same cause and it remains the uppermost cause on their hearts today [2003]. Through their influence and writings, many of us have also come to love these islands and their history. I was privileged to succeed Dr Miller at St Giles Presbyterian Church, Sydney, in 1981. In knowing him, and in the several books he has authored for the Banner of Truth Trust, we have felt something of the spirit of the Patons, and the others who were in Vanuatu before them. One thing is certain: it would have been the great desire of Margaret Paton that her *Letters*, now in print again, should be a spur to the churches to 'send ten thousand fresh messengers to the farthest bounds of the earth to proclaim, by word and example, this glorious gospel to the millions.'

IAIN H. MURRAY
Edinburgh, January 2003

A Paton Family Table[1]

Illustrating how four generations of the Paton family served the New Hebrides Church, 1858–1970:

Dr *John G. Paton* (1824–1907), Tanna, 1858
First wife, *Mary Ann Robson*, married 1858, died with infant son *Peter Robert Robson*, Tanna, 1859
Aniwa, 1866. Second wife, *Margaret Whitecross*, Aniwa

- *Robert* (1865–1911) m. *Elizabeth Margaret Brown*
  - *William Frederick* ('*Wilfred*') (1904–70) m. *Marion Isabel Reid*; Ambrym, 1933–48
  - *Francis J. C.* (b. 1906) m. *Rita Bishop*; Tangoa Training Inst., 1931–33
- *Frederick J.* (1867–1941) m. (1) *Helen Robertson*; Erromanga (d. 1905) (2) *Christina Cameron*; Malekula, 1892-1941
- *Francis H. L.* (1870–1938) m. *Clara Sophie Heyer*; Tanna, 1896–1902
- *Margaret* ('*Minnie*') (1869–1952) m. Rev. *John Gillan*, 1900; N. Malekula, 1900–14
  - *John W. P. Gillan* (1903–70) m. *Florence Hand*; Malekula, 1932; Tangoa Training Inst., Santo, 1935–47
    - *John R. P. Gillan* (b. 1936) m. *Claire Johnson*; Malekula and South Santo, 1955–70

[1] From *Live*, vol. 2, p. 31 (see footnote 5, p. ix).

Preface

In the second volume of the original edition of the *Autobiography* of John G. Paton, the ninth chapter consisted of fragments of letters from 'the graphic and gifted pen' of Mrs John G. Paton; in the single volume, or *Popular Edition*, the exigencies of space demanded the excision of that chapter altogether. Many have been the regrets that have reached me, from readers far and near, at the loss of what they regarded as 'a great enrichment' to the story; and still more numerous have been the expressions of a hope that those letters might appear entire, containing 'the full-flowing descriptions' which I had ventured to characterize as 'one of the most charming pieces of missionary literature' with which I was acquainted.

My opinion thus reinforced, I set myself to gain, and succeeded in gaining, Mrs Paton's consent to the publication of these *Letters and Sketches from the New Hebrides.* Alas, they are still only fragments! Some of the most memorable of these family letters have gone astray in the hands of careless or now unknown friends, to whom they were lent in the course of their annual rounds, and can no longer be traced. None of them were originally intended for other eyes than those of our inner circle. Hence the spontaneousness, the life-like look and feeling, which distinguish these *Letters*, and make them, in my judgment, worthy of being preserved and published. Their literary grace is of the unconscious kind—the rarest grace of all.

A further reason that has made me eager to give these *Letters* to the world is this: they present another picture of mission life and experiences in the New Hebrides from that portrayed in the now famous *Autobiography* of her husband. No feature will be found in the one contradictory to the features in the other; but many lovely and thrilling scenes of a supplementary and illuminative kind. *Here* we have the woman's delicate touch; we see with the woman's eye; and, above all, we have what has been called 'the saving grace of humour,' which, while it makes us sometimes smile where the other would make us weep, does not thereby the less but rather the more endear to us those beloved 'darkies of the Southern Seas.'

I do not pretend that my work or my anxiety in preparing this volume has not been very great. Unlimited powers were, of course, given to me in dealing with the materials put into my hands; but that only increased my sense of responsibility. From the first word to the last, I have carefully copied out the whole, and prepared and arranged every page for the public eye. But no skilful or cultured reader will need to be told that the book, as now presented, is solely the product of one pen and of one mind, that of the authoress herself; and that, beyond the merest literary setting and arrangement, no part of the writing is mine.

It is my hope that the many thousands who have read the *Autobiography* of John G. Paton will rejoice to see here the other but not less beautiful side of the shield.

James Paton, Editor
Glasgow, November 1894

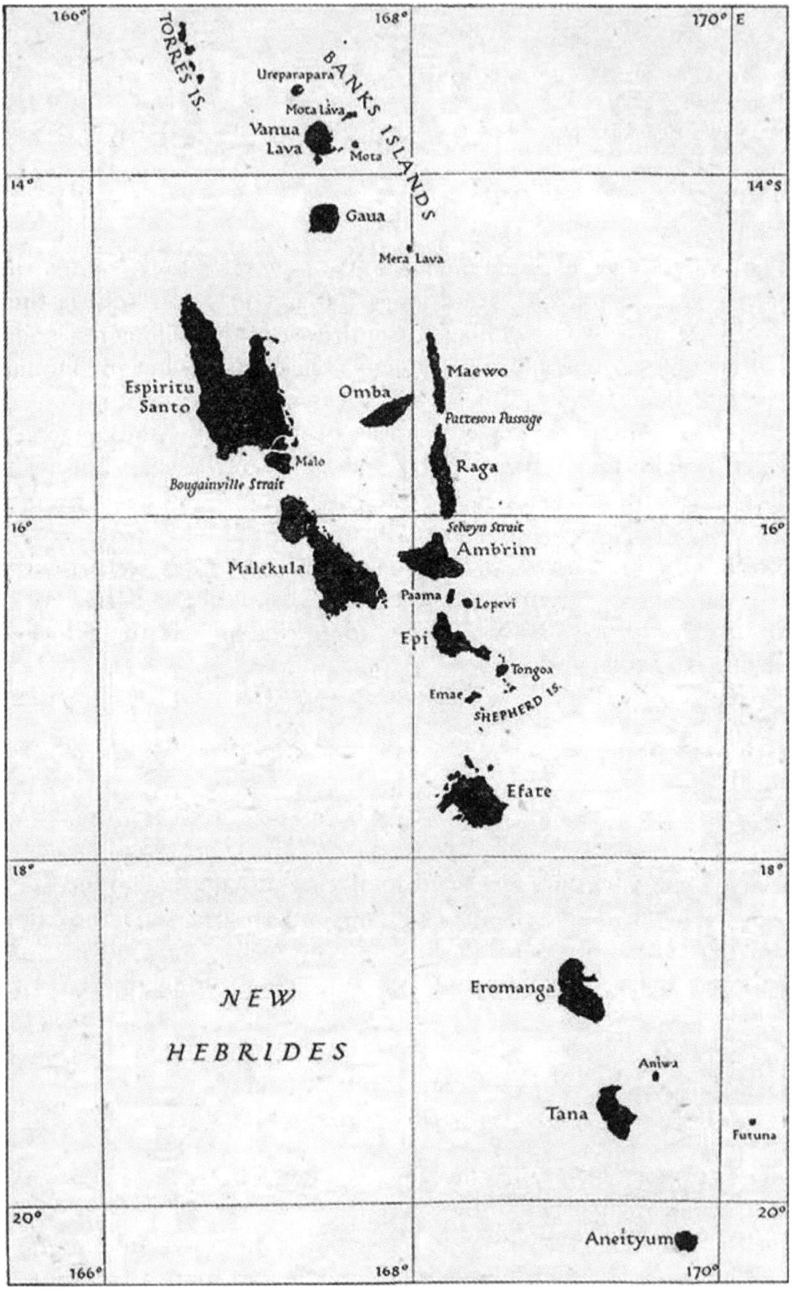

Map of the New Hebrides (Vanuatu).

I

Bound for the Islands

SYDNEY,
17 JANUARY, 1865.

MY OWN DEAREST ELIZABETH,[1]

My heart always fills, when I think of the great distance there is now between us, and how long it may be before we meet again! I began first actually to realize it, when being towed out, on the Sabbath morning we left Liverpool. I could only bury my face in the pillow, and almost groan your name over and over. By the time we got up, we were out of sight of land, until in the afternoon we sighted the Welsh coast. It was a lovely day, and the villages near the shore shone so pretty and clean, though the land itself looked rocky and barren.

I think I described to you, ere leaving, our dear little cabin. We found it very comfortable indeed; the more so, as for convenience Captain Ellis allowed us to get on deck by the 'companion' that led up from the bathroom, communicating with his room and ours. He is a fine specimen of the thorough English gentleman, and has been exceedingly kind to us during all the voyage. So has every other officer, especially Mr Friend, the first mate, who did everything for our comfort that he could possibly think of.

I have been so engaged, since coming to Sydney, that I could not settle to letter-writing; and now (January 18th) we

[1] Her sister in Edinburgh.

are arranging to go off in the *Dayspring* to Adelaide, passing round, however, by Hobart Town and Launceston. Mother and I are a little timid about sailing again, as we had a month's very severe sickness at the commencement of our late voyage. Indeed, our dear mother did not quite get over it, all the way. We lived almost entirely on deck, only going down when absolutely necessary; and we, at least I, got to be very fond of the sea life, though, alas, woefully subject to the dreaded sickness. We had sometimes almost to be carried on deck, and lay there the whole day—our meals being brought up to us, when we could face them at all!

Having sighted land only twice—namely, St Antonio and Trinidad—we reached Sydney on December 27th, 1864, after a very smooth passage of ninety-five days, enlivened by two somewhat severe but very brief gales. We entered the Heads about six o'clock in the evening. The Bay is beyond anything I had ever imagined, and may truly be said to be one of the finest in the world. I sat perfectly entranced, and wondering how I could give you any idea of it, when Mr Mitchell (the gentleman about whom J. H. wrote to us, and who has been *such* a friend) coming up asked what I thought of it. I told him that I was wondering how I could find language to describe it to my sister at home.

He answered: 'Tell her, it is indescribable. To attempt it would only be to murder it. It must be *seen* to be understood!' And I must add, I am quite of that opinion. To me, however, at that moment, it suggested only Loch Lomond on a larger and grander scale. But the hills are covered with gum trees; and magnificent houses and monuments are studded here and there, high among the trees, and far along the shore. It seemed like fairyland, with the pure and wondrous atmosphere. We had a lovely peep at Sydney, just as the sun was setting behind the spires; but, for the time at least, I had no inclination to enter the land of strangers, however fascinating. How different had it been dear old Scotland! So I opened my locket in a quiet corner, and had a good 'cry' as I gazed once more on your beloved likeness. How often have I looked at it, during the voyage; and two or three times I have caught myself passing my fingers lovingly over it, when too dark to have another look!

We have been staying with Dr and Mrs Moon, very good and very kind friends. I must tell you what we saw in Sydney by the next mail, but the pleasantest thing I met with there was your precious letter. How I *did* devour it! Kiss your darlings. Tell them they are never out of my mind.

Your ever affectionate sister,
MAGGIE WHITECROSS PATON.

2

First Impressions of the New Hebrides

MARÉ, LOYALTY ISLANDS,
17 OCTOBER, 1865.

MY DEAR FRIEND,[1]

Our visits to the different Colonies we enjoyed very much. The people were exceedingly kind to us, and some of them are now my dear friends. Hobart Town and Launceston are very like Scotland as regards climate and cultivation; but Sydney is certainly the most beautiful, or rather I should say the surroundings of Sydney, for the town itself is rather unfinished-looking, and the buildings very irregular. The harbour, however, more than makes up for any defects.

Mr Paton's work was so pressing that he was obliged to leave Adelaide the moment his business was finished, and before it was thought prudent for me to accompany him. I joined him at length in Melbourne, a few days only before we had to sail back to Sydney. It was rather an undertaking to go alone thither, with my baby only five weeks old; but he is one of those sweet charming little things that give no trouble (so his mother thinks!), and we reached Melbourne after a short and pleasant passage of only two days. I enjoyed the short stay there very much; was out driving a great deal, and saw most of the town and some of the outskirts; but

[1] Written to a friend in Stirling, Scotland.

missed seeing several of the kind friends who called for me. We heard, to our delight, just before leaving Melbourne, that the steamer with Mr and Mrs Niven had arrived. We were obliged to go, however, as our passage had been taken; but Rev. Mr Ramsay kindly promised to receive them.

We sailed for Aneityum on May 20th, but did not get out to sea for a few days, the wind being contrary. Indeed, our passage altogether was rather disagreeable, as our little vessel was uncomfortably loaded with goods for the mission families, besides our own and Mr Niven's furniture. A number of natives, too, were being taken to their different islands; but this was all nothing, had the wind been favourable, which it was not for a great part of the way. In fact, we got frightened at last to ask Captain Fraser how the wind was, the answer for so many mornings had been 'Dead ahead!'

Mrs Ella and her little son were with us, going to join Mr Ella at Wea, and we enjoyed her society very much. We encountered a severe gale, and one night we were startled into consciousness by a noise like thunder, and by water rushing in upon us. A sailor called out, immediately after, that Mr Ella's boat had gone! A heavy sea had swept over the deck right in the centre, carrying all before it; even the davits were wrenched off, and lost with the boat. Had any of the men been in the way, nothing could have saved them. A deal of damage was done to the ship, and we lost two centre tables, two beds, and some other things; but they never cost us a thought—we were so taken up with poor Mr Ella's loss. The boat was a fine large one, given by a congregation in Sydney. It cost between £40 and £50. The whole amount lost, Captain Fraser and Mr Paton estimated at £150 (or more—I forget the exact figure), and all the work of a few moments!

It was very providential that no lives were lost, with so many natives on board; but they are generally sick, and safe in their berths, when the weather is the least rough. A vessel cannot be manned with a native crew. Captain Fraser has tried it; but, had he trusted them, the vessel would have been lost. At the very time they are most required, they are sick and wrapped up in their blankets, and neither promises nor threats will induce them to turn out! They do very well for pulling a boat, but even then they require a head and guide.

I remember seeing a number of natives assembled on the deck-house one Sabbath for service, which Mr Paton conducted in what is here termed *Sandalwood English*—a sort of peculiar broken English, which traders use with the natives all over the islands. I was amazed to see how he had gained the attention of all, when not above two or three of them knew the same language. They were looking earnestly into his face, and evidently drinking in every word. I crept nearer, and, listening attentively, heard such sentences as the following: *Jehovah very good. He love black man all same white man. He send Son belonga him. He die for all man.* I could hardly help smiling at first, but soon got as interested as the natives. A few of them came to *our* service afterwards, but, as might be expected, they could not understand. At the first native service Mr Paton had a coloured audience, speaking *eight* different languages.

Three Tanna men were on board, in whom, of course, Mr Paton was most deeply interested—two of them having been 'stolen' from him there by a Hobart Town whaler. They were in a vessel in Melbourne, and, hearing that their 'Missi' was in Sydney and about to sail for the islands, they made great efforts to get to him. They got the mariners' chaplain to intercede with their captain, in whose hands they had sufficient money to carry them to Sydney. He allowed them to go. They came by steamer, met him on the street, and, coming up with a bright smile of recognition, exclaimed, 'Missi Paton!' He did not know them at first. They turned sorrowfully to each other, saying in their own language, 'Missi does not remember us.' Upon this, he instantly recognized them. They were immensely delighted, told their story, and were of course taken on board the *Dayspring*.

It was an exciting time for us all, when we came in sight of Aneityum. The natives all turned out, and went flying about the deck, seizing and hauling ropes with all their might, or doing anything they possibly could to help. The sound of 'Land ho!' seemed to inspire them with new life. We had never seen them so animated, and did not indeed know till then that so many were in the vessel. Poor things, they were delighted at getting near their own land. I assure you, it is an interesting sight at any time to watch the first grey speck, hardly distinguishable from a cloud in the horizon, and see it gradually develop into hills and trees and rocks. As we could not get inside the reef before dark, we had to lie off and on till morning, when we sailed into the harbour and feasted our eyes on this interesting island. There was the neat white church and mission house and premises, contrasting beautifully with the dark green foliage, surrounding and partly concealing them; but what I most admired were the tall cocoa-nut trees, with their feathery leaves, waving along the shore.

Mr McCullaugh, and Mr Robertson the cotton agent, soon came on board to welcome us. We found they were all well, and anxiously expecting us, as we were a month past the time. The *Dayspring* had required to be provisioned for a year, however, and as Mr Paton needed to raise the money both for that and for some of last year's expenses, it was impossible to sail at the time appointed. He had great success during this last visit also, for above £1,700 were given to him before we left the Colonies. It will take at least £1,200 per annum to support the *Dayspring*.[2] It sounds a great deal, but is not so, in comparison with other vessels of the same kind; and it must

[2] This was the 'little ship,' the first *Dayspring*. See *John G. Paton: Autobiography* (Popular Edition, p. 229; Banner of Truth Trust, 2024, p. 231).

always be remembered that, owing to peculiar causes, none of these mission ships can be allowed to trade so as to meet the cost of their own maintenance.

But I am diverging. We went on shore in the afternoon, and were earnestly invited to stay—our rooms having been prepared weeks before. Mr Inglis came next morning, and we accepted his kind invitation to go to Anami. We dined at Mr McCullaugh's, and then went round with Mr Inglis in the afternoon in his boat—a distance of from twelve to fifteen miles. We enjoyed the sail exceedingly, having a fine view of the island so long as it was light. The native teachers' houses looked lifelike. But for them I should have fancied the place uninhabited. The mountains behind stood out solitary but beautiful. The latter part of our sail was by moonlight, and was extremely pleasant. As we neared Mr Inglis's station, a bright fire on the beach guided us to the exact spot. Our boat was surrounded by a host of natives, eager to welcome us. My baby was carried off in triumph to Mrs Inglis!

We were delighted with everything we saw, as indeed we had good reason to be. It is no light matter to see a benighted and barbarous people so thoroughly enlightened and Christianized. Mr and Mrs Inglis are richly repaid for their long and laborious toil, in seeing so many devoted followers of Christ amongst those who were once savages. Next day being Sabbath, we had the longed-for pleasure of seeing the native worship. All things were really done 'decently and in order.' When we went into the church we found it full, the women sitting on the one side and the men on the other—all squatted on the floor, while numbers stood outside with their children. I could not help thinking that it was the noblest mission on earth to carry the gospel to those perishing souls, and that Mr Inglis had honours before which earth's proudest laurels pale, when I beheld them sitting there with the word of life in their mother tongue.

My meditations were, however, soon put to flight by the singing, and I found it hard to control my risible faculties! They hold on very tightly to their books, and that with both hands, but they do not by any means stick so fast to the tune. I am told that it is our common Psalm tunes they sing; but, like some of our musical composers, their variations are of such a nature that the tune is not easily recognized. They sing 'Auld Lang Syne' pretty well, to a nice hymn, which Mr Inglis composed, or translated, I forget which.

There are two services on Sabbaths, with a short interval between. My baby was baptized after the second. I felt it a great privilege to have that done by Mr Inglis, our eldest and most honoured missionary. I had hoped to have him baptized by my brother-in-law, Mr Lyall, at Adelaide, but Mr Paton could not spare the time, greatly to the horror of an Episcopalian, who declared it was 'unsafe'!

We spent such a pleasant week at Anami, and heard a great deal about mission work from Mrs Inglis, who is delightfully communicative. Both she and her husband were extremely kind. How I wish you could see the mission stations on Aneityum! They are in such exquisite order, and so complete. It takes quite a long time to go into all the different places—stores for all sorts of things, schools, workshops, etc. It entails a great amount of work on the missionaries, however, as they must personally look after everything. Natives are very willing, but cannot be trusted too much. I was surprised and delighted to see the arrangements at table so very nice, and, above all, so very like what they might be at home. All these things, small in themselves, are of worth, as part of the new life that has come with Christianity.

To our vast delight Mr and Mrs Inglis accompanied us in our voyage round the islands. We joined the *Dayspring* on Monday, the captain sending off boats for us as it hove in sight. Mr Inglis sent two boatloads of oranges and bananas, which were very refreshing during the voyage. The trees in front of his house are beautiful, with large bright oranges hanging in thousands among the dark green leaves, 'like golden lamps on a green night.'

Next afternoon, we arrived at Lifu, and found Mr and Mrs Macfarlane and their children well. The following morning, we met the governor of New Caledonia, newly arrived. He seemed very agreeable, and tried to repair, as much as possible, the ravages made by the French.

We next visited Maré, taking Mr and Mrs Macfarlane to have a meeting with their brethren there, and then returned with them before proceeding to Wea, where Mrs Ella had the pleasure of being reunited to her husband. It was a new field, and we left them in apparently favourable circumstances. But it is not right to judge from a mere passing visit; indeed we need not try, for, in general, only the bright side is then seen, the natives all turning out quite pleased to see a nice ship, and ready to promise anything. Wea, like the other Loyalty Islands, is flat; but the beach, for miles along the shore, is most beautiful, and covered with the loveliest little shells, many of which we gathered as we strolled along. A lot of the little natives followed us, picking up handfuls and holding them out to us, saying, *Welly goot!* We chose what we considered *welly goot*, and off they ran for more.

Sabbath was spent on Wea, and we had the pleasure of seeing the church filled. Mr Ella spoke in Samoan, and the teacher translated. The people seemed most attentive, and we left next morning, well satisfied that there was at least a good beginning. Romanism was the great drawback. A French priest is situated a few hundred yards from Mr Ella, and has, we have since heard, abused him fearfully—even sending his servants to thrust Mr Ella out of church during Communion Service, which they did with great violence. Poor Mrs Ella fainted! I am truly sorry for them both—they are such kind and gentle souls, and Mrs Ella is little fitted to endure these hardships at her age. She was a very mother to us younger wives, and endeared herself to us all.

I must not forget to say a word about Maré, before leaving the Loyalty group. It was there, if I remember rightly, that I first saw *a real savage.* I recollect so well, standing at the head of the cabin stair with Baby, amusing myself watching the buying and selling going on a-deck, when Baby gave such a crow of surprise that I wheeled to see what was attracting him. A naked savage was grinning over my shoulder, with scarlet and white paint stuck on his forehead and cheeks, and long white hair streaming down over his back! Instinctively, I rushed halfway down the stair; but, recalling that I must come into contact with such creatures, I returned, and rather liked the poor soul before I had done with him. In the first place, we tried to be very polite to each other, grinning and nodding and making signs though neither of us, I am sure, guessed what the other meant. He offered to take Baby, who seemed quite delighted; but I declined that civility, pretending to show him that Baby was going to sleep. He seemed satisfied with the encounter, and strutted off with all the majesty of a prince! He was, I think, the only savage we saw on Maré, as they are nearly all civilized, if not Christianized.

It was Saturday evening when we arrived; and all the gentlemen, as usual, went on shore immediately after. They found that poor Mrs Jones had been so dangerously ill, and that she was still too weak, almost, to speak. While they were absent, a number of the natives came with shells, etc., and with calabashes, which they make into water-bottles. I wanted one or two, and Mrs Inglis thought it wise to purchase them, as Mr Paton had brought two boxes, both to give away among the natives, and to procure curios for the subscribers to the mission in Australia. On asking the man what he wanted for his wares, he seized my hat, gave it a tug, and said, *All same belonga my wife.* I liked the fellow's care for his wife, not too often seen in these islands; and I determined he should have a hat, even if I gave my own. So I told him, through the interpreter, to return on Monday morning, and Mr Paton would give it to him, which he did.

The trade (for I suppose it is trade) with the natives is most amusing, and goes on from morning till night, the deck often so covered that one can hardly find standing room, while the incessant jabbering is deafening! Often did we wish for a Frith to depict these groups with their varied expressions! Numbers stood round the captain, with pigs, game, fowls, taro, etc., knowing that he requires many provisions for the ship. They contemptuously rejected some things offered in barter, and eagerly pointed to something else, long strips of calico being greatly in favour. Others would surround the missionaries, offering shells, mats, and all sorts of native productions; while one, perhaps, would be strutting up and down the deck, arrayed in some wondrous newly acquired garment, the admired of all! But the most amusing part was the *dressing*, which operation Mr Paton seemed to think quite as necessary as the giving of the clothing. I fancy I see him still, trying almost in vain to stick the great awkward arms of some delighted recipient into the right holes! This refers more to Tanna and Efaté, as trade was most lively there.

By-the-bye, I had some rather tempting offers for Baby, consisting chiefly of pigs! Mrs Fraser told me that one man offered the captain *four* last year for their little Maggie—a beautiful and darling child, seven months older than mine. No doubt the poor fellow was offering his dearest treasure. They have not the slightest idea of what we call value. They simply take violent fancies for certain things, and, like children, can be pleased with nothing else. On Aneityum, for instance, the officers of the *Curaçoa* were highly amused by the natives there taking a *penny* in preference to a *sovereign* or *crown*, offered for a pig which was sold to their ship!

I have, however, been straying far from Maré, and must return to it for a little. Mr Jones insisted on having us ashore every day, and was extremely kind; all the more, as we felt how great must have been his trouble to entertain so many while Mrs Jones was ill. I had an interview with her for a few minutes, with which I was greatly delighted, as I had seen her eldest girl (a very interesting child) at Sydney, on her way to England to be educated. They all say that this is *the* trial of the mission field—I mean the parting with one's children. I shudder to look forward to it! Our Sabbath services at Maré were particularly interesting, being the finest sight I have yet seen in the South Seas, owing, I suppose, to the natives being so much more intelligent and further advanced than the Aneityumese. Several were even 'taking notes' during the sermon; and the singing, which they took in parts, was most beautiful.

After returning with Mr and Mrs Macfarlane and their dear children to Lifu, and landing Mrs Ella at Wea, as before mentioned, we again steered our course for the New Hebrides. The first we visited was Ambrim, and a beautiful island it is. The high hills are covered with luxurious vegetation down to the water's edge. Mr Inglis and Mr Paton went on shore; but Mr Niven had not the nerve to venture! It was a very anxious time for Mrs Inglis and myself till they returned safely, for there was no knowing how the natives might be disposed. They seemed, however, to be friendly, and even restored one or two rowlocks which they had stolen from the *Dayspring* on her previous visit.

Next morning the gentlemen again landed (still with the exception of Mr Niven!), and a number of the natives came off in their canoes to our ship—fine, healthy, lively-looking fellows they were—examining everything with intense curiosity, including Captain Fraser and ourselves. They felt his hands and arms, and seemed to 'like' him, as do all the natives; for I believe that even savages can appreciate such a truly Christian gentleman as our captain is. The babies were objects of extraordinary interest to the Ambrimese, who pleaded so earnestly (by signs, of course) that we could not refuse to allow them to hold them for a little, which they did with a woman's tenderness. They could not make out whether mine was a girl or a boy, and we could not at first make them understand. Mrs Inglis, however, managed at last to do so, and they received the intelligence with shouts of admiration, calling out *Man! Man!*—for a girl is looked upon as rather a calamity by all the blacks.

I must omit much that is greatly interesting, and go on briefly. Ere leaving Ambrim, the missionaries tried to induce the natives to receive the native teachers we had brought from Maré, but without success. They would readily have taken a white missionary but the chief would not promise protection to the teachers, who were indeed disappointed at having to be brought off again. We sincerely hope that, after one or two visits of the *Dayspring*, they will be more favourably inclined.

Our next place of visitation was Efaté, which looked exceedingly fresh and lovely as we approached it in the early morning. It is a very fertile island, and I was struck with the peculiarly brilliant green of the vegetation, which seemed more beautiful than in any island of the group. Mr Morrison came off to welcome us, and to invite us all ashore. His home is on a little island off the mainland, where they live at present for the sake of a chance of health; and it is a lovely spot, with a fine garden in front. The view from the windows, too, is so hopeful; for, instead of the wide ocean, which is but suggestive, to me at least, of the enormous distance betwixt us and home, there is just a little belt of beautiful blue water, and then the richly wooded island beyond. Pineapples are plentiful there; and I was in great hope that, if we did not get to Tanna, we might be settled on Efaté, as I should feel so privileged to be near Mr and Mrs Morrison.

The Sabbath exercises were extremely enjoyable, and we could hear them singing hymns in their own homes. We had visits, also, from several of the surrounding heathen; and one day I played a few simple airs on Mrs Morrison's harmonium, to which they listened mouths and eyes wide open! I was amused, immediately afterwards, to see their mingled terror and admiration for a little *vase* on a side-table. They seemed thoroughly afraid to approach; but, at last, one bolder than the others took a very long stride, having one of his feet as near the door ready to fly on the slightest appearance of danger. He managed, however, to touch it, and that gave the others confidence to go and examine it.

Our next resting-place, being Erromanga, was of the most entrancing and painful interest to us all, from its previous sorrowful history. It was Sabbath afternoon as we drew near, and we were rather alarmed to hear the sound of guns firing. On casting anchor, one of Mrs Henry's men, sandalwood traders, came off and told us that they were in great danger, owing to a dispute between Mrs Henry and the natives. Soon we had the extreme pleasure of welcoming Mr Gordon on board. Our mission would sustain a severe loss indeed, were he also to become a victim to this treacherous people, like his noble martyr-brother! On looking round, one could scarcely believe that such murder and bloodshed had ever desecrated the lovely scene which presented itself. The little river, where Williams fell, seemed to flow from a beautiful glen, while the peaceful looking hills, rising on either side and away into the distance, were bathed in the shadowy light of the setting sun. With the exception of Port Resolution on Tanna, I have never witnessed such a lovely and deeply interesting landscape.

We remained at Dillon's Bay four or five days, till peace was restored. The murderer of John Williams met, for that purpose, with the said Mrs Henry, on board the *Dayspring.* We were all assembled on deck, and the negotiation was carried on with grave dignity. Mrs Henry delivered her speeches to Mr Inglis, who translated them into Aneityumese to a native teacher, who, in turn, translated them to the Erromangan in his own tongue, and backward in the same way—Mr Gordon not being able to be present. At last, something was said about payment for the damage done to the native plantations by Mrs Henry's cows, which roused that Madame's wrath to a degree. She suddenly dropped her assumed dignity like a cloak, and, clearing the space between herself and her opponent with a bound, she brought her clenched fist within an inch of his nose, shrieking, *'Me pay you! Me pay you with a stick!'* Which payment the man not seeming to anticipate favourably, some altercation ensued ere peace could be finally restored.

Next day we sailed, bearing away Mr Gordon, in order to have his presence at the general meeting on Aneityum with the other brethren, Mr and Mrs Morrison having come with us from Efaté. Tanna, the island I had most wished to see, at last came full in view, and we sailed pretty close to it for a considerable time before anchoring at Black Beach. In passing along, I was struck with the variety as well as majesty of the scenery. One part seemed to be pretty level, near the shore, and covered with fresh green grass—only I was rather suspicious if it was grass, as, in all these islands, truly 'Distance lends enchantment to the view.' The mountains of the New Hebrides look extremely beautiful, a little way off, with the changeful shadows of the sunlight playing upon them. The beauty, however, in a great measure vanishes, when you set foot on shore, and see broken cocoa-nut shells and all sorts of rubbish piled about; while, instead of sheep grazing (if they could graze among such stuff), multitudes of pigs are grunting in every direction, having apparently strayed from their styes, which are stuck here and there all around,—but which you find, on closer inquiry, are the habitations, not of the *pigs*, but of the *people*!

When we came to anchor at Black Beach, we found three trading vessels lying there, one of which had providentially rescued our native teachers there, some months previously, when about to be killed, and carried them to Mr Gordon's care on Erromanga, where we received them; so that Tanna was now in a dark state indeed—no missionary, no teacher! It was, I think, Saturday afternoon, and the missionaries and their wives went all on shore—except, once more, Mr and Mrs Niven. When we offered to shake hands with the women, they shouted and laughed at us. They wear little grass skirts round their middle and beads round their necks. A few of them came forward, and seemed pleased with the little things we gave them, such as strips of red calico, etc. But we took care not to trust ourselves too much with them, and did not go many yards from the boat, merely taking a look at the little church, and the teachers' houses, which they had been forced to quit. Some of the Tannese were all the while on board, whom Captain Fraser kept as hostages for our return.

Next day being Sabbath, Mr Paton had a service on shore in the afternoon. As the language on that side of the island is quite different from the language at Port Resolution, a chief, who knew both, translated very nicely, being an old friend of Mr Paton's, and making a great fuss over his 'Missi.' We sang a hymn in Tannese, which Mr Paton had translated in earlier days—he reading the line, and Mr Morrison leading the tune, *Old Hundredth*, which went bravely. One of their former teachers prayed, and Mr Paton addressed them, the chief interpreting. A few of the women put in an appearance too, and all listened attentively, till, lo! three or four boats arrived from the neighbouring vessels to 'trade,' and off they all scampered as fast as they could, leaving us the church by the shore all to ourselves!

We weighed anchor on Monday, and, on our way to Port Resolution, the vessel lay off and on near Mr Matheson's old station, while the missionaries landed to visit the natives, and next morning again we lay off and on at Port Resolution. There, however, a solemn service had to be performed. One of the Tannese lads who came with us had during the previous days sunk rapidly, evidently the result of years of overwork and hard usage in the 'traders,' from which great numbers of them die. Mr Paton was his constant attendant, being able to speak to him in his mother tongue, and fed him with wine, tea, etc. Alas, he died the night before we reached Port Resolution, and we buried him next morning, within sight of his longed-for home! It was Mr Inglis's turn to conduct worship, which was on deck, and he read appropriate passages of Scripture, after which the body was gently lowered into the deep. It was a very solemn scene, and went keenly home to me; for my youngest brother, the missionary, although not exactly buried at sea, died on entering Leith Harbour and was thus borne home from Cuba.

Numbers of Mr Paton's old friends came off to welcome him very heartily, and Baby and I had a good share. They seemed truly pleased to see us, especially Nowar, the old chief. But he warned him not to go ashore, nor let the vessel draw near, as the heathen party had shot one of his men a-fishing, only a few days before. Indeed, it is a wonder that any of the friendly party survive at all, after such incessant fighting! Some of the heathen chiefs themselves also came on board. Fine and vigorous-looking men they are, and such hair! Their heads have the appearance of being covered with twine, small portions of their hair being twisted from the root to the tips (generally half-way down their backs) with something like thread. They were in a state of great delight about the baby, and were particular in asking Mr Paton if both it and the woman 'belonga' him!

You may imagine how intensely moved I was, as we neared the scene of his former trials and persecutions. A more grandly beautiful spot one could not well conceive. The mountains rise with such a majestic sweep, terminating in sharp peaks, and covered with luxurious vegetation. The beautiful white beach is lined with cocoa-nut trees, with here and there bold brown crags jutting out and finely contrasting with the dashing spray beneath. Through the glass I could see the gable of Mr Paton's house, still standing on a rising ground in the centre of the bay; and he pointed out to me, by the different colour of the trees, that *sacred spot*, so indelibly photographed on his memory. Oh, how I longed to spend a quiet hour by the grave of her, in whose footsteps I feel so unfit to follow, and who met her trials so unshrinkingly and alone—alone, so far as regards female companionship and sympathy!

On leaving Tanna, we had a view of the *volcano* at night, with its red smoke rising and brightening all around; and we anchored, or rather lay off and on, at Aniwa next day, and were relieved to find the native teachers there safe and well. That island is not particular for anything, being a flat little place, but we nearly lost our vessel there, owing to a sudden gale sweeping round, while Mr Gordon and Mr Paton were on shore. Captain Fraser saw what was coming, and had a flag put out; but they not observing it for a few minutes, and having a heavy sea to contend with when they did set off, the *Dayspring* was almost driven into the reef; for, had the captain gone outside before the missionaries got on board, he could not have returned for them that day, and to have left them on Aniwa might have been to sacrifice them. The moment they were on deck, the boat was hauled up, both 'watches' set to work, and the vessel swung round, almost grazing the reef till we passed away from the island. It was a time of painful anxiety to the good captain, who prudently kept the danger from us ladies till all was over.

Our last island, before returning to Aneityum, and which we came up to early next morning, was Fotuna. I was greatly taken with it—it so much resembled Stirling Castle, but higher in the middle, with a tableland extending along one side, and about a fourth part as high. It seemed so homelike and healthy, having no fever and ague, which is more than can be said of any other island of the group. The people, too, were already prepared for a missionary, whose life would, humanly speaking, be quite safe, as they are not inclined for war, though energetic-looking and healthy, superior, indeed, to any we had seen with the exception of the Tannese.

This island is supposed to contain about seven hundred inhabitants, and I had serious thoughts of reigning there, as it would be a nice little field for one missionary and his wife! My inclinations were divided betwixt it and Pango, the next station to Mr Morrison's on Efaté. There is no anchorage at Fotuna, so the *Dayspring* lay off and on, while we spent a very pleasant day on shore. Rhu, one of the Rarotongan teachers there, had been some time on Aneityum, and was returning with us to his wife and children. On the voyage, he had often urged Mr Paton to go to Fotuna; and, before he left the ship, he sat on the deck for more than an hour, pleading most eloquently with 'Missi' to remain with them, and every now and again winding up his arguments with a warm grasp of the hand, and the exclamation, *Me too much love you! Me do anything for you!* I felt I would almost like to go for Rhu's sake alone; I never in all my life heard such pathetic pleading.

When we came on shore at Fotuna, we had some hard climbing, and were followed as usual by a long train of admirers. The mission premises are on the raised tableland,

and among trees. Great crowds of people came to look at us, as I believe we are the first white women who ever landed on Fotuna. The *ladies* were, in consequence, very curious to have us examined properly; and they went about it in a business-like way, as I can testify from the pokes and thumps received. They always felt themselves at the same time, to see how far we were alike! Poor things, they had yet to learn that we were sisters, resting under the same penalty and equally in need of and entitled to the same Saviour.

On their examinations becoming rather too minute, I escaped into the house, which, by the way, was a very nice one for a teacher's. The other Rarotongan teacher and his wife had been residing with Rhu's wife, during his absence. They are very nice people, and, like most of their class, rather fine-looking, with almost courtly manners, and held in great respect by the natives on account of their being so much lighter in colour. Their habitation boasted a few dishes; and they had a nice dinner prepared for us, consisting of young pig, fowls, yam, and capital green cocoa-nuts. Afterwards there was a service in the church, when Mr Inglis baptized Rhu's children. Mrs Inglis had found, on questioning the Aneityumese teacher who came round to see us, that she and her husband were not well used by the natives, who forced them to work for them, and stole their food, etc., for they are great thieves. So Mrs Inglis instructed her to run home, bring her husband and their goods, and return to Aneityum.

Mr and Mrs Inglis, Mr Paton and I, waited while the first boat's load of missionaries were being taken to the ship, and had a long and delightful walk, and then a seat on the brow of the hill, which we enjoyed so much, it being cool, and the view, though not varied, calm and pretty. On one side and far above us were the lofty grassy rocks, and right beneath the placid-looking water, with the *Dayspring* in the distance and the little boat wending to and fro. Seeing it return for us, we went down to the landing, and there Mr Paton got into conversation with a man who knew Tannese pretty well and was urging 'Missi' to remain. Mr Paton asked him why he was so anxious for that, and the man ingenuously replied that when he was over in Tanna he saw him have a number of boxes and that he gave the natives clothes and other things! But, as Mr Inglis very wisely remarked, we cannot expect them to long intelligently for Christianity before they know what it is. They see only the outside tokens of its presence.

We found, on getting into the boat, that the Aneityumese teachers were waiting at some distance along the shore; so we steered in that direction, meeting a number of great whales, which fortunately did not pay us any attention. We took up our teachers; but, at the same moment, some of the Fotunese jumped into the boat, and would not be persuaded to go back, evidently thinking it too good an opportunity to be lost for visiting Aneityum. We knew there would be no time to send them back from the ship; and if we had pitched them out into the sea, where they would have been perfectly at home, yet they might have taken revenge on the native teachers. Mrs Inglis held up her fingers and counted how many 'moons' it would be ere the ship could return; but it was all of no use! They sat grinning at her with the greatest composure, and were taken on to Aneityum. There we arrived next evening, being Saturday, after a six weeks' deeply interesting and very profitable voyage amongst the islands of our mission field.

Yours affectionately,
MAGGIE WHITECROSS PATON.

3

Settling Down on Aniwa

ANIWA, NEW HEBRIDES,
NOVEMBER, 1867.

MY OWN DEAREST ELIZABETH,[1]

I often wish you could all look in upon us in our pretty Island Home, for we have long since got into our new house. How I did appreciate the doors and windows here, after living two or three months without them! The natives gave us, or *me* rather, so much more of their company than was quite agreeable; for Mr Paton was generally away, building the house with the Aneityumese who had come with us for that purpose. I fear I had not too much confidence in the black faces that were always peering over my shoulder, when I was getting home-letters ready, and eagerly inquiring, *What for you make paper about man Aniwa?*

Now I am writing in our large airy parlour, free from interruption by the natives for at least a little while. The house is not, of course, like a home one; though I think it a model of simplicity and comfort, with smooth white walls and broad veranda. The roof is thatched with sugar-cane leaf, and the doors and windows (of French type) were brought from home. The foundation is raised high, and it is so pleasant to look out on the ground which slopes gently to the gate. There would be fine scope for a landscape gardener

[1] To her beloved sister at Edinburgh.

here; but the space is being simply, and, I think, prettily laid out, with an oval patch of beautiful grass just in front, and a broad coral walk winding on either side down to the gate. The sides are planted chiefly with bananas, as much for their useful fruit as for their beauty, and they *are* pretty, with their great long leaves stirring gently with the slightest wind! The background is equally nice, though differently laid out from the front; and the kitchen and similar premises are built to the side. The fence around is made of reeds, and looks like light basketwork. Altogether, you would think mine a lovely and inviting home, and you see it can't possibly suffer from comparison, as there are only the native huts all around!

Mrs Inglis provided me with excellent servants, and we have two good Christian men as native teachers. The one living beside us is a valuable helper to Mr Paton, and an enlightened character too, having been about eleven years at Melbourne, working at all sorts of things, making good use of his eyes during that time, and learning to talk English of course. Kanathie, his wife, is one of Mrs Geddie's trained women, and does everything thoroughly. She too talks a little English, and approaches more to a companion on that account.

I am sure Kanathie can never know what a thrill of comfort and hope her presence gave me, that day we landed on Aniwa! I was eager enough to step out of the *Dayspring*, into the little boat that was to carry us ashore; but as we neared it, and saw black faces peering at us from among the reefs, with not the flicker of a smile of welcome on their faces, I really began to tremble with a sort of dread, and wondered if they were thirsting for our blood. They seemed such a terrible contrast to everything around, for it was a lovely morning, and the beautiful light blue waves were sparkling in the sun as they slowly chased each other along the beach. I tried to hum a tune, to keep up at least a cheerful appearance, but it was harder work than I had anticipated! When Mr Paton stepped ashore, and began to lead the way with our little boy in his hand, a nicely dressed woman in a pretty buff jacket and straw hat came forward and took my hand to guide me over the reefs. I stood still, gazing up in very amazement at the sight of anything so civilized; and Mr Paton had to explain to me that this was the teacher's wife, whose very existence I had forgotten. I scarcely ever felt such a clinging to anyone in all my life as to that poor woman; and I began to walk with a firmer tread, when I thought how she too had given up home and friends and everything, to come here for Christ's sake, with her husband, where there was not a soul to cheer and comfort them. These native Christian teachers are really the true pioneers of the mission, and deserve far more sympathy than we do!

How anxiously did I watch for a smile from any of the women that day; and really they were very kind and civil, and did not refuse to shake hands, although I rather think I am the first white woman that has landed among them. Indeed, they would certainly have taken my heart by storm with their bright smiles, had I not been already sufficiently inclined to love them.

We commenced our establishment, as you are aware, in the little native church, and a considerable body of the people turned out to stare at us. Just fancy me, perched on the top of several mattresses, holding quite a *levée*, while Mr Paton was at the boat-landing, receiving our boxes and getting them sent up to the house. Messrs. Cosh and Neilson were busy putting up a bed; and I would have preferred some active employment too; but it was thought necessary for me to keep a sharp lookout, just to prevent our chattels from walking away!

The *Dayspring* left us that afternoon, and we all gathered round for our first meal. We had plenty of provisions, but as yet nothing was unpacked to cook with; so we made an attack upon a barrel of biscuits, and, thanks to Mrs Geddie's kind forethought, cooked salt beef and bread; while Mrs Inglis, fearing little Bob might have to rough it more than was good for the wee man, had sent a basket of eggs and sponge cake and nice things to last for a long time. Kanathie brought a huge roasted yam too; and, one of the Aneityumese having taken off his hat and reverently asked a blessing, we all proceeded with a will; for our appetites had been sharpening since morning, and all things tasted sweet. Mr Paton and I made boxes do duty as tables and chairs, and the rest squatted beside us on the ground, there being no separate tables that day! It is not the way, exactly, that people commence their housekeeping at home, but I think it far better; at least, it had all the freshness of novelty, and I thoroughly enjoyed it.

After finishing our repast, we got one end of the building screened off with matting, and made up our own snug little bedroom. The other end, where our boxes were piled up, was concealed with bedcovers; while the middle space was left for a great variety of uses—sitting room, sleeping spot for the Aneityumese, and place of worship! Then we set about getting unpacked what we barely required for cooking, etc.; but, in the thick of our operations, darkness fell, and we had to make the best of our way to our beds, having stupidly forgotten to provide lights while we could still see to find them! So ended my first day of mission life.

What a protection I felt that little band of Aneityumese to be during those early weeks, for I thought the natives would hardly attempt any harm while they were with us; and I had always one or other of them with me, while Mr Paton was away building about half a mile distant. Nay, the first morning I awoke on Aniwa, just before daybreak, after listening a moment or two, in terror, for a stealthy footstep or any sort of unwelcome sound, the stillness was broken by a hymn of praise from those sable worshippers, who had already begun their morning devotions! You can imagine how sweetly it sounded in these surroundings, lifting my thoughts upward; and I soon fell asleep again, feeling the music of those words, 'God reigneth.'

A few weeks served to place us on a more confidential footing with each other—I mean the natives and me; for Mr Paton seemed to take for granted from the first that they were all his *dear friends*, though most of them received us with a great deal more sauce than was palatable! They are shrewd, and a number of them really clever fellows; but those who have been in trading vessels are awfully *knowing*, and very impudent. It is really rich to hear them talking in their sandalwood English, pretending to know all about everything, and putting on such a serious face when telling some of their more outrageous lies, invariably adding, with a grave shake of the head, *That no gammon!* I used to find it extremely difficult to sit with a solemn face, under these circumstances.

Indeed, the trial to my *risibles* I found it hardest to bear was that which befell me especially on Sabbaths. The first of these days, in particular, presented a ludicrous scene in the way of dress; and it was only by a most desperate effort that I could manage to keep a long face, while watching the natives coming into the church. We had arrived on the Tuesday; a number of garments had been distributed among the people, and from twenty to thirty turned out to the worship. One man, I remember, came prancing in, looking so delighted with himself in a snow-white vest—absolutely nothing else! Another came stalking majestically, with a woman's skirt pinned round his throat, and the tips of his fingers appearing at the bottom of it. A third had a native bag done up so as to represent a hat, which he took off with quite the air of a gentleman as he entered the door. One man had on a nice little jacket I had presented to his wife; and, indeed, everyone who wore any clothing at all did so in the absurdest fashion.

The effort at self-control was fast becoming unendurable, when the worthy Missi unintentionally proved 'the last straw.' His face was a picture of adoring thankfulness, and his prophetic soul—unconscious of anything grotesque—saw them already on the way to glory. He whispered, 'O Maggie, shouldn't we be grateful to God to see them all coming out to church, *so nicely dressed*!' He was adding something about 'jewels' and 'trophies,' but I was already halfway out of the church, under cover of a convenient fit of violent coughing, and just managed to slip round a corner before going into prolonged convulsions! Pray forgive me; I loved them nonetheless; but that phrase—*so nicely dressed*—was rather more than my woman's soul could withstand.

The women were not quite so grotesque in their attempts as the men; though, even yet, they prefer putting on a dress, as they would a shawl, with the sleeves crossing in front. It is to be hoped that soon they will all wear clothes; but they have made less advance in this respect than in any other, since we came. They do so like to go about in their native state, though most of them put on *something* when they come to the worship. A few, very few, perhaps a score, always wear clothing; but, oh, it is sickening to see so many of them coming about with nothing but paint stuck all about over their bodies! The dark colour of their skin softens off the effect a very little, though; and there really is a look of free independence and dignity about them, as they stalk along so erectly, one after the other, for they never walk two or three abreast; and they are much better off, in many respects, than your poor at home. Properly speaking, they don't know what poverty or labour is! They have no one to oppress them in any way, each man being his own master; and, as for the chiefs, their power is more nominal than real. Of course, one glance at the home privileges, which the poorest may enjoy, shows how infinitely superior is their situation, viewed as a whole.

Aniwa, however, does not seem to have some of the horrid customs practised on Tanna and some of the other islands. There are *widows* here, and the women generally are more kindly treated. Indeed, I was quite delighted to hear one of them scold a man most energetically for some offence, two or three days after arriving; not that I think it woman's most beautiful function to be always attempting to bring the lords of creation into subjection, but the fact that she even dared to speak her mind so revealed a great deal.

Life, humanly speaking, is perfectly safe here; I mean more particularly our life, for the natives don't scruple much about shooting each other, though no murders have occurred lately. I would not be much afraid to meet almost any of them alone, for really they are a most desirable set of savages, although it was some little time ere I could feel safe among them, and, about a fortnight or three weeks after coming to Aniwa, I had a thorough fright. I happened to be alone in the house one day after dinner, and, hearing a noise in the end containing the goods, I lifted the curtain and looked in; but it was some time before my eyes became accustomed to the darkness, as the boxes excluded nearly all the light. At last I saw *a pair of eyes* glaring at me, and dropped the curtain in terror, wondering whether it could possibly be a wild beast; but the owner of the eyes soon made his appearance in the shape of a fierce-looking little man, in a great rage! Kagaru came right behind him, with some tools in his hand, which Mr Paton had sent him to search for; and this man had been looking on, and evidently thought I was watching lest he stole anything. He exclaimed, in a voice trembling with passion, *What for you look me?* 'Because I did not know who was there,' I replied. *You plenty lie! You 'fraid me se-teal. Me no se-teal, me come worship. What for you look me se-teal?*

I assured him he was mistaken, but he could not understand me well, and strode off in great indignation, coming back again, just after Kagaru had gone to carry his message, and with him a party of about twenty. Of course I made sure I was going to be dispatched at once, but thought I should die first of fright, as they all came in at the door! I tried to appear as unconcerned as possible, and, Bobby being brought back by his nurse, there was a fine excuse for taking my work outside while he played about, for there I thought I might have some small chance of escape.

There was a little cleared space in front of the house, and they all followed me out and sat down right opposite on the verge of the bush, with a dozen yards or so between us; and there we sat, hour after hour, sewing, and amusing the child, all the while that man never lifting his eyes off me, but shouting every now and again, *You plenty lie! You all same Tiapolo!* etc., etc. I did not mind the compliments, but had a wholesome dread of the ugly looking club that he held. I thought Mr Paton never would return that day, and, when it began to get dark, I could stand it no longer, but, catching up the child in my arms, sauntered carelessly along till I had a little of the bush between us; and then I did make a run for it, never looking round till I landed at my husband's side! Poor Bobby thought it grand fun, and made the woods ring with laughter.

I might have saved myself, however, this little escapade. The man, I have since learned, meant no real harm. He is an excitable fellow, though, and very forbidding in appearance, having one side of his face polished black, and the other always daubed with white paint. Have they not strange ideas of beauty, to disfigure themselves with such stuff when they want to look their best!

About a week after this, we had an opportunity of seeing them in full dress, at a heathen dance which they made in honour of the burning of the coral to make lime for our house. I was along, one day, looking at them building, and we were amazed to see a long procession of men and women coming, with a wild and fantastic appearance. On hearing there was to be a heathen dance, I remained till it commenced, anxious to witness the scene; and really it is a blessing one does not see such things just at first coming, for, if I had, I fear I could not have remained on the island five minutes! It began so very suddenly; and, though of course very differently carried out, it greatly resembled the principle of a ball or dancing party at home. The women are painted, though not with rouge. Flowers, too, or rather beautiful variegated leaves, are their ornaments; but they wear such an enormous quantity, that they look like moving shrubs. The men have long waving plumes, fixed in the top of their hair, with shells, and everything they fancy as ornaments stuck all over them.

When they reached the *Imrai*, the sacred cleared ground, where they were to perform, close to our house, I waited to see how they would arrange themselves; but they suddenly commenced with a horrid yell, rushed furiously round the lime-pit for about five minutes, and then stopped as suddenly. After that, they took it more leisurely, three or four of them sitting apart to keep up the singing, which was almost fine, but more like chanting than dance music. They go through the dance in a pretty orderly manner, but with much more energy than grace. They don't 'walk' through the figure, but literally beat the ground with their feet, every now and again yelling and rushing round the lime-pit in the way they commenced. I fancy it was kept up till morning, for we heard the shouting all through the night.

There is always a great feast on these occasions, consisting of pigs and all sorts of native fruit; and the whole affair is attended with many evils, for the people get so excited that they don't care what wickedness they commit. A number of them came to ask Mr Paton if he was very angry, or if it would *break the worship.* He thought it best, however, not to interfere too much with their old habits, till he had engaged them with something better. All the same, he faithfully showed them the evils arising from such a thing, and they have given it up long since, being now interested in what is higher; illustrating Chalmers's famous phrase, 'the expulsive power of a new affection.'

The Aneityumese with us were much interested, as I saw, in the festival and dance. No doubt, it brought to mind many things in the former days of their own heathenism. They were, to the people here, a living epistle of the fruits of Christianity; and those of them who could speak in Tannese, understood by many Aniwans, gave very telling addresses at the worship, contrasting their present condition with the past. When they left us, at the end of five weeks, I never felt so lonely in all my life. The *Dayspring* came to pay us her farewell visit for the season, and bear away these voluntary helpers back to their own island. I longed to go on board and see dear Mrs McNair, who was ill with fever: but the sea was too rough, and I could only stand on the reef and watch the little vessel, as it rose and fell in the stormy distance. The Aneityumese went off in the little boat that took our letters, and, as we waved our last *adieus,* I felt for the first time the utter desolation of being the only white woman amongst untried heathen; and oh, it is desolate! I can't describe the awful feeling.

I looked at Kanathie to see how she was bearing up, when her countrymen were all leaving, and I thought that really the woman's heart was made of stone; she was chewing a stick of sugar-cane, and laughing heartily! But, now, I think my own heart must have turned to something of the same sort, for, whoever comes or goes, it creates so little emotion there. I have never known what it was to have a long day, or five minutes, to indulge in melancholy—except during the time I was so ill. I never knew, till coming here, what a healthy thing it is for both mind and body to have plenty to do; especially when, since the dry season, we have not known what it was to feel ill.

That evening on which the *Dayspring* left, it had brought us a large mail; and, I think, letters never were so precious, but they are always precious here. We sat far into the next morning, devouring their contents. A few weeks after that, we got into our new house, and have been so comfortable; though, as yet, it consists only of two rooms; but they are large, with a wide lobby between, the kitchen, etc., being outside. I never appreciated a house as I do this one, having seen the labour it cost, and, positively, I felt a compunction about putting down the matting, for then the evenly laid floors could not be seen! The great drawback is that we have no view, and you know that I admire a good one. But the people were intent upon us buying this ground, instead of any other, it being their sacred ground where they performed their heathen ceremonies, offered sacrifices to the devil, etc. Kagaru and Mr Paton have dug up ever so many of the bones of these victims while levelling the ground. The natives think it a clever thing to have chased Tiapolo out of his headquarters, and taken possession. Some of the most superstitious are under the impression that he has taken his final departure from Aniwa; and they dread every affliction as a punishment for sending him off.

The advent of the little *white chief*, when our home was ready for him, caused tremendous rejoicings. It softened me wonderfully to the forbidding-looking savages, when they figured as *baby worshippers*—especially when it was my baby they adored! They would watch by the house for hours, on the chance of getting a look at him. Every movement of his little hands was a new wonder, and brought down showers of applause—for was he not a *man baby*? The Aniwans look upon him as their very own, and call him their white chief. Bobby's Aneityumese nurse is quite jealous of the compliments given to his wee baby brother!

I got new insight into native character, during those weary weeks of convalescence, learned many things regarding them, and have come to the conclusion that they are the veriest mixture of contradictions in all creation. One day, you are wound up to a pitch of enthusiasm, feel that they are your mainstay, and that you might learn at their feet (I mean the Aneityumese teachers and servants); the next, that they are as little to be relied on as children, and that you must be at the beginning, middle, and end of everything. Now, for instance, Kagaru gave me more solid comfort through his prayer, on the night I was so near death, than it has ever been my lot to receive from any white minister. John, feeling he must have some human sympathy, sent to tell him I was fast dying. His wife and he were in the room at once; and a score or two of savages trooped in behind, choking up the place almost to suffocation. John instantly manufactured errands, to get a few of them quietly outside, while doing all that mortal man (or indeed the cleverest of doctors) could do to save me. Amidst all the din and bustle, clearer even than my own husband's frantic appeals, came Kagaru's low and earnest tones as he prayed in Aneityumese; and the words that he often slowly repeated to the Lord—*Aminjinaig, Aminjinaig* (= take care of, take care of) *Missi Paton the woman*—gave me more quietude and comfort than I can ever express. There was One, then, who could and did 'take care' of me!

But then, weeks after, when I was able to take an intelligent view of my surroundings, this is what I first remember seeing:—John, sitting by my bedside, with an old straw hat on the back of his head, and a huge tin basin between his knees half full of what tasted like very sweet thin porridge, with which he was feeding me lovingly from the cook's large iron spoon! He assured me that it was water gruel; that he had got into the way of making it nicely now; but that he could not find a clean dish on the premises to put it in! He was so proud of his cooking that I asked for the *recipe*, and you have it here: Equal parts of meal, sugar, and water (a cupful of each for one dose); boil all together, till there is a smell of singeing, whereby you know it is sufficiently cooked!

We had first-class faithful servants, and my cook could dress and truss a fowl, and make 'gravy' fit for any table, as he always does for our own; but sickroom cookery was beyond him. It never occurred to the others to wash dishes, so long as there were clean ones to be had; hence they went through the whole stock, leaving an ample dinner set, two breakfast and two tea sets, waiting to be cleaned when I was ready to take command again! Yet, they were very, very kind in many ways, and would sit fanning me by the hour in the hot sultry weather, when they might have been enjoying themselves outside. My baby throve splendidly, and we both got a right royal welcome when we made our first appearance at church.

Our fine new church stands close to our house. The building of it is the most interesting work that has taken place on this island. The very manual labour (which some might think regrettable) was, however, a special means of bringing the people under the influence of the preached word; for when Mr Paton used to go visiting the different villages and urging the people to come to church, he found them at such variance with each other, that, if a man from one district came, it was sufficient to keep the rest away; and for a long time our congregation only numbered from about six to twenty. The persons from different tribes could hardly meet without bloodshed. There was nothing but rumour of wars, though numbers of the natives seemed willing rather to worship than to fight.

The feasting and dancing season was drawing near; and Mr Paton thought that, if he could get them all actively employed, it might draw them together in a friendly way, and prevent a great deal of wickedness; so he proposed the building of a new church. He found it very inconvenient to have the old one at such a distance from our house; and, besides, it was too small for the number of people that Mr Paton intended and hoped to see at the worship. He laid his plans before them, one day, telling them he wished all the people of Aniwa to come and build a house for Jehovah, at their old sacred ground, being nearer the centre of the island; that he wished every man to bring a stick to help to put it up, and every woman to plait some cocoa-nut leaves for the roof; that it would be a great work, and take many days to finish it; and to bear in mind that they would receive no payment for this, as they had got for the printing house and the other houses they had built for him—for this house was to belong to all the men of Aniwa, not to the Missi; but that he himself would work with them, and give all the nails or other things they could not provide.

They had several pigs killed over the subject; for two or three of them never meet to talk over any important matter, without discussing a pig at the same time! The greater part agreed, and soon had a commencement made; but it might almost be said that, while they wrought with one hand, with the other they held their weapons. Indeed, the most deadly enemies worked at the farthest possible extremes, glaring occasionally across, as if they would dearly like to do something!

One man, in particular, owed the safety of his life to taking part in the work of church-building; for he was in danger from more quarters than one, being a troublesome and bad fellow. He had been hiding about for some time, but made his appearance when this work began; and he toiled from morning to night with a will, for, as he triumphantly informed the Missi, they would not dare to kill him while he was building Jehovah's house. One of his enemies came also, and said in Tannese: *O Missi, you should not have begun this, till the men of Aniwa had done fighting; for I wanted to shoot Nelwang, but now I dare not break the worship.*

As the building of the church, however, advanced, their interest deepened, till all their jealousies and quarrels were absorbed in the excitement of the work, and the greatest enemies would stand side by side, passing the tools, and talking cheerfully to each other. It was really a treat to see them all, after a hard day's work, gathered around outside the cookhouse, and enjoying a large kettle of tea—a thing they are very fond of! When carrying any heavy load, or doing any hard work, they always give peculiar shouts. It seems as natural for them, as for sailors to sing out when pulling ropes; and the most gladsome sound I ever heard was the shouting when they were bringing the pillars to support the roof. We would hear the noise in the distance, gradually waxing louder and louder, till thirty or forty men would appear, hurrying along with an enormous tree on their shoulders, and making a deafening noise as they passed the house—lots of them looking out at the corner of their eyes to know if they were seen! Of course, we always took good care to be at the door, to show our admiration and to cheer them on, and that seemed to please them amazingly.

The heavy end of all the work, as you may imagine, fell to Mr Paton; but he was right glad to do his part for such a work, and more. It does not suit him to be encased in a pulpit, so he made a nice platform; and his desk is covered with crimson velvet and tassels—a present from one of the Australian congregations. You will be apt to laugh at the incongruity of velvet drapery in a native building, nevertheless it looks pretty. My seat is made opposite; and the entrances to the building are on either side of it. There are eighteen windows, but really I don't know the number of feet. The ground is laid with small white coral, and the natives sit on plaited cocoa-nut leaves.

How proud the people were when the church was finished! And we were no less so, I can assure you. I think few home churches can ever have been opened with such intense feelings of interest and hope; but, strange to say, instead of the good turnout we expected, *there were fewer even than usual*—for they are so dreadfully afraid of offending his Satanic Majesty, although they profess to hate Tiapolo. When they saw, however, that he did not wreak his vengeance on those who did come the first two Sabbaths, the others gained courage; and since then, the attendance has steadily increased, till now it averages about a hundred and twenty on Sabbath and sixty on Wednesday. Their behaviour, too, at the worship, is very good, and some of them give nice addresses, for Mr Paton generally asks one or two of them to speak or engage in prayer.

Their prayers are usually most reverent. But they might be more polite to each other in their addresses, for the speaker generally begins by telling his brethren that they are *like pigs, dogs, serpents, etc.*, and winds up by asking them, with great indignation, how long they mean to continue *their black-hearted conduct.* They possess the advantage of knowing all that has been going on; and, if any flagrant wickedness has been committed during the preceding week, the perpetrators do get the benefit of it; while, if the speaker happens to have been himself one of the worst, he is conveniently oblivious of the part he acted! This seldom occurs, though, as it is only the best men who are asked to say a few words.

One Sabbath, some time after we came, when the people were in a very disturbed state, owing to one or two deaths that had occurred, Mr Paton asked Pavingin, one of the men that had been on a visit to Tanna just before we came to

Aniwa, and whom the *Dayspring* had picked up and brought on with us. We were much struck with the attention that his speech elicited. We could not tell exactly what he said; but we noticed him pointing once or twice to the shells he wore on his arm, while talking very impressively. We learned, afterwards, that he had been telling them an interesting incident that occurred on Tanna, when the *Dayspring* called on her way hither. It seems that, when dear old Nowar found he could not have his old Missi back again, he took Pavingin aside and told him that he now gave Missi Paton into his charge, and begged him earnestly to do everything he could to make him comfortable, and to tell the people of Aniwa to be strong to do the worship of Jehovah; for the Tannese had treated Missi Paton so badly that, though he and his people wished him back, the other *Missis* were afraid to let him come alone, and now they were all left without a missionary. Nowar then finished up by taking the white shells from his own arm,[2] binding them round Pavingin's, and telling him to wear them, and every time he looked at them to remember his words about being kind to Missi. We did not know of this at the time; but the narrative did great good to our impressible Aniwans.

It occurs to me, however, that I have never told you of that interesting visit to Tanna. We had to go into Port Resolution, on our way here, for shelter over the Sabbath; and though I enjoyed getting inside the bay for the first time, it unsettled our minds about coming to Aniwa afterwards. I, at least, had got fairly reconciled to it. Nowar was intensely disappointed, when told that the missionaries would not consent to Mr Paton's coming alone. He said comparatively little, but his venerable and expressive face showed how he felt it, as he sat mute on the deck with the tears in his eyes. Oh, how I loved

[2] See *John G. Paton: Autobiography* (Popular Edition, p. 344; Banner of Truth Trust, 2024, p. 348).

and respected him!—this man that risked his life to save my husband. I had read of such devoted love, but have never seen another living specimen; and deeply did I feel for the disappointed old chief, as he at last silently disappeared over the side of the *Dayspring* into his canoe,—but binding us to be sure and come to see his place that day.

You may imagine how it stirred Mr Paton's old memories, especially when we went on shore; and Nowar, having at last found the use of his tongue, made one grand effort to keep his friend. He must, somehow, have got it into his head that I was the hindrance, for he directed all his eloquence to me. Of course, I did not know more than a few words of the language; but there was no mistaking the meaning of his earnest and pleading gestures. He took me to see the places where Mr Paton and he had lain concealed in the bush—sometimes for days; and he showed me the very scars on his body, where he had received the wounds intended for 'my Missi.' Then, he held up his arms to show how strong they were to protect him still; but assuring me there would be no more fighting, for he would stay on his own ground; and he had chosen a lovely spot for our house on the brow of the hill, and commanding a fine view of the bay. What could I say to the dear old chief? I got Mr Paton to explain that I was as anxious as himself to live on Tanna; but that all the other *'Missis'* thought it was not good for us to go alone to such a large island, and that Captain Fraser had no orders to land our goods there. Nowar, however, removed that difficulty too, at least to his own satisfaction, by telling us that if we could just get the things pitched overboard, he and his men would land them all ashore in a few minutes! A number of Nowar's followers, old friends of my husband, backed up all these appeals, and joined earnestly in the entreaty of their chief.

Was it not very, *very* hard to leave them? Mr Paton, feeling it most keenly, was decidedly of that opinion, and, indeed, had his mind firmly made up to stay, and risk a vote of censure or sentence of excommunication, or whatever else the next annual meeting might, in its wisdom, see fit to pronounce! Experience, however, has proved that it was well that we followed the decision of the meeting. Mr Inglis, also, in one of his kind letters, has been assuring Mr Paton that he believes him to be doing more real work for Tanna here, than by labouring unaided amongst the dense masses there. We hope this may truly be the case; for the Aniwans can nearly talk the language of the Tannese, and have thereby great influence on their neighbouring islanders. On this account, particularly, Mr Paton has set himself to get some of the best of them instructed and trained to go thither as native teachers.

The fact that the Aniwans understand Tannese has been an unspeakable advantage to my husband's work, and is, I believe, one main cause of the people here having improved so rapidly. Mind, I don't mean to infer that conversions have taken place already, though the conduct of a few of them is almost everything that we could wish. But it is matter of great thankfulness to have so many willing to be instructed, and coming so regularly to church. The chief, who lives in the village near, is our firm friend. I regard him as really 'one of nature's gentlemen.' He does not know how to be rude. He talks so quietly and gently to everybody, except when anyone has been *breaking the Missi's word*, as he styles it, and then I don't care about being too near him! He digs his great toe into the coral and sends it flying round him like hailstones, while he relieves his burdened soul by pouring forth a perfect torrent of abuse on the guilty party.

Our chief is an intelligent-looking old man, and often regrets to Mr Paton that his *arms are too weak* to let him help in building or anything of that sort. But it is his great delight to go at night and catch the flying-fish, which he brings to the cookhouse early in the morning, giving Kanathie strict orders to have them prepared for our breakfast. His eyes really glisten with delight as he sees us enjoy them, for he makes himself our unfailing guest every morning and evening. He is not strong, and he so much enjoys a cup of tea and the soft bread. He always comes in before the worship on Sabbath and Wednesday, takes in Mr Paton's Bible, and lays it on the reading desk. Every evening, also, he collects the people for worship, which we have under a large banyan tree, in the meeting ground of the people, just outside our fence. This service, above all others, I enjoy. The quiet hour, the gorgeous sunsets, reflecting everything in that brilliant yet mellowed light, and the distant murmur of the waves, make the whole scene most enchanting; so much so, that, after the worship, we often sit still and sing all our hymns over and over again till all is dark.

The natives, indeed, are extremely fond of singing, and of music of any kind. I was most amused to see the power it had one day over a poor superstitious woman. She had ventured to come and look round the place with her little boy; but nothing would induce her to come near the door. She always drew back, saying she was frightened; and, when I patted her little boy on the shoulder, she drew him quickly away. I thought to try what effect music would have, and, slipping into the parlour, I began to play very softly the *Tyrolese Evening Hymn.* In a moment or two she came gliding in, all her superstitious fears forgotten, with a wistful and eager expression in her large black eyes, and she sat down by my side. When I finished, she lifted both hands imploringly, crying in her own language, 'O Missi, make it sing more!'

I have such a fine large class of women and girls; and I never expected it could be such delightful work to teach them—they are so amiable and pleasant and willing to learn. There are about fifty of them; and you can imagine that it is no light work preparing seams for them all, especially as they are so fond of sewing. But I shall soon be able to vary the occupation, by teaching them reading, for Mr Paton has finished printing our first Aniwan book, greatly to the delight of the natives! I hope my women will learn to read, and will like it as they do the sewing and singing; for, at present, after sitting for two hours and a half, they would like to go on still longer. Some of the mothers bring their babies, and sew and nurse alternately. It is a fine sight to see them all, some of the old ones with their spectacles, sitting in rows round the parlour floor, the spectacles having given them 'new eyes' and a new lease of life.

Mr Paton had a nice schoolroom built, at the first, but we have seldom got into it. It has been very much used as a sort of hospital; for, when anyone is sick, we find it almost impossible to get the friends to come, even once a day, to carry to them a little nourishment; and it is often *that* they want more than medicine, as food is very scarce on this island. Once or twice, having brought a family to live here in which there was an invalid, we found it so much easier to give good food—when it was being prepared, at any rate. One dear little girl, who had been reduced to skin and bone when carried here, went away from us fat and strong. A case like this tends much to promote the interests of our work, as every little incident connected with us is noted and talked of over the whole island.

Much illness might be prevented, if the people would but cultivate more. They don't plant enough to last them more than half the year, and the other half they live almost entirely on cocoa-nuts. Indeed, we were reduced to something like that ourselves, for two or three weeks before the *Dayspring* came from the Colonies this year. Though we had stored a great quantity of provisions, we had an unexpected number of natives to feed, entirely with our European food, and the *Dayspring* was two months longer in returning than we expected. It did us no harm, however, and, had it not been for the anxiety about my little ones, I believe I should have rather enjoyed the variety than otherwise. How it used to go to my heart, though, when dear Bobby would ask, every morning, 'whether the *"Day-'ping"* (as he called it) would come today, and bring a "bikkie"'!

The natives were very frightened that I might not be able to nurse the baby properly on such hard fare; for, being a *man of Aniwa*, they are under the impression that there is not such a fine child in the whole world and, of course, I quite agree with them! Their love of children is a beautiful feature of their character, and their own little things are in many cases very tenderly nursed. For my part, I almost think them really prettier than white children, with their brown velvet skins and large brilliant black eyes.

Yours ever affectionately,
MAGGIE WHITECROSS PATON.

4

Glimpses of the Aniwans

Aniwa, New Hebrides,
December, 1868.

My Dearest Mother, Sister, and All Friends,[1]

Quite a number of events have happened to us this year! Two rooms have been added to our island home: one, a little study, which John badly needed, and which has to serve also, in the meanwhile, as a drawing room, when we have visitors. Our native servants get so utterly confused if strangers are sitting in the dining room, while they are laying the table. The Aniwans call this the Great House, and are perfectly lost when they get inside—four rooms being quite too much for their comprehension! And, although they saw them being built, they ask in each room, with bewildered faces, whether they are north, south, east, or west?

We sometimes have to take them through several times in a day; and it is genuine fun to watch them—a perpetual play, without the wickedness of attending theatres! Some of the scenes are truly dramatic. One fellow, the other day, got so fantastically excited, when I set the sewing machine a-working before him, that he performed a war dance in the middle of the floor, flung his arms all about, and called lustily for his dead father! We get the real acting here.

[1] To the family circle.

A skeleton timepiece, under a glass shade, comes in for a very large amount of interest. *The Path of the Sun* was what they called it, after we explained how the hands and figures indicated its course in the heavens. I tried yesterday to explain that it was the earth, and not the sun at all, that was going round, but was promptly informed that I was a *liar*!! So I won't trouble them any more with my physical geography for a bit. They are just about as unripe for it as were the learned Italians, when Galileo propounded his theory, a couple of centuries ago. They will stand and watch the pendulum go for ever so long, and ask all sorts of questions, exactly like inquisitive children, whose minds are beginning to awake.

Everything about this house is wonderful to them; and the more initiated ones give themselves very important airs, when explaining matters to the *Atamtahu (= Man Bush).* A helpful young fellow living near us shows off one of the smoothly plastered walls as his 'bit of work.' He had taken trowel in hand, when the Aneityumese were putting on the second coat, and was ordered to stop and 'not disfigure the Missi's walls.' He appealed to John, who declared he was 'doing wonderfully' (so he was!), and let the poor fellow go on till it was finished. But, at midnight, when all was quiet, he himself took a lantern, and carefully smoothed over again the whole surface of the wall.

It will be so nice when the building is all complete; and I am trying my very best to make it the prettiest and most inviting home I know—as refined, as civilized, and as nearly what we have been accustomed to, as our limited resources will permit. We must not let ourselves 'down' because we are among savages, but rather try to lift them up to our Christian level in all things. One's home has so much influence on one's work, and on life and character; and it is due to our two wee boys to make it a bright one. We should do our life-work all the better, for having a home in harmony with our tastes. At least, it is no part of my creed to believe that there can be any religion in ugly surroundings, or that everything pleasant is sinful; though one old witch, a regular Mrs Grundy, did tell me, before leaving Australia, that missionaries' wives were expected to live and dress in the most primitive way, and to set an example of great gravity and solemnity, else they would get to be talked about. The old Adam in me felt like choking such insolence; but I controlled myself to retort, that in my Bible there was no separate code of rules for missionaries' wives, any more than for other Christian gentlewomen!

It is an increasing wonder to me that anyone can think that Christianity has anything to do with such fads; much more, that anyone can be blind to the fact that our kind Creator has given us such wealth of beauty in nature. He might have restricted himself and us to useful and nutritious cabbages; but, on the other hand, he has scattered flowers everywhere. The foliage plants here are exquisite, and the scenery is surpassingly beautiful. There is an indescribable charm and softness, too, in the atmosphere, which makes one feel, especially on going out in the early morning, that to *be*, just to exist, is a transcendent joy.

But what puzzles us excessively is—to understand how these poor natives can be so utterly at variance with their surroundings. Nature neither raises nor refines them one iota—in fact, it seems to take no hold of them whatever. If nature alone could regenerate us, one would expect to find nymphs and fairies inhabiting these 'gems of the Pacific'; instead, the most degraded savage in war paint presents himself. I once heard the New Hebrideans uniquely described by their oldest missionary, who read solemnly the terrible first chapter of the Epistle to the Romans, and then capped the apostle Paul by adding: 'The heathen here have all that, and they have *cannibalism* into the bargain!'

To look, however, from our poor natives, still heathen, and gaze on the almost saintly faces of the Christian Aneityumese, our assistants, keeps us from dreaming of despair. There you have a grander view of the transforming power of the glorious gospel of Jesus Christ, than I think it can ever be possible for anyone to feel in a Christian land! And, oh, how those poor savages have helped us to realize the meaning of the Incarnation! We have often felt, in living near them, that we might thereby understand, in some faint degree, what it must have been for the Lord of glory to leave his home on high and to dwell with us. The difference betwixt the best of us and the savage is as nothing, compared with such transcendent love; and yet the bare idea of living with them (not merely near them) is too awful. We do, of course, live with them, in a way; but not as really one of themselves; for we can always, at will, shut to the door of our own home, and retire into the sanctuary of dear family life—an infinite recompense and joy.

In all this, I am referring to the Aniwan savages on the whole; for we have some dear old pets amongst them already, who are most lovable, and form a kind of outer family circle of darkies living on the premises. After nearly despairing of getting any of the young folks under our care, a bevy of eight fine bright girls unexpectedly presented themselves one afternoon, and asked where they were to sleep, as they had come to stay! Some of these were fine looking, marriageable girls (at a marriageable age *here*), but I thought it my bounden duty to prevent that till they were older, and their constitutions more confirmed. But they were full of life and animal spirits, ready for any kind of pranks (and pranks here are not always innocent), and years seemed added to my life with care for them. I did indeed wish that I were a wise woman of, say, thirty, instead of an inexperienced girl (that burden has since rolled off, and I am willing to 'bide my time'), and

I used to lie awake half the night planning how to keep them fully and pleasantly employed.

I ransacked female missionary literature, but found little help there. *Numbers*, as to converts and classes, were brought prominently forward; but they all seemed to fight shy of practical details for their training, and that was exactly what I wanted. At length, dear Mrs Inglis of Aneityum came to the rescue with her clear practical wisdom, common sense and long experience. She and Mr Inglis paid us a flying visit, as they passed in the *Dayspring*, and I proudly marshalled my flock, arrayed in their best pink dresses, to *alofa* her. There was a bright and hearty shaking of hands, with words of encouragement which I translated; but, the moment they were gone, she said: 'Mrs Paton, you do wrong in keeping those big girls. It is high time they were married, and under the care of their husbands. You have too many, and the responsibility is too much for you. Don't you feel it to be so?'

How thankfully I told her all my difficulties, but added that I thought I had no business to feel this a burden, when other missionaries' wives seemed to rejoice in having large numbers. She replied: 'It would be a great deal better for the thoroughness of mission work, in its ultimate success, if they had not such large numbers. They can't possibly do justice to them. And as for our natives marrying too young, we must to some extent take things as they are, and of two evils we must choose the lesser. If those girls were in civilization, and hedged round with its restraints, or even on one of our Christian islands here, it would be different. But natives are adepts at cheating, even while you think you are watching them! Oh, my dear, I know how you feel, and did exactly the same thing at your age; only I carried the burden a great deal longer, for want of some kindly and experienced counsel.'

Her wise advice was promptly acted upon. The three eldest were married in the church to the husbands betrothed to them from infancy. They live near us, and come constantly about us; so that we can, I hope, still influence them for good.

The younger girls are more easily managed, and, we are only too thankful to get them young. What sharp little monkeys they are; too observant by half; and I am just finding out how very careful and guarded I must be, as absolutely nothing escapes them. John has been reading me such long lectures lately, about taking sufficient rest, that for a quiet life I wait till his back is turned, before flying round to do the hundred and one things that only the Mistress can, and then get on the sofa to rest before he reappears. I never dreamed that this little bye-play was noticed, till, the other day, a dear wee girlie rushed in excitedly, whispering, *Quick! Quick, Missi! On to the sofa! The missi-tané is coming.*

Of course, everything they say is in their own language, at which we are getting a little bit more fluent, under great difficulties. No dictionary, no grammar, to refer to; nothing but our own ears to instruct us; and the natives do gabble at such a rate! At least we think so; but they say it is we who talk so fast that all our speech runs into 'one long word.'

For a very long time, we were puzzled to find *the sign of the future tense*, and were much at a loss in translation work, as you can imagine. We often heard the natives say *Ka*, and asked what it meant; but they declared there was no such word; and it did not occur to us that it might be a prefix. At last, one day, I was doing something in the dining room with my baby in my arms, when his nurse came forward, saying, *Avau Ka-takoia, Missi.* She spoke very distinctly, and I saw that *Ka* meant 'will.' I put my baby in her arms, and flew out by the back, the shortest cut to the church, where John and some of the natives were working. I met him, on the way, rushing home, hammer in hand, to make known his discovery, and we both shouted to each other in the same breath, '*Ka* is the sign of the future!' We laughed so heartily, that the joke had to be explained, as well as we could, to the wondering bystanders; and they were amused and deeply interested.

The study of the language began to be quite fascinating, after we knew enough to ask questions but I shall never forget the half-comical agony I endured, when I first wanted to give some natives a regular scolding,—and not a word of the language would come to my relief! Talk of repression of pent-up feelings; wait till you have an experience like that.

We did not go to the Mission Synod this year, as John thought things here far too encouraging to be left even for a little; but I had a delightful trip (barring the sea-sickness) to Port-de-France, with our dear friends Mr and Mrs Sim, who had come down in the *Dayspring* for a short visit to the islands. They could only stay one night with us, and it was so delightful to have them, that we sat up the whole of it talking! It was thought too good an opportunity to be missed for consulting the French doctor about little Fred's arm; so I was off with them, next morning, after a busy packing up in the small hours, and arranging things for John's comfort in my absence.

This little peep into civilization again was simply delicious—a lovely drive into the beautiful surrounding country, well named New Caledonia, being more like Scotland than anything I have ever seen (the British were noodles not to take possession), and then back to a sumptuous dinner, which Mr Sim had ordered at the hotel. Captain Fraser and Mr Robertson were with us, and I think a happier party never sat at a table.

Next day, we were stopping at an English store, when I suddenly missed Freddie and his nurse. On going outside, I found Mistress Litsi giving characteristic expression to her first impressions of civilization, to the intense amusement of some French officers on the opposite pavement. A large cartload of pigs had just passed, and Litsi was letting off a string of ejaculations, flipping her fingers in the air, and hopping from one foot to the other. Fred was nowhere to be seen; and, after rushing up and down, I found him in a store whirling things from the counter, unceremoniously, and as fast as a child's mischievous fingers could! The shopman was hasting to the rescue; and I had to apologize and explain, in the best French I could muster, probably not less broken than some of the things now scattered on the floor.

Your loving daughter and sister,
MAGGIE WHITECROSS PATON.

5

Early Mission Days

To the Rev. Dr Macdonald, South Melbourne.

My Dear Sir,

How much I enjoyed your kind letter, which came by the *Dayspring* last month! I was delighted, indeed, to hear that your parish now extends to the New Hebrides,—rather a scattered one certainly; nevertheless you are bound to look after your flock, and we shall soon be expecting *a pastoral visit.*

In the meantime, I shall try to answer your letter as fully as time permits. We were so delighted to hear of all the Victorians are again doing for the *Dayspring.* The Copelands and we are almost entirely dependent on the *Dayspring* for communication with the civilized world, as it is but rare that trading vessels call here, there being no proper anchorage either at Fotuna or Aniwa.

We indeed rejoiced, for we had a little taste of starvation last summer; not much, but just enough to give variety to our quiet life! The poor natives suffered more severely, for they do not plant enough to last them half the year; but they take it very coolly, subsisting on cocoa-nuts or anything else that comes their way. Indeed they seemed far more concerned about us, than about themselves. Some of the old people and invalids, whom we had been supplying, absolutely refused to take any more bread to their tea, when they found that our flour was getting done, declaring that *they* could eat roots and leaves like our *nannie nannies* (= goats), but that we could not. They will, I think, be better off in future, for they have plenty of good ground lying waste, which Mr Paton is urging them to cultivate.

You were, I daresay, surprised when you heard that we had been sent to Aniwa instead of Tanna. It was a blow which Mr Paton has hardly got over yet; but all the brethren were decidedly opposed to us going there alone, and we feel now that we have been divinely led hither. Mr Inglis, in his last kind letter, said to Mr Paton that he believed he was doing 'more real work for Tanna,' by bringing the Aniwans to a knowledge of the truth and thus fitting them for by-and-bye spreading the gospel among the Tannese, than if he were now labouring alone among that dense mass of people. We are encouraged, therefore, to hope that there may be many 'ambassadors for Christ' from this little island, for the Aniwans are a superior people, and the work has made steady and rapid progress of late. I don't mean that half the people are converted—very far from that! There is a great deal to be done before the soil is prepared even to receive the seed; they cling so to their old prejudices and superstitions. I believe, to many of them, it is like taking a great leap into the dark to risk the anger of their gods by coming to the worship. For what proof have they, at first, that we are leading them into the right way? True, they see we wish to be kind; but the idea of anyone coming among them simply for their good is a doctrine they cannot understand.

We are very thankful to have so many regularly at church; and Mr Paton possessed a great advantage in being able to address them from the first in Tannese, which some of them speak freely; hence the double hope of training them as helpers for Tanna. You would be surprised to see with what propriety the services are conducted. The native teachers, two devoted men from Aneityum who have been here for years, try to give short speeches. Then Mr Paton usually invites one or other of the more enlightened of the Aniwans to speak, which he does by invariably pitching into his brethren in the most energetic terms, comparing them to pigs, dogs, serpents, etc.—the speaker not generally including himself—and asking how long they mean to continue their 'black-hearted conduct'!

They are never at a loss for a text, and for a long time after we came, it sounded to me something like *Missi Paton and Teapots.* I supposed it to be, 'Missi Paton *versus* Teapots'; but by-and-bye I discovered that it was not Teapots, but *Tiapolo* (= Devil), against whom they stormed. Lately they have been choosing more sacred subjects, generally a repetition of what they have heard from Mr Paton before, or been helping him to translate during the week. Last Sabbath, we were much struck with the gentle persuasive tones of the old chief who was addressing them. Mr Paton noted down two words he did not remember having heard before, and asked for the translation after worship. The man took him by the hand and said in Tannese, *Missi, I was only telling them what you have been teaching us all this time, about Jesus pouring out his blood to wash away all our sins!*

Taia, and Namakei the chief, two of our firmest friends, give very telling speeches sometimes. The former is a tall and powerful fellow, quite a notoriety on account of his loquacious powers. He has a great deal of ready wit too; and, though he does little else but talk, it is wonderful what influence he exerts. Some time ago, he prevented a violent quarrel ending in probable bloodshed. The party who thought themselves insulted ran home, seized their arms, and were rushing past Taia's house, where he was lying outside basking in the sun and enjoying his pipe. He saw something was wrong; for they don't continue the habit of carrying their arms constantly now, and he called out to them (of course in their own language), *Stop! stop! let me see what you are carrying. Is it the book that Missi has been busy making?* His sly hit set them all a-laughing, and they turned into his house; there he had a long and serious talk with them, and got them to give up the idea of fighting, at least for that day. The next being Sabbath, he came to Mr Paton before the service to ask him to let him speak; and, having both the offending parties present, he *did* give it them, finishing up by reminding them how difficult it had been to get a missionary, and how he, Taia, had gone to Aneityum to plead for more native teachers after they had murdered Nemeyan and tried to kill Navalak, and how he had always been careful to give them food to do the work of Jehovah! In that part of the speech referring to his own conduct, there were a few embellishments which in strict regard to truth might have been omitted, but his advice seemed to do good, for we heard no more of that quarrel.

Taia, however, does not always do as he professes; and Mr Paton sometimes feels it incumbent on him to call Taia to account; but Taia's equanimity is never in the least ruffled. He sits listening with his chin resting upon his knees, looking up now and again with a bland smile and saying, *Ah, very good talk that, Missi! Very good talk that!*

Namakei, the chief who lives close beside us, is a very different character—a dear old man, one of nature's gentlemen, who could not do an unkind thing to anyone; and yet his influence is felt more than that of anyone else on the island, for everyone seems to respect the dignified and pleasant old man, who makes it his special business to attend to Missi, and see as far as he can that his wishes are carried out. He often complained, when the house was being built, that his arms were too weak to let him help; but he did what he could, by being kind to our Aneityumese servants and the men we had helping us to build, and providing them often with native food. He is our guest morning and evening; and it is a great pleasure to see the old man sipping a cup of tea with such evident relish. Namakei never fails, when well, to take Mr Paton's Bible and lay it on the desk every Sabbath and Wednesday before the service; and to get the people in the village assembled for the worship, which we have every evening under a large Banyan tree in the *Imrai*, the great place of general rendezvous, which is close behind our house.

I particularly enjoy this evening service, when all nature is at rest and looks exquisitely beautiful, everything reflecting the gorgeous sunsets, and nothing heard but the soft rustle of the leaves and what Longfellow calls 'the symphony of Ocean.' I think the natives too are inspired with it, for none of us seem inclined to move off after worship, and often, but especially on Sabbath evenings, we sit still and sing over all our hymns. They never tire of this, being all of them intensely fond of music.

I could not but admire the power that music had over a very superstitious woman who came one day to have a look round our premises. No amount of persuasion could induce her to come inside. I was anxious that she should, for I thought I might get her coaxed to come to my sewing class; but she looked towards the door with a kind of horror, saying she was *weak with fear*; and, when Mr Paton patted her little boy on the shoulder, she took fast hold of him and drew him away. I bethought me to try what effect music would have. I went in and played something over softly. I had only played a few notes, when she came gliding in, all her superstitious fears forgotten, gazing with an intense and eager expression in her large black eyes, and sat down at my side. When I stopped, she held up her hands in an imploring manner and begged for more.

I was heartily amused the first time I was called upon to perform on Aniwa! We had just unpacked the harmonium, one day, about a fortnight after our arrival. The news must have spread like wildfire; for, towards evening, about forty or fifty people came marching towards the church (the house where we stayed till our new home was built), the foremost shouting in broken English, *Missi make him bokis (= box) sing! Plenty man come hear you make him bokis sing!*

I must not omit to tell you about my peculiar charge, and a very pleasant one it is; I mean my own sewing class. Nearly fifty women and girls attend pretty regularly every morning, except Wednesday and Saturday; and we spend about two hours (often more) together sewing and singing. They are very tractable, and willing to learn, having taken a great fancy for sewing. I never dreamt it would be really such delightful work teaching them, but my heart was drawn to them from the first, and I shall always feel grateful to them for the kindly way they behaved to me, when I landed amongst them, timid, and rather frightened at feeling myself the only white woman on these lonely shores!

Mr Paton took the matter much more coolly, seeming to take for granted that, they were all his 'dear friends'—though most of the men, really fine fellows we have since found them, thought it advisable to receive us with a good deal of impudence, trying how far we could be imposed upon! Plenty of them talk a little English; and really it was almost laughable, to hear them telling the most monstrous lies with such a long innocent face that one would suppose they believed them themselves, and then gravely adding, *That no gammon!*

How thankful I felt for the friendly protection of the Aneityumese, during those first few weeks of uncertainty and fear! Mr Paton took care always to leave two or three of them with me while he was away building. Mrs Inglis, too, provided me with excellent servants; otherwise, I would not have been able to commence teaching so soon, for a few women came two or three weeks after we landed. Their attendance, however, was very irregular, and for months no more than three or four would come at a time. I was getting almost disheartened, when one day the wife of our oldest chief came to look at the house, and Mr Paton whispered to me that if I could get her sympathies enlisted others would be sure to follow. It turned out to be the case; for, though she laughed heartily at a half-blind old woman like her learning anything, she changed her mind on Mr Paton fitting her with *glass eyes*, and she has since come regularly every morning. From that time, I had fresh scholars almost every day, till now about forty-eight attend.

I feel the sewing, however, to be only a stepping-stone to something far more important. It brings me into contact with them, so as to learn their language. I so long to be able to talk freely to them; but it is slow work with me! How the apostles must have appreciated the gift of tongues on the day of Pentecost! I wonder if it was accorded to their *wives* as well! It is so provoking, when you think you have mastered enough to venture on a little conversation with them, to see them looking at each other wonderingly. Some time ago, in talking to a girl, I plunged a little deeper than usual, thinking to astonish her with my wisdom, but she looked up innocently and told me she *did not savvy talk Biritania*! I must have made awful blunders, at first. But some of the women can talk Tannese, as well as the men; and I got Mr Paton's help in any great difficulty—though he did not at all times enjoy the interruption, especially if the point in question turned out to be only about a needle and a thread, while he had been called away when setting up the type for our first Aniwan book!

The book is almost ready, and would have been long ago, but for the horrid old press which Mr Paton got the loan of being completely out of repair. He has got it coopered up so as to do, however, and all are eagerly longing for the book—myself among the rest, for I shall begin to vary the occupation with my scholars by teaching them to read; partly for my own benefit, as well as theirs, as I could not long continue this work of sitting up half the night to prepare so many seams.

One of the women, Kamani, who looked forward to getting a book, has been suddenly removed, and I have missed her sadly. She was such a kind and affectionate creature. She always sat before my seat on Sabbath, and was the first to shake hands. I shall never forget that night she died. When I went to see her after the worship, she was lying on a mat just outside their house for air, and a little flickering fire lit up the sorrowful faces of the dark group around her. The breeze was low, and there was nothing to break the solemn stillness, but the heavy breathing of the dying woman, and the sobs of her little girl. We sang softly her favourite hymn, one of the first Mr Paton translated, but with difficulty got through it, for there was not a steady voice that night—she was so much beloved. Mr Paton offered prayer. I never felt any death so much in all my previous life.

We would have liked more evidence that she was saved. Mr Paton had been very often talking with her; and when he asked her if she loved the Saviour she answered in the affirmative. But we must not build too much on that, for almost everyone on Aniwa would give the same reply—most of them being under an impression that they are very good Christians indeed! I could only feel that it was a terrible warning to be more diligent in the future. When I felt I must go to my little ones, and took her hand before parting, they told her who it was, and she pressed it again and again, and with a dying effort brought her other hand round to close upon mine. I could not have believed her capable of such deep affection; for I never did anything for her, that I remember of, except ministering a little to her bodily wants when she was ill.

An hour or so after we came home, we knew that her spirit had passed away by hearing the wailing begin. That expression of grief is, I think, more real than affected. I saw more of it next day than ever before, as I went to see Kamani buried, at the urgent request of her husband. All her friends were there; and, though they might have made a little less noise, it seemed to be for the most part sincere. They evidently considered it a duty too, and spurred each other on; for if there was like to be a calm, a dismal howl was sure to be heard from some far-away corner, which would set them all on with renewed vigour.

Before closing this long epistle, I want to tell you about our *first Christian marriage* here, especially as the bride was decked out from your Emerald Hill box, last sent—at least partly so. It was a deeply interesting occasion. Kahi, the bride, was one of my scholars, a pretty young widow of about seventeen; and Ropu, her lover, was such a nice fellow too, a great favourite of Mr Paton's. They seemed really attached; but Kahi's father-in-law demurred about giving her away, as he considered her still his property, having given a high price (present?) for her, when he bought her for his deceased son. One morning, however, Ropu appeared with such a number of fat pigs, that they quite took the old man's heart by storm, and he declared that he might have her that day, if the Missi thought it was right. The Missi did not object, but advised them to get married in church; and I determined to give Kahi a nice present, in order to tempt her young companions to follow her Christian example—not a very high motive, to be sure, but if the prospect of a good present will induce them to alter their habits in regard to marriage, I have not the slightest objection that it should be so. It's about the highest motive some of them can yet appreciate; and there is no vital principle, after all, at stake in the mere form.

We made the event as public as the time would permit, and there was quite a little gathering to witness the ceremony. Poor Kahi was brought to me in tears; but when we put on her nice skirt and jacket, and she caught sight of the pretty hat, which happened to be trimmed with orange blossom, she seemed to think she had indulged long enough in sentiment, and dried her tears quite briskly, looking out from under her long eyelashes from side to side with great admiration; and when, at last, I put a flaring red handkerchief into her hand, she fairly laughed aloud! There was a little trouble with them in church, as they would not come near enough to join hands till they were pushed; and then the poor girl got her marriage vows repeated to her on the deafest side of her head; for, being too bashful, or something of the sort, to give the response, it seemed to be the public opinion that Mr Paton was letting her off too easily; and the men, taking up the question, thundered it in such a manner as to elicit a pretty quick reply!

I suppose Mr Paton will be telling you all about the building of the church, and how pretty your pulpit hangings look in it. Velvet drapery in a native building sounds rather incongruous; but I like the contrast; and Mr Paton thinks his platform desk quite a triumph of joinership. Oh, I earnestly hope that the Saviour's presence may always be felt with the preaching of the word; and that, in regard to many, it may be said, 'This man and that was born (again) there.'

December 6th.

Please send the *Dayspring* quickly down, this season; for I have found this morning, to my horror, that our whole stock of flour has gone useless; and not a bit of bread shall we get, till the vessel returns! I suppose we are indebted to the climate and the weevil together for this. We have plenty of other food—so no danger of starving.

Faithfully yours,
Maggie Whitecross Paton.

6

The Church of God on Aniwa

ANIWA, NEW HEBRIDES,
NOVEMBER, 1869.

MY DEAR FRIEND,[1]

So far as our work is concerned, this last year has been one of the happiest we have spent on Aniwa. Certainly it has been the most encouraging. Formerly we were cheered by our natives giving up one after another of their grosser heathen customs, and a very few adopting civilized habits, such as wearing clothing, etc. This year, we have the intense joy of seeing a little band of them come out from all their heathen superstitions, and declare themselves for Christ.

To spend such a day as we did a few Sabbaths ago, when our little CHURCH OF GOD ON ANIWA was formally constituted, we felt to be worth more than all the sacrifices connected with our isolated life. We had a very good attendance, one hundred and eighty being present, and an unusual solemnity and interest pervaded the church throughout the whole services. The communicants, twelve in number, were arranged in rows, from the platform to my seat, so that they occupied the space in the centre; and, as they stood up to answer the Form of Questions Mr Paton put to them before receiving baptism, you could scarcely have conceived of a more intensely interesting group. Vasi, our eldest member, must, we think, be near to ninety;

[1] To a lady in Australia.

but aged and infirm as he is, he came every day to school with his spectacles on, and is one of Mr Paton's best writers as well as readers. Our old chief, Namakei, was there, with his daughter Litsi. She is his only child living, and is almost as great a comfort to me as to her father. She was the first girl who came to live with us; and, being the eldest on our premises, she sets a good example to the others. Her devotion to Mr Paton almost amounts to idolatry. She seems as if she never could be grateful enough to him for being the means of her conversion. But the one I felt most interest in was Namakei's sister, a very gentle and delicate-looking woman. I knew what it had cost her to profess her faith in Jesus, and how her husband and son were even then jeering and laughing at her!

If I had time, I could tell you something interesting about each of them; for, of course, it was our knowing all their little histories that made it so intensely a gratifying sight to us. I could remember when one began to wear clothing, when another cut off his long hair, and when one whom we had thought a very hardened character came one day with the last of his idols, saying, *Now, Missi, these are the very last. I have no more.*

It was a beautiful sight to see these all standing up neatly clothed, in the midst of their benighted brethren, to declare themselves on the Lord's side; and more than we could witness without deep emotion. Never did I feel happier in any society on earth, than when partaking of our Saviour's body and blood with those dark sisters and brothers, now united with me in Jesus. It was a day long to be remembered. I trust it will be so even in eternity, with thanksgiving. Our dear friend and sister missionary, Mrs McNair, was with us, paying a long promised visit; and I felt so glad she happened to be here at the time, for she says she never witnessed a more beautiful and affecting spectacle.[2]

[2] See *John G. Paton: Autobiography* (Popular Edition, p. 375; Banner of Truth Trust, 2024, p. 380).

We have every reason to hope that the true work of grace is begun in their hearts. Mr Paton had much satisfaction in them, while attending his candidates' class; and their own earnest inquiries were what delighted him most. How often have we had cause to set up our Ebenezer, since coming to this far-off land; and this is but a small beginning, yet we have most emphatically reason to thank the Lord and take courage.

Since I wrote last, Bia, my clever and faithful Rarotongan woman, left to go in the new *John Williams* to her own land. She has been waiting this opportunity ever since her husband died here about a year and a half ago, and I can't tell you how I miss her. She was so thoroughly perfect in everything that I never saw a white woman to equal her. When she left I was for the first time entirely dependent on our natives for help; but my girls had been so far trained, and I got Mr Paton to ask a nice boy to come and be my cook. He agreed, after hearing that he would not be obliged to marry one of the girls! I don't know what had put that into his head; but he seemed very much relieved, when Mr Paton told him that he did not come here to 'make matches'—he left that for themselves to look after!

Mungaw was so disgusted at having to wear a kilt, that I did not dare to mention about cutting his long hair; and Mr Paton does not wish the natives to be forced to these things; for he always says that, when their hearts are changed, they will be sure to give up these things of their own accord. I know that this is very true; but, as I don't see that there would be any harm in having the short hair first, I coaxed Mungaw to cut his, and he looks very much more civilized.

We have quite a gathering of boys now on the premises; for Mungaw had not been installed into his office two days, before a few others came, and asked quite humbly that they might be allowed to do something for the Missi. We were truly amazed as well as gratified at this unexpected proposal;

for the boys here, as a rule, are the idlest and most impudent set I ever saw. They seem to be the 'masters' too, for no one thinks of contradicting a boy. Of course, Mr Paton told them he was very glad to have them come, as he wanted to teach them a great deal they ought to know. They are really doing tolerably well; and I feel so thankful to have a man-cook, as there are so many things connected therewith that men or boys require to do, and that they will not do to help a *woman*—for instance, chopping wood and black-leading the stove.

Their abominable heathen notions often trouble us, though not more than we might have expected. For the last two days, there has not been a boy on the premises. They all bolted yesterday morning at daylight, on account of something about the girls. I expect to see them all skulking about again, tomorrow or next day; for they like best to show face gradually, after absconding in that way. Meanwhile, I can hardly regret it, as it has shown what an interest and care our little band of church members have over us. The moment those of them who live near us heard of it, they came and told the girls just to go on with their regular work of doing out the rooms, etc., and *they* would do the cooking! So three men presided over the porridge pot, while two old wives infused our tea. And they all managed their work so well, that I knew nothing of our absentees, till I wanted to give our cook directions about the dinner. Our church members seem to think it incumbent on them to come between us and any annoyance that may occur; and if love and kindness to their missionary is to be a test of their love to Christ, they already have it!

What a rich year this has been for our mission! We have had the extreme pleasure of welcoming two new missionaries; and, what is of most interest to us ladies, their *wives*. How eagerly we look forward to any additions to our limited circle, and how many questions we ask each other about the expected sisters, which usually cannot be answered till we have the pleasure of seeing them for ourselves! We like Mrs Watt and Mrs Milne so much, and I hope they may find our society pleasant.

The fact is, however, we have to like each other, for we can't choose our society down here exactly. You ministers' wives in the Colonies can visit with as many or as few of the sisterhood as you choose; but I can tell you, we should feel pretty uncomfortable if we had to wait on board the *Dayspring* for a formal invitation to 'dine,' or 'spend the evening,' when we have the opportunity of visiting each other. We are only too glad to get off in the first boat, leave the *mal-de-mer* behind us, and get a hearty welcome from the missionary and his wife on shore; and as we gather round the well-furnished table (for the very best in the house is produced to grace such occasions), what a social, merry, delightful entertainment it is! We are all so thoroughly delighted to see each other, and have each so much to say and to hear, that the time speeds like lightning; and we fancy we have hardly been seated five minutes, when we are assured it is time to go on board. If it is a harbour station and we can remain all night, we find that a mission house is very elastic, and that none of us will be allowed to sleep elsewhere.

How these little yearly visits, on our way to and from the Annual Synod, animate and cheer us, as well as our pleasant and more lengthened stay at the station where the meeting is held! And we all come back to our posts with new life and vigour. I never was, I think, so benefited by anything as by my short visit this season to Aneityum. Mr Paton was delighted to see me so much fresher-looking, when he came back from Santo, and I have been feeling stronger ever since.

The *Dayspring* is a great blessing to us all. There is little fear of any missionary now, on the most savage island, being ill treated, if they see that he is well looked after. Of course,

I mean 'humanly speaking' the fear is *nil*; and, if we be kept in safety and our work in the end begins to prosper, that dear little vessel and her supporters have more to do with it all than might by some be imagined. Two of our natives, one of them the wildest character on Aniwa, were engaged by Captain Fraser to go as boat's crew, the trip before last; and they came back in ecstasies, declaring there never was such a captain as the one on board the *Dayspring*. He was so kind and good to them; for when they came to any island without a missionary, he would not let them go on shore for fear of being killed, and that would have damaged our work on Aniwa. Then they counted on their finger ends, with great glee, the things they had received in payment; and as these are good and useful articles, it engenders a love for such things instead of the paint and stuffs they get from the traders, while their huge ambition for sailing and sight-seeing is gratified.

I trust you will excuse this hurried epistle. My little ones are continually bothering me to explain about the pictures, which I gave them in the hope of keeping them amused and allowing me to have a little quiet, so I find it hard to write at all.

Ever yours affectionately,
Maggie Whitecross Paton.

7

Death and the Dayspring

New Hebrides, South Seas,
Havannah Harbour, Efaté,
5 December, 1870.

My Dear Mrs H.,[1]

I cannot express to you how much I valued your dear kind letter; and what a relief it was in the bitter grief of hearing about my precious sister Elizabeth's death, to know the particulars of her latest hours. But for yours, I should have been left in dreadful suspense; for, in her dear husband's last letter, there was no particular account of her fatal illness, as he wrote in the full belief that the letters sent to Adelaide had already reached me, while they only came to hand as we came on board.

Yours came the day after Frank Hume was born, along with her husband's and others; but Mr Paton kept the sad tidings from me for ten weeks, till I was better able to bear the awful trial. And it is only, as you said in your letter, when we have a hold of Jesus' hand that we can breast the billows that surge over and threaten to drown us. I had to lay down the letter, again and again, and pray for strength to read on to the end—you brought the closing scenes all so vividly and so really before my mind. May God bless you for what you have been to her! Fervently have I uttered this prayer, when reading your letter, in very bitterness of grief at the idea of her

[1] A lady in Edinburgh.

having died so far away from us all. But I felt so glad, also, to learn that you and our darling Elizabeth had become so dear to each other,—my ever beloved sister!

Will you please give my kind love to B., as I shall not be able to write at this time? We have had, unexpectedly, to take a voyage at the end of this season, the time usually set apart for writing our annual letters, and making up our orders for the Colonies. For our little Frank's sake, we have asked Captain Fraser to run the *Dayspring* over to Lifu, that we may consult the French doctors there. We have come round the whole voyage, however, as it was thought advisable to go first to Santo, on account of our missionary, Mr Goodwill, who, we heard, was dangerously ill; and we are now, on our way back, locked in here by head winds. In the first place, we were driven in by a rough gale; and I have such a horror of sea-sickness that I am very glad; though I grudge the time, which is specially precious at this season; and it is not much writing one can do on board, with natives constantly coming and going, and, in the circumstances, you will excuse this disconnected epistle.

We go to Lifu, as soon as the wind changes, where we fondly hope to get good help for our little one; as I really would not like to have to take him to the Colonies, even although the *Dayspring* is going to Adelaide this year. I feel I could not stand much more parting, and would much rather forego the intense joy of meeting than endure another farewell; and Mr Paton does not see it to be his duty to accompany me, and leave our beloved work for a season. Then I have another little thought in the background, and that is—that they might take my bairns from me! My judgment says, the sooner they are in a civilized country the better; but I don't think, more than I can help, of this heart-rending trial—time enough when I have to face it in the swiftly coming days.

How often my mind reverts to that happy time, the year I spent in Edinburgh, with which you all are in memory so closely associated! I think it must have been the tenderness of your nature that mainly revealed itself to me; for once or twice I have indulged in a *guid greet* (*Scotticé* for weeping heartily.—Ed.), when looking at your name and that of your dear husband, in the book you kindly gave me. The tenderness, however, would not be worth much without the firmness which forms its solid background, and makes the other stand out in beautiful relief on the pages of memory and love.

My four bairns are all thriving, despite those little ailments, and I think we all shall be much benefited by this short voyage. Captain Fraser says that I look like another woman already; for I had got so weak and thin, after the tidings of Elizabeth's death, that my husband became seriously alarmed. It seemed as if I could never get over the shock; and the one thought always stood out before me, like a great blackness, whichever way I turned, that my precious Elizabeth was gone! I cannot tell you what a sister she has been to me, nor how I loved and admired her—she was so noble and true and unselfish. If ever woman was sincerely mourned, she is; and not by me only, but by many hearts. I feel as if death would not be so terrible, now that she has gone before; and that helps me to understand what happy Christians mean by not being afraid to follow Jesus through the Dark Valley. Oh that I may be prepared for the call of my God, and, meantime, may reap the full benefit, that this sore affliction is intended and is fitted to draw forth, within my soul!

I ought not to trouble you with my feelings, but you write so kindly, and you were so dear to her, that I could go on telling you everything; still I must reluctantly close, as this is among the first of my replies, and I have many letters still to overtake.

Believe me,

Ever gratefully and affectionately yours,
MAGGIE WHITECROSS PATON.

8

To the Children of the Dayspring

ANIWA, NEW HEBRIDES,
JULY, 1871.

MY DEAR LITTLE FRIENDS,[1]

Grown people, as well as children, have to do as they are bid, sometimes; and that is the reason why I am writing this letter, instead of someone abler, and more accustomed to the task.

It is about your beautiful mission vessel, called the *Dayspring*, that I am to say something; and I will do with you, as our friends in the civilized world do with us. They do not fill the *Dayspring* with letters of wise advice, telling us how diligent we ought to be, and how little we are doing compared with what we might do; else, we might turn round indignantly, and want to know what business it is of *theirs* to preach to *us*, from their safe and comfortable homes! But they take a far more effectual plan to make us feel how diligent we ought to be; for the little vessel comes to us every year, full of precious and loving messages from kind friends who do all they can to help us, and tell us how much they sympathize with us and pray for us; till we really feel humbled, and begin to think, *What have we been doing to deserve all this; and how have we been attending to our share in this labour of love?*

[1] To children whose gifts helped to maintain the *Dayspring*.

Now, if I tell you how really grateful all the missionaries are to the children, who give their money so willingly to keep the *Dayspring* in nice order, and how the little vessel actually helps to keep the missionaries alive, as well as those so dear to them, by bringing them food and medicine and all they require, I am sure you will not grudge having denied yourselves many little gratifications to help in so important a work.

No ship in the world has been more highly prized or more eagerly longed for than the *Dayspring*; and we feel very much like children bounding out of school, to have unrestrained freedom with their companions, when it arrives and we meet with our missionary friends; for, then, we can talk in our own language, saying whatever comes uppermost, without fear of being misunderstood or of setting a bad example—as you can easily understand, we are in the habit of acting so carefully before the natives, who might so easily take wrong meanings out of what we say or do. The visits of the mission vessel are bright days in our lonely existence, which we think and talk about afterwards, as you do regarding holiday pleasures after you return to school.

But, if the *Dayspring* has been prized by the missionaries, when things went well with them, oh how their hearts have gone out in gratitude to God, when the little white-winged messenger of mercy has been seen approaching at a time of sickness or danger! I know of at least two mothers, in this mission, who have gone to the shores of their lonely islands day after day with aching hearts, and eyes strained to catch the least little speck of hope on the horizon—for their babies were lying so sick that they feared they might die, ere the *Dayspring* came to carry them away to see the doctor.

Further, last year, when the vessel was too long in leaving Australia, our dear missionary, Mr McNair, used to pace the shores of Erromanga, looking for her in vain! He was reduced to greatest weakness by the fever and ague of the climate; and, the natives having been unusually sick also, the store of medicine was exhausted; so that their only hope was in the return of the vessel, with the medicines they so much needed. Sometimes, after returning from the beach, he would throw himself on the chair and say, 'I think I shall be in my grave, before the *Dayspring* comes!' And he did die, as you have heard—one of the most godly and devoted missionaries that ever came to tell the heathen about Jesus—not, however, before the vessel arrived with all fresh supplies, but then it was too late to do him any real good.

It would be easy to talk for hours about what the *Dayspring* does for the mission; and, if you had been on board last year on the return from the annual meeting of the missionaries, you would have seen some brisk work going on in the way of house building. I was very much amused with the little I saw at Erromanga. The *Dayspring* had to wait there for two days; and all the missionaries united to improve the time, to the utmost, by putting up a cottage for Mr McNair in a healthier situation. Captain Fraser himself wrought like a common sailor, and spared a couple of men to help; so, the moment the anchor dropped in Dillon's Bay, we were ordered into the boat. The eager missionaries dispensed with the ceremony of paying their respects at the mission house, first of all, and, leaping out of the boat, as we passed the site at the entrance of the river where the new house was to be erected, they threw off their coats, turned back their shirt-wrists, and, in less than five minutes, were making brushwood and trees fall before them in their zeal to prepare for the foundation. They worked like that for two days, and managed to get up the wooden framework of the house—little dreaming that their beloved brother was never to enter it; for, in less than a fortnight, he was taken home to the beautiful mansions above! The last we saw of him was at the boat landing, where he stood looking so bright and pleasant, wishing us, as we shoved off, a hearty 'Godspeed!'

I have told you a little of what the *Dayspring* does for the missionaries; but just think of what it has done for the heathen, by bringing these missionaries to them. I have not time to dwell on this; but there will be ages and ages in eternity for these redeemed Ethiopians to show forth their praise and gratitude to God for sending us to tell them of him who died for them. Remember, however, that it is the missionary, and not the mission ship, that brings souls to the Saviour; for important as the *Dayspring* is, and it is of vital importance, it cannot make known to a single individual the way of salvation through Christ. We must have missionaries, who will go and live among the darkies, learn their language, teach them to read, and show them what it is to live as Christians. Will not some of you, who have done so well in giving your money to the mission, do infinitely better by giving *yourselves* some day?

May I close this letter with one little word of advice?—and it is this: whatever you do, let it be done 'for Jesus,' who values even a cup of cold water, when given 'for his sake.' You might possibly be disappointed in your mission vessel, if you saw her; and if you came to be missionaries, you would find it uphill work indeed, to be sacrificing your whole life merely for the sake of those who could not understand your motives, and who know not what it cost you to give up home and friends. But Jesus regards every sigh, and whatever is done for him will meet with a sweet reward even in this life; for he who has promised can *never* disappoint!

You may not be able to come and teach the heathen, or even to give money to help them, but every one of you can pray for them and for us. Do this always, like dear children, and believe me to be

Your loving friend,
MAGGIE WHITECROSS PATON.

9

A Trip to the Colonies

ANIWA, NEW HEBRIDES,
1871.

DEAREST FRIENDS, ONE AND ALL,[1]

How utterly helpless one feels here in a case of sudden emergency! We fancy we are getting on independently of all the machinery of civilization, when, some little hitch occurring, we realize what we owe to it. Not for ourselves so much do we feel it, but it cuts deep to see our little ones suffer. A severe cough and influenza epidemic having swept over the island last September, our little three-weeks-old baby caught it, and, after his severe tussle with the cough, needed special skill. Hence our trip to Lifu in the *Dayspring*, only to find that the French, to our most bitter disappointment, had cleared out, just one week before, leaving only a resident official. They don't want to be scattered, in case the Prussians come down on them at Port-de-France!

It was thought by all that I ought to take Baby to the Colonies, but a more inconvenient time could hardly have presented itself. The Annual Missionary Conference was to be held at Aniwa, after the hot season, for the first time (it has always been held on Aneityum hitherto), and I had all sorts of preparations to make for it. John could not possibly leave his work, now so successful and so intensely

[1] To the family circle.

interesting; and the thought of being away from him three or four months without hearing was unbearable. The want of postal communication makes us feel so completely shut off from the civilized world—only getting letters once a year by the *Dayspring*! There are stray chances; but they are so very rare, especially on Aniwa, where there is no harbour, that we cannot count upon them.

Our dear baby, however, dispelled all hesitancy, by a violent return of his complaint; and, in five days thereafter, we were on our way to Australia in the *Dayspring*, John accompanying us on board to put us under Captain Fraser's kind care. I had my own way about bringing our boys with me; but our pet lassie, the ex-baby, not quite two years of age, John determinedly refused to part with, imagining all sorts of evil would befall her by the way. Her nurse is an experienced Aneityumese teacher's wife, who won't let the sun light upon her to hurt her. The little cloud of white was the last thing my eyes rested upon, as the shores of Aniwa receded from view; and the first, on our return four months later, as her father held her high in the air to let me see that she was all right!

I don't think I ever told you of the tremendous sympathy—of the wrong kind—that I received at the birth of my baby girl. It was on a Sunday morning. I was in perfect ecstasies that my long-cherished wish had been realized—I had now a daughter of my own! John joyfully announced the advent, after the morning service was over; with a gentle prohibition against anyone visiting me for a fortnight at least. A white congregation might be rather scandalized at such personal and domestic references. But the mission is altogether a family concern; and family life on Christian lines is quite its most conspicuous feature. In church, you must be prepared to hear your full name popping out, right in the middle of a native's prayer, and then each name of all your family, and heaven's richest blessing invoked on them and you, especially when there is any sickness or trouble. Is this, after all, not more sensible than a minister in civilization petitioning 'for thine afflicted handmaiden'—losing for you all sense of worship in the immediate speculation as to who the *handmaiden* may be?

Well, on that delightful Sabbath evening, John and I had a lovely and quiet little chat about 'our many mercies.' Indeed, we had more to be thankful for than may at first appear, as, though a digression, I may here record. Four months before, I had inadvertently partaken of a very poisonous fish, which dear old Namakei the chief had unwittingly brought to us. (And didn't he have to stand a storm of abuse from his *heathen* brethren! They had not *taken the worship*; but, then, they did not try to *kill Missi's wife*!) The poison got a terrible hold upon my system. The two natives who partook of the same fish after it left our supper table (what a merciful providence that John took no supper, and that the bairns were in bed!) both got sick, immediately came out in a rash, and were quite better in a few days. I was almost dead before the emetic took any effect; the brandy I drained seemed of no more consequence than water; and, indeed, I have never properly rallied. We did not dare show the natives that I was ill so long, lest they superstitiously thought the worship was bringing new disease amongst them. So I managed to get through the teaching and the outward duties in a kind of way; and John shortened our services, whenever he saw me getting very faint, without the natives knowing why. No watches here!

Well, as I was remarking, before being interrupted by this fish-digression, on that glorious Sabbath evening my dear husband poured out his heart in a prayer of thanksgiving, before going to his study to mount guard and keep out intruders, leaving the door open between my room and it. Several times he heard a slight rustling, but, when he listened again, all was still. It turned out to be two dear elderly native women, creeping on their hands and knees, determined to get close to me by fair means or foul, in order to console me in what they thought my misery! They seized my hand sympathetically, and said, *O Missi, Missi, you are young, and will live to forget this day!* A panic seized me, as I heard their words, about my husband and my boys, though I had seen them only a few minutes ago; but their next remarks reassured me—'You must not fret about having *only a girl* this time; you know you have had two sons already, and will have many more before you die. We have all had to bear the same disappointment. We cannot always have sons!' I used the most forcible language which I knew, in their vocabulary, to make it very clear to them that their sympathy was entirely wasted. I made them exclaim with delight at the fat dimpled face and hands; and they left the room comforting themselves that they had seen 'a real white little woman of Aniwa.'

That same *little woman of Aniwa* has done more to reconcile those poor unfortunates here, who have obtained only daughters, than a hundred sermons could have done. They see what a treasured pet she is to us, as God's precious gift, and our actions speak louder than any words. All little girls of Aniwa will be more lovingly treated in the days to come, for the love we showed to this little woman of Aniwa.

Fools, who have had no experience of the many-sided influences of Christianity in saving and in civilizing the heathen, may chatter against missionaries marrying, and shake their heads about the distractions of a family. We who are in the thick of the work, and know all sides to the question, feel overwhelmingly thankful that God has given us these children, not only for our own happiness, but even for our work's sake. How often are those wonderful words suggested to us, *A little child shall lead them!* Our bairns are little missionaries, every one. They have called forth in the natives a softened feeling towards us, and in us towards the natives and their children. Strange to say, too, they have given us material help in mastering the language. They do not, of course, know nearly as much of it as we, who study it grammatically; but they seem to imbibe the *idiom* with their very breath. Their language is polyglot. They speak to us in English. I strove hard to keep them from learning Aniwan, for the sake of their morals, but could not manage it, with native servants all about. So they always talk Aniwan in their play; and the natives are so proud to hear them lisping 'the language of Aniwa.'

The life of the Christian home is the best treatise on Christianity—a daily object-lesson, which all can understand, can 'read, mark, learn, and inwardly digest'; in fact, it is the only Bible which many of them shall ever read! It wakens a terrible feeling of responsibility to see how they sometimes look up to us; not that many of them appreciate in the very least our motives for coming to live amongst them. They cannot rise to the feelings engendered by the cross; and, as 'every man imputes himself,' they take for granted that we must have in view some ulterior and selfish object. We were struck with this very specially, one day, when a brazen-faced embodiment of the Evil Spirit, the wildest savage on Aniwa, came to demand something or other, and John gave him a lecture on his evil ways instead. Rangi tossed his head, and threatened *to go to hell*—if he might not get doing as he liked. John rebuked and appealed to him. But I, not being the missionary exactly, felt free to express my mind, hinting pretty broadly that that was the place for him, that he would find suitable company there, and that it need not affect us whether he went upstairs or down! Whereon he turned in amazement, and asked, 'If it doesn't make any great difference to you then, for what did you leave your own land and come to us?'

It is hard to believe sometimes that they can get any good, proportionate to the sacrifice made for them; and it is at this stage that one's faith and obedience are put to the test. We have got to believe that the Lord meant what he said, when he commanded that the gospel should be given to 'every creature'; and I can understand now why Paul, the greatest apostle, was not kept as a sort of splendid figurehead at Jerusalem, but sent 'far hence' among the Gentiles to assault the strongholds of Satan. The Lord showed what he thought of the importance of foreign missions by sending his best man to be the first missionary to the heathen; but I think he gets precious few, even of his own followers, to agree with him in this. They say (and I was often met with the remark on our late visit to Australia), *Anyone will do for these heathens*; and seem to grudge a man of burning enthusiasm and magnetic eloquence going to the foreign field, as if it were so much power and genius being wasted. We, from our point of view, think that it is here, in the foreign mission field, that such a man finds warfare worthy of his steel, in trying to break off the time-riveted fetters of idolatry. Undoubtedly it is the very men who are most needed and best qualified to fill the higher posts in civilization, who are also wanted, indeed, who only are fit to be trusted with the overthrow of Satan worship in the darkest places of the earth.

One hears and is asked so much about the qualifications needed for missionaries, by people who can't be got to understand that all that tends to make a good and true man anywhere tends to make a good missionary for the foreign field; and *ditto*, with double emphasis, for the missionary's wife! Sanctified common sense, and high culture, are means of grace among savages, as among others, when they are laid upon the altar to God. Though they have not such gifts themselves, they are capable of detecting the want of them in others. But, highest reason of all is this: no missionary can have too many resources within himself, or accomplishments, to bear up against the down-dragging influences of heathen surroundings. If one had only time, there is splendid scope here for certain branches of study. The beauties of nature are such that artist cannot capture nor poet depict them. The brilliance and the colouring of sky and of water would drive a painter to despair. Conchologists, botanists, and naturalists would find food for endless and delightful speculations.

The natives have a rudimentary knowledge of botany, and their own names for every tree and plant on the island. One morning, as John was setting out to a distance with some of his lads, he saw a pretty little fern which he thought I might like for the rockery, and, cutting it out by the roots, he sent one of them back with it. Farther on there was another beauty, which he examined, but remarked that, as it was exactly the same, he would not uproot it. 'It looks the same, Missi,' they replied, 'but is not'; and they indicated its minute points of distinction, which ranked it in an altogether different family of ferns!

They have also names for many of the *stars*, but don't attempt to number them—as they can count only up to ten! When they want to impress you numerically, for instance, with any person's great age, they say *he has lived more yams*, *i.e.* years, than all their fingers, counting them, then their toes, pointing to each; then impressively pointing to their heads, they add they are like their hairs and more than can be numbered! John makes them count in English, and simple addition and subtraction are to them the deepest mysteries of learning, to which only the most advanced can hope to attain. The strain of having to exercise their minds to think in foreign words is too much for them. It would be dreadful to risk their soul's salvation on the chance of their understanding the little smattering they might get of English; though many well-intentioned wiseacres gave us brilliant advice about teaching them the English language, giving them the English Bible, and throwing open to them the glorious treasures of English literature!

If they could only show us *how to throw open their minds to receive it*, they would indeed be doing us a service. They seem to think that our islanders have no mother tongue of their own, and that they are standing all agape, ready to drink in instruction. Would people only exercise a little common sense, and consider whether they would thus eagerly learn a foreign language from longing to be instructed about a new God! Or, even, how would we like to go back only to pre-Reformation days, and have our Bible practically a sealed book, by seeing it exclusively in the Latin tongue! If a Chinaman wanted to come and instruct us in the doctrines of Confucius, he would certainly begin by learning our language, and adapting himself to our modes of thought, not by trying to teach us Chinese and throwing open to us the treasures of Chinese literature. Of course, it would be very nice for that Chinese missionary, if we would learn his language and save him the trouble of learning ours! But, then, we wouldn't; and no more will the South Sea islander, who can date his beloved mother tongue as far back as any of us. The Tower of Babel! They say the New Hebrideans came directly from that scene of confusion of tongues, and I verily believe it.

All the same, it would be splendid if our islanders could speak English, and we heartily teach them all we can. Mr Inglis says the only way to bring it about would be to take all the children and babies away from their mothers, and to bring them up entirely with English-speaking people! Many a good laugh they must have had at our expense, in our efforts to speak Aniwan. It is so difficult at once to think and to speak fluently in a foreign tongue, to say nothing of speaking idiomatically; and I can tell you, my sympathy now flows out to foreigners. Although we can gabble away to the natives, and understand pretty well what they say, they could easily cheat us; indeed, they might be plotting our destruction, by our side and in our hearing, by simply concealing all the meaning in a well-known parabolic style of their own. They have borne with us very politely, and not laughed at us half so much as they might have done; for they do enjoy a joke, as children do, and are a merry-hearted race—often laughing so heartily that they work it off by rolling on the ground!

These cheery natives were not long in finding out my provoking sense of the ludicrous, which has been a great trouble to me in my missionary life here—there is so much to evoke laughter. By desperate efforts, even in church, I had kept my risibles under some sort of control; but I lost any reputation that way achieved, on the celebration of a most comical wedding. The bride was rather an old girl, say fifty odd years, and as she had gone through the same ordeal three or four times before, *à la native*, she could not see the use of making an exhibition of herself this time in the church. At any rate, she would *not* 'rise' to the occasion, when her young bridegroom stood ready to take upon himself the vows of matrimony. After sundry whispered admonitions, and more vigorous kicks from those around, she was at length got on her feet; but, on finding that she was expected to take her partner by the hand, she flopped down again determinedly; and the Missi, with a helpless and puzzled look on his face, had to go on with the ceremony, on these conditions. I confess I heard nothing more, being obliged to duck my head and give in, almost audibly pleading that the number of times I had successfully *resisted* should be counted in my favour! It was noised abroad, immediately after the service, the happy pair having at once bolted out at different doors and in opposite directions, as if they never meant to meet again, that the *Missi finé* had been *dead* (*i.e.* gone into fits) in the church!

I have rued that day ever since, as they have made it impossible for me to reform. Of course, there are no more scenes like the above, as we are now getting too 'civilized.' But if anything out of the way, or the least bit comical, takes place in the church, a hundred pairs of merry twinkling black eyes and mischievously expectant faces are in an instant turned eagerly towards my seat—sufficient of itself to upset my not too heavily weighted gravity.

How charming it was to be in a civilized church again, and to listen to an excellent sermon in one's own language, after nearly five years among the darkies! Geelong was our first destination, which we reached on a Sabbath afternoon, and went to the evening service at St George's. We were quite a large party—Dr and Miss Geddie, Captain and Mrs Fraser, Mrs McNair and I, besides some of the *Dayspring* crew, looking so respectable in their Sunday 'rig.' The church, internally, looked chaste and beautiful; the pulpit artistically so, of light grey stone, draped with coloured velvet; and the rails were bluish green. Mr Campbell's subject was *Jesus and His Disciples Talking of Heaven*, and one could easily imagine the scene on that lovely summer evening. The second last hymn was 'O'er these gloomy hills of darkness,' and it came home to me with such power that I could not venture to sing a line—my thoughts were all on Aniwa! When the collection was being taken, they passed our seats (doubtless thinking we had done fairly well in giving ourselves!); but Louis, one of our sailors, made a very decided flourish of his arm in the air, so the plate had to be brought back. How kind everybody was, and what a cordial invitation we had to the manse—boys, nurse, and all!

I had often, while on the island, pictured what my sensations would be, if ever I again trod the streets of civilization; but I had none at all! It all came so natural, that I quite forgot I had ever been away, as we flew round 'shopping' all next day—a very necessary prerequisite to our appearing anywhere. It was great fun getting Litsi into shoes, for the first time, before we all went on shore to stay; and she was so unsteady on her unaccustomed leather feet, that I had to carry the baby, for she needed her outstretched arms to balance herself, as she went clamping along and squealing, *Missi, Missi, I'll fall! I'll fall!* The native language quite interested the genteel crowd that began to gather around, while I felt disposed to register an inward vow that the next walk I took with Litsi would be 'a moonlight flitting.'

It was, however, an abiding joy to me that, during all our stay, everyone was so kind to poor dear warm-hearted Litsi. The servants, at the different houses of our friends, made quite a pet of her; and, in the coasting steamers, the ladies made no objection to her sleeping in their cabin. Litsi had exalted and very exaggerated expectations in going to the *white man's land*, the land of the missionary, where she would see only what was pure and good and holy; but, to the credit of those with whom she met, and her not being able to read the daily newspapers, she was *not* disillusionized. When we arrived at Adelaide, and she saw the royal welcome I got from my own mother and sister and all the dear ones there, it struck her in a peculiar way, which she could never get over. I was, of course, wild with delight, and flew from room to room, all talking merrily, as we were being shown over the pretty new manse, and the cousins making friends with each other. When, at last, I went upstairs to my room, there I found Litsi sitting on the floor, and sobbing like to break her heart! As I anxiously inquired the cause, she burst out: 'Missi, I never knew what you had given up to come to our dark land! I never knew you had given up a mother like that, or such a sister and brother-in-law. We did not know you lived in such beautiful homes. *I fear, I fear, you will never go back to our dark land again.*'

In truth, Litsi's remarks about civilization showed more

wide-awake intelligence, than did as a rule the white folks' remarks about heathendom. She once asked me if the Adelaideans had all quarrelled, as hardly any of them *alofa-ed* each other in passing; and, when told that they had to wait for 'introductions' before speaking, said, 'Was it not enough that they knew each other as Christians?' At one minister's house, she came to me in great consternation, and said, 'Didn't you say that Mr Blank was a Missi?' 'Yes; why?' 'Oh, you must be mistaken. Look, *he has a pipe in his mouth!*' There, sure enough, was the worthy divine, enjoying a quiet whiff in his garden. I knew that tobacco was tabooed, and for strong reasons, as an evil by the missionaries; but, not being at the moment ready to explain how it was wicked for a black man and not wicked for a white man to smoke, I mumbled something about people having sometimes to smoke 'for toothache!' And what an amount of needless sympathy poor Litsi, from day to day, lavished upon that sorely afflicted man!

To prevent misapprehension, I may here add that the *tobacco question* was brought up at the Synod by-and-bye, by the younger missionaries. They urged that it was setting up a false standard of Christian living to forbid smoking, when that was the first thing the natives would see among professed Christians whenever they visited civilized countries. The embargo was accordingly removed from the *Dayspring*, and the 'weed' may be used as an article of barter. The elder missionaries had, in their more trying conditions, good and sufficient reasons for prohibiting tobacco, specially owing to trading associations of a demoralizing character. But a time had come, when most were agreed that the prohibition was to a certain extent a hindrance to the gospel. It may, possibly at least, be reduced to harmlessness; and really, there is so much of crying and unquestioned sin around us which must, at all hazards, be forbidden and denounced, that what is not in itself *sinful* may well, in regard to practice, be relegated to the category of open questions! I gave in, long before John (if he has really given in yet!)—and it has occasioned a great deal of innocent pleasure for me to make a very modest weekly gift to my cook and herd, all the while renewing the strict injunction, 'No smoking on the premises.'

What a lot Litsi had to tell of the wonders of Missi's Land, when she returned! And all so different from the savages who had gone up with the slavers, and seen only the evils, which they are quick to imitate—for they understand, as with lightning flash, what appeals to their lower nature. Litsi has, like her father, dear old Namakei, a refined and gentle nature; so much so, that her sweet and intelligent face won all hearts. I can never be grateful enough for the ever kind and ever respectful way in which she was treated by our generous friends in the Colonies. Helen's servants used to teach her hymns, and sing them with her in the evenings in the kitchen, so that she felt quite at home. How instinctively she at once detected the difference between an intelligent interest in her, and that of those who petted her like a favourite pup that can appreciate nothing but food!

Litsi's mistress, also, experienced a mighty difference in the numerous and varied inquiries into mission life. Some such stupid questions were asked by people. My patient and praiseworthy husband set himself unweariedly to enlighten everyone, worthy and unworthy alike; and, in reply to the most outrageous questions, poured forth his soul on his beloved mission and his dear islanders. No one could imagine what may be encountered even amongst the friends of mission; once and again I heard bloodthirsty females soliloquizing thus: 'Only four missionaries murdered on Erromanga? I quite thought it was more. But they were cooked and eaten!—weren't they?'

The homecoming was just delicious. Everything that John and the darkies could think of was done to welcome us. The word WELCOME shone in great letters over the front gate. The lawn and all the grounds were in perfect order; and several alterations beautifully carried through, which I had long desired—among the rest, a day nursery and extra bedroom had been built. And withal, there was on everything that flavour of originality which only the natives can bestow—for instance, sheets spread out for tablecloths, and *vice versa*, toilet covers for towels, etc., etc.!

I had six weeks to prepare for the Mission Synod here. It passed off splendidly; for, in truth, the good men, one and all, were easily pleased and easily entertained. Seven missionaries, including the captain, came as guests; and my cooks and servants were up to the mark. Mr Inglis wrote playfully afterwards, to one of his friends, that 'they were like to die the death of Dickens—hard work and high living!' They did a great deal of solemn and important business, and needed to be well sustained, which we did to our modest best. Their meetings were held in the study, and all went happily.

My baby's baptism was, to us, the most interesting event, of course. Dear Mr Inglis, who has baptized all our children, baptized him at the close of the first Sunday service. The natives were intensely interested in seeing the first white baby baptized on their island (the others were baptized at Aneityum). But, if the stark truth must be told, the killing of a bull, next morning, carried away the palm for interest. Half the island turned out before daylight to be in at the death—which, alas, they made, as tragical as possible by firing six shots at the poor animal, and then scampering off after each, with the animal tearing after them! Mr Nelson fired the last, and the only effectual shot.

Dayspring in sight! Goodbye!

Ever yours affectionately,
MAGGIE WHITECROSS PATON.

10

Family Life and Church Life

Aniwa, New Hebrides,
1872.

Dearest Home-Friends, and Others,[1]

In the end of March last, we were greeted with awful tidings—poor Gordon killed on Erromanga! We had got over the hot season, and were eagerly preparing for the arrival of the *Dayspring*, with our yearly mail and supplies, when a boat brought over the shocking news, with a pathetic letter to John from the Christian natives there. Ataulo, Mackie, Naleen, and some other poor fellows, came in the boat, brokenhearted, and wanted to stay here altogether.

Sad to say, dear Gordon was tomahawked by a superstitious native, who regarded him as bringing disease amongst them, though they were indebted to a trading vessel for that. A confederate went along with the murderer, to give him his moral support! And that noble fellow, whom we knew and loved, has been cut down in his prime. I cannot enter upon the horrid details. A certain type of so-called *'religious'* paper will dilate on these. For us, it is all too near, and too real, and he was our brother missionary! What a difference it makes to hear of such an event from a safe distance in civilization, and to have the tragedy enacted close to your home, and by the very people, or their kindred, with whom you are every day

[1] To the family circle.

surrounded. It begets such an *eerie* feeling; and, for the time, it bred a distrust of black faces in general.

A few evenings thereafter, John having occasion to go to the boat harbour, I was too frightened to stay behind (nurses and bairns had gone on before, always in the thick of everything!); and, as we strolled home arm-in-arm in the quiet moonlight, John tried to persuade me how nice it would be to take a little time for the same thing every evening, how it would do me good, etc. He was astonished, when I informed him that he was indebted to poor Gordon for this quiet walk and talk! We have since heard that the dear Missi Gordon was just translating the *Acts of the Apostles* at the stoning of Stephen, and that, when his murderers smilingly called him out and sent him to join the noble army of the martyrs, the ink was still wet on the page at these heartbreakingly tender words, *Lord, lay not this sin to their charge.*

Our work jogs along pleasantly here; none the less so, that we—I, rather—have made a very few stern rules that must be kept. The natives about have got into our ways. I have not to chase round, as I used to do, to prevent them plucking the fowls for table *before* they are killed. This they were very fond of doing for the mere pleasure of hearing them scream! From almost the first day, I made rules about not allowing the natives generally to come into the house during our meals; or ever to go into the cookhouse, under any pretence whatever, as I don't care to have suggestions of their personality in our food. If they want to see the cook, he goes out to them. By the way, he is quite a character, that cook of ours; knows a few words of English, which he is fond of airing, and says, 'Yes, sir,' and, 'No, sir,' to me. I can't feel in my heart to bring him down from his pedestal of politeness, by correcting his mistake, and John won't, pleading that the fellow shows great penetration and knows exactly who rules the roost! One nice old man, eager to imitate the Missi in everything, began addressing me as 'Maggie, dear!' but his Reverence promptly interfered, and put a stop to that.

Our natives are very amusing in many of their ways; and, though often provoking and disappointing we do not lose heart, as we might do with white people, remembering that in these respects they are only children after all. We manage to keep our bairns, in a large measure, separate from the native children, for weighty reasons, but it requires a little engineering to prevent them from feeling it. The front of our house is quite fenced off, and the side gates are locked, so that they play about by themselves, or with their nurses; and, on Sundays, we are entirely free of visitors. On this latter subject I had more bother with the Missi than with the natives. He maintained, of course, that we are here for their benefit, which I heartily agree to, and for six days in the week I am their devoted servant in Christ, at their beck and call; but, in his name, I claim this one day, so far as its domestic life is concerned, to be unreservedly given up to our little ones.

We, thus, can preserve *our family life* even in the midst of heathendom. After church services and Sunday Schools are over, and the natives who prefer to remain are supplied with piles of picture books, which they immensely enjoy sprawling at full length on the grass, the Paton family have a sweet and blessed time under our shady front veranda. Books for our bairns are read aloud, followed by question and hymn and happy talks; and we ourselves, bathing in these fountains of love human and divine, are rested and refreshed for the duties of an approaching week.

In fact, we keep far better friends with our natives, by getting rid of them occasionally, and doing so without hurting their feelings. We explained tenderly how much we enjoyed their company, sometimes; but asked them to think, if they were in a foreign land and had to talk incessantly in a foreign language, whether they wouldn't like to have part of one day in the week to themselves, with their own family, and speaking their mother tongue; and to this they heartily agree. I fear I am regarded rather as a *law* unto these poor people around us; but then, you see, John is the embodiment of the glorious *gospel*; so their theological surroundings are tolerably complete!

Another rule I fought for, after being three years on Aniwa, was—that no one should enter the church, without what appeared to me a decent covering. John was unfeignedly thankful to get them there to hear the gospel, in almost any condition; but I maintained that we too had a right to church privileges, as well as the natives; and that I could not worship the Lord in his sanctuary, with practically naked people stuck right in front of us, nor was it good for our children. So the Missi was at last induced to fire off another of my bullets amongst his 'beloved flock.' He solemnly announced in the church assembly, that the few who still came unclothed would, in future, have to put on something, were it only a fathom of calico, which they all had, or could easily secure by doing a little work; that, a month's warning being given, thereafter no naked or painted person would be allowed to enter the church. There were only three or four natives who were in the habit of coming unclothed, and it wasn't fair to the others to let them ride off in that way, and defy our Christian custom.

When the month was up, and we were assembling in the church, there slipped in a heathen, clothed in nothing but the most startling war paint! I spotted our friend, and vowed he should not escape the missionary's notice either; so, when John had finished reading the hymn, and looked across for me to begin, he found his harmoniumist leaning calmly back with folded arms. His amazed face said as plainly as possible, 'What's the row?' I gave a slight inclination of the head in the direction of the painted individual; and John at once took action by requesting him to leave the church, since he had had full notice to quit this heathenism in the house of God. The gentleman, however, had no more intention of leaving the church than I had of beginning the hymn. It was a question of which would win, and soon began to be exciting. Had I been 'given to betting,' as they say, I would have backed 'our side' to any amount!

John repeated his request firmly, but very kindly, setting forth the reasonableness of such a regulation; this was enforced by earnest whisperings all around, while our young hero sat complacently grinning, with his chin resting on his knees! The Missi then began quietly to collect his books, saying that he never made a rule that he did not mean to be obeyed, and would therefore now leave the church, and worship with his family in the mission house. That, however, would not be tolerated, as the young man gathered from the ferocious looks directed against him; and, on the chief of his district being seen to move with serious intentions of ejectment, the big fellow swung out of the building like lightning, carrying his dirty nakedness with him, and the service went on with something of Christian seemliness.

That same afternoon, John being at a preaching in this man's village, the poor savage had got one side of his face washed, and turned it to the missionary; but he was told to sit right round and make himself quite comfortable, as there were no rules to exclude any one from open-air services. To do him justice, he joined heartily in the laughter that greeted this sally; and he has become one of the very best fellows we have, since coming off second best in this little tussle.

I have my sewing and singing classes on our front veranda, which is a vast improvement for me, there being a constant current of air, which wafts away the odour of Ethiopia. It is quite pronounced enough in the open air, and was overpowering in the schoolroom. I have used more *Eau-de-Cologne* here, than I did before in all my life (I disliked scent in civilization), and would have ruined my poor husband if I'd had to buy it; but kind friends, who evidently knew better what I was coming to than I did myself, loaded me with gifts and have kept me supplied ever since.

We have had a rare influx of missionaries this year, actually four new ones; three from Nova Scotia, and one from Melbourne, who made a romantic marriage with Dr Geddie's daughter on Aneityum. They had plenty to do, at the mission conference, locating them; and the children and I spent the time with dear Mrs Watt at Kwamera; Mrs Milne, a gem of a missionary's wife, being also one of the visitors. She and Mr Milne happened to be on a visit to us, when she came of age; and there was great joking about being independent of her husband now!

The three weeks at Kwamera just flew past. Everything was so charming, the perfection of a mission station in all its workings. And what a magnificent island is Tanna, with its majestic mountains, rich vegetation, fine rivers, and last, but not least, its grand old volcano—a huge pillar of cloud by day and of fire by night (the best lighthouse in the world, the sailors say), and as restless as the ocean, sending up tons of lava into the air about every ten minutes, with a rumble that often shakes our house even on Aniwa! The seascape here is a perpetual study—Kwamera being on the weather side of Tanna, the breakers are the grandest I have ever seen. I wish I could describe them as we saw them. We used to sit for hours (mind, we were on holiday!) watching the majestic progress of the mountainous waves, as they rolled obliquely along the reefs, the pale green deepening into shadow as they curved round before breaking, with mighty roar into a sea of boiling surf.

We made a charming visit, one day, to a village three miles inland. The scenery was romantic; and we chose to go a part of our way right through the river, which flows swiftly and gently down its broad bed, forming a lovely vale between towering heights, covered with luxuriant creepers, ferns, and foliage down to the water's edge. It was such fun to leap from one great flat stone to another, with the clear water flowing all around us; but we often paused to look up at the grand heights above, and drink in the beauty of the scene; there was strange power, too, in the silence over all! Here and there, where the glen narrowed, were beautiful waterfalls. Mrs Watt and I got through all, springing over the ground like wildcats; but Mrs Blank kept us in great merriment, accompanying her slower progress with a succession of shrieks, and frantic appeals to the natives for help; and, finally, she capped the events of the day by tumbling off a Tanna man's back flat into the river! The spirit of girlhood was on us, and Mrs Watt and I sank helpless on the nearest stone,—and went off into fits of mischievous laughter.

A scene of a very different kind was being enacted, that very afternoon, on the same island, as we heard a few days later by letters from Port Resolution. A trader's vessel had anchored there; and the notorious Captain H. went tipsy to Mrs N.'s, knowing her husband to be absent at the mission conference, and tried his best to insult her. The Aneityumese servants were away cutting wood, and she fled to the *Imrai*—a Christian lady seeking the protection of the savages against her own degraded countryman! They guarded her well, and drove the wretch back to his boat. In rage, he declared that he would return at midnight. But the house, and the boat landing, were loyally watched by night and by day; though that did not prevent Mrs N., and her young sister, the bride, from being kept in misery and terror, till, three days after, the vessel and its hateful captain cleared out to sea.

Our return to Aniwa was a sad one, owing to dear Namakei's death, while away at the Mission Conference on

Aneityum. There was hardly a dry eye, when John preached his funeral sermon next Sunday; and his was, I suppose, the largest mission funeral on record in the New Hebrides, the captain and the whole Synod having followed the remains of the grand old man to their last resting place. We do so miss him here; he was such a lovable friend; and his passionate devotion to the 'little white chief' was really pathetic.

The mission settlement that stirred our hearts most was that on Erromanga. It is very brave of Mr and Mrs Robertson to tackle that martyr island, all alone. We had a delightful visit from them in September. They came in their boat, a distance of over forty miles, and had a stormy and perilous passage; they lost their rudder, and, when they should have been landing at the mission station toward evening, they found themselves on the wrong side, the weather side, of Aniwa, and had to battle with the breakers the livelong night, rudderless and tempest-tossed. Right thankful were they to reach this, next morning, as it was all that Mr Robertson could do to keep up the courage of the natives, and prevent the boat from being smashed among the reefs. They say here that 'a special providence watches over fools and *missionaries*'—and we have often much reason to think it true!

Those visits of our brother missionaries are truly like angels' visits, in more than in their rarity. It is so delightful to have intercourse with kindred spirits (by the way, does that suggest that *we* are angels? Well, let it!), and with whom we have so much in common. We do not by any means 'talk shop' all the time; but it is so uplifting to have enlightened converse about our work, get the benefit of each other's experience, and compare the traditions and legends of our respective islands. During one of these visits, from the Watts, I think, we were comparing notes, and I called in our girls for further information. To my intense delight, the younger girls, who had grown up mostly with us, knew nothing at all about them, showing that our teaching had really taken the place of their heathen superstitions. So we called in some elderly Aniwans who immediately waxed eloquent, and greatly interested us in their traditions. They have, for instance, one about the Flood; and this not only tallies strangely in some details with the biblical account, but, what is more striking, it points exactly the same moral, or nearly so.

You can have no idea how companionable the natives are, when once you can talk to them freely. Their faces light up with such intelligence; and they are eager both to hear and to communicate. Pictures they are wonderfully fond of; we spend many an hour explaining them, and can get a good deal of gospel truth into them, in that way, without seeming to preach. But they don't, by any means, take everything on trust. They must be convinced, before believing all you say. Once I described to a lot of women how water got so cold in Britain that it froze, and became so solid and hard that the people ran about on the top of it. I saw perfectly in their looks that they did not believe it, though too respectful to say so. It so happened that the *Dayspring* called the very next day; and what should Dr Geddie bring on shore, but a huge block of ice! Some kind friends in Melbourne had put a refrigerating machine on board; and Dr Geddie had some ice prepared for each mission station, well knowing what a treat it would be to us, as well as an interest to the natives. What crowds came to examine it! They touched it; they howled wildly over their first experience of real freezing cold; and they eagerly yet sorrowfully marked it melting away. I made the women confess their unbelief of the evening before; but they added, with pawky grace worthy of a Scot, *We did not believe you would lie, Missi! We just thought that somebody else had told you crooked.*

John has been trying to make the 'crooked' paths of the Aniwans straight, shortening the distance betwixt us and the boat harbour by clearing a direct road for the hand cart, instead of the very circuitous one they had been accustomed to travel. When, however, it was finished, they simply howled with disgust at the awful *length* of it! It was in reality one-third shorter; but simply because they could now see it all at once, they persistently argued that it was ever so much longer, nor could be convinced till Missi tested it by a walking match. He preached a good practical sermon to them, next Sunday, about God's tender wisdom in hiding so much of our earthly future from our view—we see not all the road we have to travel in dust and pain!

Nearly all the natives wear clothing now. This is a great index of change; for, in the heathen state, they are positively as ashamed at the idea of wearing anything, as we would be at the idea of proposing to go naked. But the men have not yet donned the 'nether' garments, as they say they are frightened for them! There is nothing they so much covet as a warm blanket or bed quilt, for they feel chilly at night (I wish we could, instead of feverish!), and they love to roll themselves up before going to sleep.

One day, a dear child was brought to us, evidently in the last stages of croup. There was not a moment to be lost, in getting her into the hottest bath. In my eagerness, I snatched the blanket off my own bed, to keep in the steam and to wrap round the sufferer. This, in a cooler moment, I would not have done, as it was my very best, and one of the fine downy ones bound with ribbon that Aunt E. gave me as a wedding gift. I would not undertake to say, whether these parents were more pleased about the care of the child, or the possession of the blanket. The sequel was characteristic. A greedy old fellow over six feet, with shoulders to match, presented himself spontaneously as a patient, and demanded a hot bath from the *Missi-finé*. We laughed, and assured Taia that there wasn't a vessel big enough to hold him, unless he went into one of the tanks. As he still insisted on a bath, we began to fear he had gone crazy; but light dawned on the method of his madness, when he ingenuously added, 'Well, if you won't give me the bath, the same kind of blanket you gave the child the other day will do!'

You would laugh to see that great huge-framed Taia—our native orator, and right glad of any decent excuse for wagging his beloved tongue. He rolls out the sentences in a grandiose style. He has just to let himself go in delivering an oration, and you immediately see that the Aniwan language can give scope for elocution and relief to pent-up feelings. Our own little boys seem to take after Taia, for they grow amazingly eloquent, gesticulate at a great rate, and act out everything they narrate—helping their English talk with an Aniwan or Aneityumese word, to enforce their meaning, which certainly colours brilliantly what they say.

We were talking, the other evening, about the Last Judgment, and what the Bible says about the world's being 'burnt up.' Our little Frank interjected, 'And won't it *Kopuko*, Mamma?' That means to 'go off like a cannon.' In these circumstances, his main concern turned out to be this, whether his favourite wheelbarrow would 'go off' in the general conflagration; and he argued, very decidedly, that in such a case it was only fair that he should 'get a new one in heaven!'

But you will see that I am as weak as mothers elsewhere, when I assure you that it charms me to hear the Bible stories we have taught them represented to us in the language and in the ideas of childhood. One day, after talking about our Lord's death and burial, little F. said so earnestly, 'But he *rised* again, Mamma; 'cause he said to Thomson (? Thomas), Look what the naughty peoples did to me!'—and he pointed to his hands, with a suggestive expression in his eyes.

They have decided ideas of their own on theology; and our little three-year-old flatly refuses to be charged with Adam's transgression. I was, for example, reading *Peep o' Day*, and trying to explain how that sin of our first parent had made us all wicked; but it would not go down in any form I could present it, and the child ended the lecture at that time by a positive protest, *I'se not naughty! I did never eat de fruit!*

I fear I could go on about these things *ad libitum* but, fortunately for you, my time is not inexhaustible, though your loving patience may be. And so, as our natives would say, *My word is ended.*

Ever affectionately yours,
MAGGIE WHITECROSS PATON.

II

The Shipwreck and the Angel-Child

Port Jackson, Sydney Harbour,
29 September, 1873.

My Dearest Mother, Brothers, and Sisters,[1]

I address you all, as this is to be the 'big' letter, and to go the rounds from Adelaide.

We arrived here last night, have all packed, and are ready to go ashore. John is much better, and everybody declares he will soon be able to dispense with both his crutches, or rather sticks!

I suppose I had better go back and narrate things in order; but I hardly know where to begin; especially as I did not get letters written for last December, when the dear old *Dayspring*, left us, and got wrecked on Aneityum, four or five days afterwards. John and the boys, Bob and Fred, had been with her in the trip north, never dreaming it was to be her last voyage round our islands.

While they were away from us, we had quite an exciting time, one way and another. For one thing, there was a welcome visit from Mr F. A. Campbell (son of the minister at Geelong), who came down in the *Dayspring* for his health, and stayed with us a fortnight, before going to the

[1] To the family circle.

Watts at the beginning of the season; and, as John had to go in the vessel on 'deputation work,' we begged of the Watts to accompany him over here, since the natives would not have thought it proper for me to receive him alone! So they all came in Mr Watt's boat, towed across by a wee trading steamer, which was subsequently smashed to pieces in the hurricane. We all enjoyed ourselves so much; rather too much, for my correspondence fell behind. I was so tempted to chat endlessly with dear Mrs Watt, knowing that I had the whole year round to write letters, and so seldom a lady visitor to enliven our solitude. Mr Campbell is fond of music; and so we had the old harmonium in from the church, and he brought music out of it indeed. He copied also my painting of the *Dayspring*, and made some fine drawings of island scenery, to be reproduced in illustrating a volume of his tour, which he intends to publish on his return. Altogether, we spent a very pleasant fortnight, which would indeed have been perfect, if only John had been at home.

Again, just before these visitors came, Litsi had her firstborn son and heir, which put us all here into a fever of excitement, she being such a universal favourite, and having been too weak to walk for months before. I was, of course, apprehensive of the consequences. It proved to be a very lingering affair; and there was a good deal of extemporized telegraphing betwixt her house and ours, a five minutes' walk; and not a little dodging to keep all quiet from the native boys, and yet get the cook to keep up the fire and hot water after tea. When I told him that I expected the boat (Mr Watt's) would come over in such fine moonlight, though I really did expect it, the girls rushed out to the veranda to let off steam! Of course, it would be enough to tell a civilized servant that you required hot water kept, but our natives would open their eyes very wide and ask, *What for?* And as, in the circumstances, I could not say what it was for—you know it would ruin any fellow's character here for life to be thought so weak as to help a woman—the boat served as a good excuse and a true one, for we had all been looking for it the evening before. But during my writing class, which I have in the evenings for those natives on the mission premises who can't go to John's morning school, I had very hard work to keep grave, while the girls kept on asking, every now and again, with a mischievous twinkle in their black eyes, *if the boat had arrived*!

I kept away from the seat of war, though sundry hints reached me that my presence there would be very acceptable; and I contented myself with sending warm drinks. But, in the middle of the prayer at worship, when one of the head boys was praying, poor Litsi's husband, a great fellow of over six feet, came tapping at the window of the next room, and pled with me to go to Litsi or she would die! There was nothing for it but to slip off with him, though I would rather have gone ten miles the other way. I found Litsi well looked after by her female friends, and bantered her about having a fine young son when she said she was going to die, adding, for her encouragement, that I said the same thing myself before Bob was born. Suddenly, a man's voice close by me said in very interested tones, 'Did you, Missi?' I could have annihilated the fellow, and, you may depend on it, I was rather more scarce of my experiences, with a male audience so unexpectedly near. I saw there was nothing which I could really do for Litsi; and, being a little nervous, I suddenly remembered that no one else could be trusted to make the gruel at the mission house for her. But she persisted, *Pray first, Missi!*—and, seizing my hand, affectionately held it all the time.

Walking back in the clear moonlight, thinking anxiously and praying for dear Litsi, I heard shouts of merriment from our half-open windows, and someone stalking out to the back, as if he would knock the floor through, at every step.

I hastened in, and found Telmonoutha, the boy who had prayed at worship, disappearing through the pantry-door and the girls leaning over the table in fits of laughter. They told me that he had uttered a very long and a very beautiful prayer (oh, how those boys' prayers during John's absence used to bring the tears to my eyes, the way they asked God to let nothing in the seas hurt their Missi, and nothing on the land hurt him etc., etc.!), but that Telmonoutha was awfully enraged for having made it all for 'these black-hearted girls,' as he contemptuously called them, and for not letting him know that I had gone! They demanded, in turn, how they could have let him know while he was praying; and, having no answer ready, he strode out in bursting indignation.

After another visit or two to Litsi, her uncle and aunt came rushing to tell me that her baby was born, and was a boy! I uttered a very fervent 'Thank God,' to which Kalangi, the uncle, responded so earnestly, 'O Missi, that's the very thing I said myself—for, you know, it might have been a *girl*!' I let them know pretty roundly that it was not the gender I was thankful for; and then ran back to Litsi whom I found sitting clasping her firstborn, as if she would never let him go; and *greeting* [*Scotticé* for weeping] indignantly at the remembrance of her sorrows, like a bairn after a thrashing. Poor Litsi, she had to lay her child in the grave, three months after, as sweet and lovely a child as mother ever loved; and, next Sabbath thereafter, at the Communion, the father looked so broken-hearted, and wore so pale a face, that I can never forget him.

This was in the middle of February; but I have not told you of the *hurricane* on January 6th. Of course, you have all heard about the dear little *Dayspring* having been lost in it; and some missionary will explain to you all about the atmosphere, the barometer, etc., so I shall limit myself to how we got on in Aniwa. John and the boys had just returned. The

Dayspring had taken off our visitors a few days before, along with our yearly order and mail, and we had enjoyed a quiet Sabbath all together again. The boys and girls had been looking over all sorts of *British Workman, Pictorial News,* etc., while John and I explained them, and all went off to bed, thinking of anything but hurricanes, our barometer having been broken some time before, and had left books and everything lying about. We generally make special preparation for threatened hurricanes, by tying down thatch, propping walls, and so forth; but we had not begun this year, as hurricanes were never known before January 12th, and so we hoped for secure and peaceful sleep.

Shortly after we had retired, the wind began to rise, and continued to rise very high; and, by midnight, we resolved to escape from the mission house. It was shaking ominously, the roof gave signs of falling in, and so we all took refuge in the cellar, the girls carrying blankets with them, and a large mattress for the children. What an exciting journey that was, out at the study door and down the steps to the cellar, for we expected to be crushed to pieces by something or other falling, and we had to shout into each other's ears, the noise of the wind was so deafening! But we felt comparatively snug, when we got into the cellar and had a lamp lit and placed in a sheltered corner, hearing the wind roaring outside like distant thunder. Litsi with her baby, then three weeks old, and a lot of people took refuge with us; while John kept me in painful suspense, taking down pictures, securing doors and windows, and trying to cover his precious bookcases with blankets; but even he was forced to desist, at the risk of life. The children, realizing no danger, were delighted at the novelty; and I myself felt rather jolly too, when we got John safely beside us; and then the natives began spinning yarns about the last hurricane they remembered, while the door was being opened, now and again, to admit some poor drenched character, with his head buried between his shoulders, and a roaring gust of wind that deafened us all for the moment, or letting someone out to reconnoitre.

About four o'clock, John took me up from the cellar to have a look at the hurricane, and really it was appallingly grand! The spray dashed blindingly in our faces, a quarter of a mile distant from the sea. Trees and branches were lying around, piled up in mountains, and the tall cocoa-nuts were swinging like slender willows before the awful gale. But the most disagreeable experience of all was in the cold grey morning light, when we put out the cellar lamps, and crawled up to our house. The wind had spent its fury, but its work had been effectually accomplished. Everything in our dear home was soaking wet, and covered inches thick with thatch and all imaginable rubbish. Windows were smashed in with branches of trees hurled against them; and there was not one spot within the whole premises on which you could sit.

I set to work, at once, with my girls, and got the dining room made habitable. We said to cook that we would not mind for breakfast; and that, if they could only manage to milk the goats, we would just take bread and milk; as the cookhouse door had been blockaded, and not a bit of dry wood could be found anywhere. But hardly had we finished this apology when the good soul appeared with the coffeepot steaming; so we had a hot breakfast after all, and were all greatly comforted.

After this, I went on to the front veranda to have a look at the *débris* outside, and never had I witnessed such a scene of devastation,—great trees torn up by the roots; bananas and fences laid level with the ground; hardly a green leaf anywhere to be seen, the salt spray having browned everything, and caused them to droop; and scarcely a yard of clear space anywhere to walk upon. One sight, however, made me clap my hands with delight; for there, in the near distance, the tremendous waves were dashing on the reef, and I had a seaview at last!

We had got an apology for one before, but it was soon hidden again. I got it enlarged afterwards, by appealing to the owners of that spot to continue the work of the hurricane by levelling a few more trees, and so giving me a sight of the *Dayspring* when she passed; for I was always so busy, getting food ready for the expected visitors, that I had no time to run with the rest to see the ship, when the cry *Sail ho!* gladdened our ears. I made my appeal to the man whom I considered the softest but he was rather obtuse, until I hinted that there would be good pay for every tree cut down. Then he understood all my sentiments thoroughly, and loudly declared that it was a shame that *Missi the Woman* could not see her own vessel, when she was working for them all the year round; but that it would not be his fault, if she did not get a sight of it very soon! Others followed, when they saw what Taia got. About forty trees, I think, were cut down. So that we had the first view of the *Paragon* from our own veranda; and we see the sun setting there in glory, from April till the end of July.

John was not at all ambitious of the view of the *Paragon*, and had often assured us that, if the *Dayspring* were in Aneityum Harbour during that hurricane, we need never expect to see her, as nothing could save her (which, alas, proved to be the case!), but that if she were in the open sea there might be a chance. The natives, however, all had the firm idea that the *vessel of the worship* could never go down; and I too hoped with them, till we heard by Mr Watt's boat, on the last day of February, that it had during the hurricane gone on the reef in Aneityum Harbour. Our natives all cried about it like children for weeks on end, and they often take fits of doing so since; while my girls went to the study and wailed for a whole evening before the photo of it hanging there, and this they have kept up, going periodically. I had great difficulty in taking in the sad news and John was distressingly sad. The *Dayspring* had become part and parcel of ourselves, and none of us could imagine the New Hebrides Mission without its little ship—'to wait on him,' and do his work still as of old. Still, even in this 'severity' there mingled 'goodness'; for it could never have been wrecked at a better place or time. All were saved, and our mail too; besides, she was going for provisions, instead of returning full of them, which would have made a mighty difference to us all.

By the way, we had our first appearance of a home spring, after the hurricane; for, when all the dead leaves and branches were cleared away and pruned, everything began to bud—so refreshing and homelike, after the perpetual green of these isles. I do not know, also, whether the greater exposure from the want of trees made us more susceptible of cold; but, certain it is, we have since all suffered severely from ague and fever, before comparatively unknown here. Several times, before his attack of sciatica, dear John was raving with delirium, while the hot fit of the ague was on him. Nearly all the natives, too, were ill, and our quinine went 'like snow off a dyke.'

But our experiences are not exhausted yet. We had a terrible *earthquake* on the first evening of February, nearly a month after the hurricane. There can be no upturn in nature so awful as an earthquake. The hurricane was nothing to it, in the feeling, though in our case much more serious in the consequences; for the earthquake did nothing worse that I heard of than knock down the chimney of Mr Inglis's cook-house, though it shook all our islands. We had just retired to bed, very exhausted, and leaving the boys and girls to finish their copies in the dining room; when, suddenly, the whole house began swaying from side to side, and the floor heaved below us for fully two minutes. John sprang out of bed at the first movement, but I, brave woman that I was, held on to him like a vice, so that he could not move to do anything! The natives rushed in upon us without ceremony, and we could hear others shouting from their houses. One of the boys, who was in the act of writing, determined to finish his letter, but the motion sent the pen sprawling across all his copy. Little Litsi, big Litsi's cousin, and a dear child, had the presence of mind to seize the lamp as it was falling. John, as he was held a prisoner himself, directed the natives to open the windows, always the first thing to be done, for fear of them being jammed up and we unable to escape! We really expected the Judgment Day to follow; but our little lambs slept calmly through it all.

Oh, how often, in our last hot season's experiences, have I thought of Elijah and the great wind, but the Lord was not in the wind, and the earthquake, we too were to hear *the still small voice* in another way! This brings me to the subject that is ever uppermost in my heart, and which I felt ought to be written about first of all when I sat down; but I would fain pass over it now, for it opens the wound afresh, which seems as if it never would quite heal here below.

Our angel-child was given to us on March 28th, and oh, what joy she brought to the whole household! We thought Frank would have kissed her to pieces in his delight, and none of us ever saw such a beautiful child. I so wish you could all have seen her, for anything I can say now will very naturally be attributed to our sacred remembrances. And yet we wondered at her beauty, when no one dreamt of her being taken, as she seemed the strongest of them all. We had great joking about who she got it from; and bantering each other about her very wee mouth, which seemed buried in her fat cheeks. Everything seemed to go on nicely; and though we were both very weak, I had arranged accordingly, and got a teacher's wife to come for a month, and had everything in order, not omitting, of course, many lectures to our girls, as to keeping true to their posts, etc.

On that Saturday forenoon—the last, I fear, of our bright days on Aniwa—we were congratulating ourselves on the quiet rest we were having, after the advent and the excitement of the previous day. John was lying on the sofa, with blankets round him, trying to stave off the fever and ague, and getting a rest after all his trotting about and anxiety; and the cause of it all was lying peacefully in her nurse's arms, being told what a wonderful little woman she was. The house itself looked like a new pin, as I had stopped my sewing class nearly a fortnight before to get through with the great annual cleaning; and what a cleaning that was! I was not allowed to do anything in it, having suffered from haemorrhage all the hot season; so I sat, and *tatted*, and directed—only putting to my hand when my careful little man was out of the way.

He himself, indeed, had far more to do than he ought; and, that very Saturday night, he was struck down in the most awful agony, in an instant; but, as I got a fright about something a few minutes after—or, just let me explain what the something was. A great ugly rat fell on the top of my bed, from the thatch, and, knowing that that was enough at any time to drive me frantic, he sprang up and killed it. That was his last action for weeks—not a very sublime effort, if he had died in the succeeding illness; and the exertion did him very great harm, for he was unable to get back to his couch for several minutes, and stood holding on to the corner of my bed, his face perfectly livid with excruciating agony. He did get to the sofa, somehow; but the groans, which he could not suppress, were heart-rending; and there he lay, without daring to move one inch, for two full days. At the end of that time, one of the native teachers tried to get him undressed; but, though he was kindness itself, his movements suggested the idea of a bull in a china shop, so I did not press him into service again!

What we would have done without Bob, I know not; for

he was a perfect treasure for attentiveness to his Papa, till I was able to be up again. That night he took ill, I thought we were all going to die; for I got into such a fever of nervous excitement, I really felt the blood coursing along my veins, while my heart beat so wildly that I thought it must soon burst in twain. I would have given anything for some white person to come and take care of us. But, in the midst of all, I felt that God would watch over us; and I prayed for a quiet mind. I resolutely set myself to look at the bright side only; and, to aid me in this, I counted over my blessings, one by one, like a child, and, as I remember, *Lena* (Helena Elizabeth Whitecross, but Lena was the pet name) came in as one of the biggest and sweetest!

Next morning, Sabbath, I felt delightfully calm, and was enabled to become comforter to my dear husband, who was still in awful suffering. The native teachers conducted the worship—that being the first Sunday that John had been absent from church, on Aniwa, unless when from home altogether; and he did not get back to it for ten long weary weeks. So I set myself to what appeared to me then a most formidable undertaking, the washing and dressing of my baby; and, propped up with pillows, I got through with the help of the natives, without the little lamb crying at all, which was considered quite a triumph! My girls too were very kind and attentive, and seemed suddenly transformed into old women; they brought in our meals, and superintended our children in the dining room so nicely, making Bob sit in his Papa's chair and 'ask the blessing.' Truly God 'stayeth his rough wind in the day of his east wind'; but the worst was yet to come, and we had to part from our newly found treasure, on the sixth day after she was born.

On the day before that, the Tuesday, I fainted while washing the dear baby; and we think she must have then caught her fatal cold, for she was exposed, while poor John from his helpless couch was directing the natives how to bring me round; and that night she refused the breast. I thought her mouth was sore; and, after a great deal of bungling with the natives, they brought me the borax and honey, with which I rubbed her mouth. I thought my heart would have broken, about a fortnight after, when I found the paper of borax as I was tidying up the room!

Towards morning, we heard a stifled sound through her nose; and John, forgetting his pain, struggled on to his elbow, and heated water in the spirit lamp, while I roused the natives to prepare a hot bath. I wrapped her in flannel after it, and did everything we could think of, fondly hoping she would soon be all right, as it evidently was not croup, being all in the head. John feared greatly from the first, though he did not tell me, alarmed by her stoutness. I got her to take her natural nourishment, and felt so delighted, the last time I fed her in the afternoon that she took more than she had done that day. She looked about her so peacefully, and opened her dark blue eyes wider than ever I had seen them; but I told her Papa that her features were getting a pinched look. He said that was not to be wondered at, as she had taken so little food during the last twenty-four hours. I just thought that might be so, as I could not see plainly in the darkened room; and I sat with her awhile on my knee, before giving her to the nurse.

About half an hour afterwards, they brought in our tea; but I put mine to a side, saying, 'I'll feed my baby first.' I took her from Nurse Williang's arms, who had her in a snug corner at the side of my bed; but, oh, the cold chill that went to my heart the first look I got at her face! There is a look about death, that is not to be mistaken; and it almost made my own heart stand still, before I could believe it true. The eyes were shut, and the little mouth open, and no sound when I put my ear close. In an agony, I felt for the little heart, for the skin was burning hot, and I could not believe that the life had gone; but all was *so* still! I looked twice at Williang, being unable to utter a word; but she was watching me with such mournful eyes; and, when I clutched her arm, she sank down on her knees, crying, *I know it, Missi, I know it! She gave two sighs and died just before you took her.*

What a death-knell that sounded in my heart. But, even then, I could not give up hope, and tried her with a few drops of milk. That was enough—it was like dropping it into an empty cup. How the sounds around me struck on my ear, even in that anguished moment, as being so unlike such a time! The children were shouting and laughing on the veranda, the girls singing about the house; and John, feeling a little relieved, was talking carelessly to a native teacher; while I was trying to realize, and all in one dread moment, that my child was actually dead. I took a few instants to follow her little spirit into the Unknown Land, gave an inward cry for strength, and then began to break the news to John, in his helplessness, as gently as I could. It was truly a night of anguish. I could have borne it better, could I have had a clasp of my dear husband's hand. But it was a blessing that he was at least in the same room; for his prayers, and his words of comfort, were most precious to my soul.

The children cried themselves sick; and I envied them, poor things, for I could get no tears to come! I thought not then of my own loss; but felt as if I had let my child go away alone, out into the dark, where I could not follow her. Perhaps it was as well that I had no time to indulge such thoughts; for I had to rack my brain to find out how, in the circumstances, we could get her decently buried. We might as well have asked any of the natives to make a ship, as to make a coffin. So, at grey daylight, Bob took one of the teachers away to the empty box-house, to look for one suitable; but Fred brought his clothes box that his Papa had made him; and, as it was the thing above all others that he valued, I liked to see him give it up to his little silent sister. Bob had given his before for her little outfit.

The church members and the natives around all came to the funeral, dressed in their best, and were let in to near the grave by a side gate, as we sent word that we were both too weak to speak to them. We had prayers in our room, before the precious remains were carried out. And then, for the first time, after all my matter-of-fact planning and arranging—even to telling the man how to dig the grave—my natural feelings would assert themselves, and I had to get back the little coffin into my bed! The native teacher laid it at my side, and fell down on his knees sobbing; while I got nearer to my God over my child's lifeless body than ever I had done before in all my life.

Poor Fred was exhausted with sheer grief; and when I begged him to go with Bob to his little sister's funeral, that some of her own might be there, he sobbed out, 'Mamma, my knees won't carry me!' He brightened up, however, and went, when he heard it was in our own premises—a lovely quiet corner, not seen from any approach to the house, nor indeed till you go up to it. We distinctly heard the singing at the service over the grave, the hymns being our translations of 'There is a Happy Land' and 'Oh, May We Stand before the Lamb.'

What a desolate home, and what desolate hearts, the little unconscious lamb left behind her, and how effectually she had established herself in our love, without ever trying to do it! I kept thinking about the German pastor, and that story of the parents who would not go into the fold, till their lamb was taken and put there first; and, though I hope I have been there already, yet our Lena constrained us to think of the world unseen, in a way that I, at least, had never done before. It all came on us so suddenly, illness and death; and oh, it is truly the King of Terrors—that mighty power, so silently

Dr and Mrs J. G. Paton and family, around 1887.

The chief and teachers of Aniwa.

The church of Aniwa.

Mission station and group of Christians,
Erromanga.

Margaret Whitecross Paton.

The Rev. Frederick Paton (1900).

The Rev. Frank L. Paton and Mrs Paton (1907).

The grandchildren of Dr John and Mrs Margaret Paton.

Dr John G. Paton and grandson.

The new *Dayspring* (1895); the original was wrecked in 1873.

doing its awful work by our very side, and we knowing it not till our little treasure was gone!

I felt sometimes as if I did not know where she had gone—for awful doubts assailed me in regard to infant salvation, and I came nigh to losing my reason over it. I never doubted, till I was tried myself; and it is not so easy to take things for granted with one's own. John managed, somehow, to get me *Logan's* book out of the study; but I felt like smiling at the bare idea of any mortal satisfying me on such a momentous subject. It was a question that I must settle with my God and my Bible; and at last I got perfect relief by resting it all on the compassion of my Saviour. He loved her, and loves her, infinitely better than I; and he could not be unkind. I mean to read *Logan*, however, too; as it will really be a comfort to know how other Christians felt in like circumstances; or, in like bereavements rather, for I hope not very many have been situated as we were.

We used to long so for some kind Christian friend to look in upon us; for, in time of affliction, the natives are exactly the opposite of white people; and, instead of sympathizing and helping in trouble, they shy off, and fear that Jehovah or Tiapolo is fighting with you, if they happen to be advanced enough to have lost faith in witchcraft, and that it is therefore prudent to look on from a safe distance! I do not say that this is the way our natives acted by any means, for they were truly kind; still it is their pervading feeling, and we felt that through all our troubles there was a damper on the worship.

Hitherto, there had been everything to commend it, in the eyes of a native. The Missi had been strong. His family were thriving. The Missi's wife had had more children in her time than any other woman in Aniwa, and most of them boys too! Then, there was no comparison in regard to his and their wisdom and worldly possessions. Now, all was different. The Missi was laid low; and his *Tavai Biritania*—that is, British Water (= Medicine)—could not save him. Death had entered his family, and he was powerless to prevent it. Even the very elements seemed to conspire against him, to prevent his being able to send for a brother missionary from Tanna. And, at a feast, one of the darkest-hearted fellows, one of the very few who didn't come to church, got up and proposed they should throw off the worship, as it was only bringing sickness and death among them, after all they had given up for it. Fortunately, however, the gospel had now too good a footing, and his motion was not even seconded. Nay, if our church members could have shown their indignation by bringing fire down from heaven, Tupaia, for that was his name, would have had small chance of escape.

They were truly kind to us, and would come in and say, 'Missi, we are crying about you, and praying all the time!' One day, a dear old woman, one of our first church members, came into the bedroom, with the tears streaming down her withered cheeks, just a day or two after I had got up, and held John's hand, taking no notice of me for a while, though I was sitting on the bed; and I hoped she would not speak to me, for my heart was fluttering at the sight of her, being one of my sewing class that I had given up to attend to the little lamb that was gone. At last, she turned right round to me and said, in Aniwan, *'And your baby died, Missi!'* There was such mother-like sorrow in her voice, that I burst into a great flood of tears, and the dear old body clasped her arms around me and held me to her heart.

Dear John got back to his own bed, when I got up on the tenth day. But the fatigue of being moved—the natives were awkward about it, and I had no strength even to stand upright—did him no good. Still, what a blessing I felt it to be able to do even ever so little to nurse my own husband, and relieve poor little Bob, who was worn out with his exertions! My first effort was to crawl into the study for a medical book.

It had been most tantalizing, during our illness, to see the study door standing wide open, with the bookcases almost in sight, and no one able to fetch us the right volume. John got rapidly worse; and, a fortnight after he took ill, when I was in great anxiety to get word to Tanna, the natives rushed in to say there was a white man in the pantry!

Like Rhoda, I could not believe at first for gladness but wrapped a shawl round, and went to welcome him, as never white man was welcomed. He was a known *murderer*; but that mattered nothing just then, for he was a countryman, and spoke our tongue! He subsequently, indeed, shifted his birthplace over to America, when a man-of-war came to inquire into his misdeeds. Besides, he had just come from Tanna in his boat, and would be delighted to take letters back from us—and was he not as a messenger from God to us?

John would not let me ask either of the missionaries there to come, in case it might be difficult for them to get away; but I knew I had only to tell them how we were situated, and that one or the other would surely come. The day after this trader left, my dear husband seemed to be sinking. For two days, he was unable to speak; and I had to listen very intently even to hear him breathe. He could get no sleep, though I made the children all go barefooted—to their intense delight. He lay with his features sunken, and his eyes wide open. He had not got ten minutes' sleep since he took ill; and he heard the most faint and distant sounds.

I remember the Wednesday, when he was lowest of all. It was literally a day of watching and prayer. I kept guard on my knees, at the door most likely to be invaded. All the children were away from the house, and I had planted sentinels to watch the approaches; and, oh, how thankful I felt, as I slipped in on tiptoe now and again, to observe that at last the Lord had given his beloved sleep! He slept for four hours, and woke greatly refreshed.

A few days later, we had the extreme pleasure of welcoming dear Mr and Mrs Watt from Tanna. I will leave you to imagine, for I cannot express, the joy and gratitude their presence gave us; and to estimate their kindness in coming off at once, in an open boat, at a time when they could ill leave their station. Further, they made arrangements to be entirely at our service, and stay if necessary till the mission vessel arrived, and take us back with them. They brought all sorts of good things with them; and Mrs Neilson actually robbed their own home of sugar, when she heard that we were like to run short. They stayed with us a month. John was again able to come into the dining room for two or three minutes, the day before they left. How thankful we were! But oh, how different he looked from what he had done the last time I had seen him there! He was full twenty years older in appearance, very emaciated, and leaning heavily upon a crutch, which Mr Watt had manufactured, and a staff of his own, and his steps were about an inch long. Yet we were thankful to the Giver of all good.

The *Paragon* came about six weeks later. John was then able to meet friends in the drawing room, but with great difficulty; still, when she called on her return journey, a month after, he went off with her to the Synod! He was carried, part of the way, to the boat harbour; and there was some missionary or another attending to him, the whole time. In fact, he was really greatly the better for his little voyage. The children and I were dropped at Mrs Watt's; and the other missionary sisters stayed with one another. John was to have remained on at Kwamera, for a little change, after the Synod; but it was there decided that he ought to go to the Colonies, and it took us all our time to prepare for joining the *Paragon*, a month afterwards.

That was a sad, sad day, when we left Aniwa, even for a six months' absence. I believe neither the natives nor we knew how much attached we were to each other till then; and there is one little spot that is very sacred now and forever! I cannot tell you what a trial it was to leave to strangers the care of that small white coral grave, that I have so often watered with my tears.

We were a few days on Aneityum, and saw the wreck of the dear old *Dayspring*. It lies on its beam-ends, exactly as Mr Campbell sketched it; and it looks so melancholy to see it always before one's eyes. We are delighted with the *Paragon*, but the accommodation at present is wretched, and must be altered to suit the mission. Captain Jenkins very kindly gave up to us his stateroom, as John was so delicate, and it was a great comfort indeed.

Yours ever affectionately,
MAGGIE WHITECROSS PATON.

12

Home, Sweet Home, on Aniwa

ANIWA, NEW HEBRIDES,
JUNE, 1874.

MY DEAREST MOTHER, SISTERS, AND BROTHERS,[1]

I really feel as if I could scarcely have the hardihood to date this letter from Aniwa, after the terrible letters of warning our last home-mail brought us as we were leaving Sydney. I think, however, I will leave John to defend himself—a thing he's not altogether incapable of doing! I merely beg that you will not, any of you, look upon our return to the island as foolhardiness; for we have come, in the meantime, only until December, and do not even require to remain till then if I should feel worse, for the *Paragon* makes two trips this season. And, to crown all, here we are in our beautiful island home, feeling stronger and better than even in the Colonies amongst all the kindness that was heaped upon us!

I must, however, arrive at Aniwa more by degrees, as this is to be the journalistic family epistle, and you have heard nothing of us since we left Sydney on the 4th of April with dear Dr Steele on board, who seemed like a link between us and civilization. I felt 'strong to go,' as our natives would express it, for I realized as I never before had done the 'Lo, I am with you,' and some of God's dear ones with whom we have had such precious Christian fellowship were with

[1] To the family circle.

us till the last. Dr Steele was very near the truth too, when he said to someone who was bantering me about keeping so cool, 'Ah, the bitterness of her grief was past, when she left Adelaide.'

We had a roughish passage of twelve days, sighted numbers of vessels on first setting out, and 'Ball's Pyramid' five days thereafter, and lastly, but for the first time in my experience, 'Walpole Island,' two days before arriving at Aneityum. We passed it on a fine star-lit night, and could see the dark outline and the water breaking on the shore. It seemed like Aniwa in appearance, but higher and smaller, with no vegetation and of course no inhabitants.

The usual amount of things blew overboard, I losing a good hat; and John had to bewail the destruction of his boxes and pots of flowers on deck, for there was a goat on board which unfortunately had as great a taste for them as himself, and ate up nearly every one of them!

You were hoping, Helen, that Bishop Patteson's *Life* would be put on board, and it was, along with a number of other new missionary works, which the missionaries eagerly perused on the voyage down. I devoured Jones *On the Trinity*, a precious little book given to me by a dear friend in Sydney, and which it took me the whole voyage to get thoroughly read and digested. I was too sick, and weak in consequence, to do anything but lie and read on deck, not being able to go down even to worship or meals till a day or two before we landed at Aneityum.

We were all heartily thankful, when we cast anchor in Anelgauhat Harbour (Dr Geddie's old station), but were so sorry on Dr Steele's account that it was such a dull drizzly wet morning. Everything looked its worst, and not a native was to be seen. Even the beautiful mountains were half enveloped in mist, and the doctor was evidently disappointed, though he took care not to express it in words. He missed, exactly as I did on first seeing the islands, the sight of native houses along the shore, for they all live a little in through the bush. It is so nice to watch somebody—I mean somebody worth watching— coming fresh to the islands, and to see one's own first impressions reproduced!

After an early breakfast, we got into the boat, and had such a warm welcome from our kind friends Mr and Mrs Murray, who would not hear of our return to the vessel again. We planned to go round to Mr Inglis's station next day, being Friday, as I knew it would be my only opportunity of seeing Mrs Inglis, and they had urgent letters of invitation awaiting us. The Murrays were determined that we should remain; and the wind seemed to favour them, for it blew almost a hurricane during the night, so that we were rather amazed to see the captain come ashore for us after breakfast. He was obliged to see Mr Inglis on business, and Dr Steele was also anxious to get round, so we thought we might venture. When we went on board, however, before finally starting, we were met with a perfect chorus of objections from all the missionaries for setting out in such weather! 'Every man to his trade,' thought I, and placed my confidence in nautical affairs on the captain rather than on the missionaries. John felt he must go, if possible, he had so much to say to Mr Inglis; and, as I was quite as full of news for Mrs Inglis—'gossip,' the wise call it—and certainly more able to rough it than he, I hastily reduced our luggage to very small compass, as there was some probability of our having to walk part of the way, and the natives would have enough to do in carrying the youngsters, Minn and Frank. Dr Steele had been fairly frightened out of going, but I felt sure he could not hesitate if I went. The worthy doctor, however, had too much respect for his tabernacle to be led into danger, even by a woman, and contented himself with looking wistfully over the stern of the vessel till we sailed out of sight. It was with fear and trembling that we committed ourselves to that little shell of a thing, jumping up and down on the great waves—and I envied the bairns their high spirits. But we were most agreeably disappointed. The wind died off, as the captain had predicted, and we never had a pleasanter sail round to Anamé.

We got there in about four hours, in time for a late dinner, which we did full justice to; and had such a fine quiet time with Mr and Mrs Inglis, who have been truly as father and mother to us. It so happened that I had not been to Anamé since before Frank was born; so I had to go through all the rooms and premises, just to make sure they were still in the same place after all the earthquakes and hurricanes. The damage that had been done during the '*Dayspring* Hurricane' was frightful, though there is little trace of it now. Mrs Inglis showed me a great wooden safe, or press, which had been carried bodily some miles up the river, but the door was fastened so well that nothing inside was broken or spoiled! The orangery of twenty years' growth was in its most tempting beauty, and we did pay attention to the fine large oranges—Minn and Frank were never to be seen without them.

The weather continued wet while we were there, and the missionaries had a dreadful day for landing when the vessel brought them round on the following Tuesday. It really was with danger to life and limb that the boat cleared from the vessel and brought them off. Mr Inglis's goods could not be landed, and we had anything but comfortable sensations at the prospect of going on board that afternoon. The vessel could not be kept waiting, however, so we packed and bade *adieu*, and got a few yards from the gate, when one of those tropical downpours came on, and John felt, as we all did, that it was as much as his life was worth to go out in it, so we turned in to the Institution to wait till it was over. It was agreed, however, after some consultation, to send a letter to the captain in name of the missionaries, asking him to send in a boat for us next day. And right glad were we to turn in again, and gather round Mrs Inglis's comfortable tea table—which little Minn evidently regarded as a foolish proceeding, for she demanded indignantly why we didn't go right off after she had kissed all the people!

Next day was worse, and, when Mr Arthur, the mate, presented himself on the veranda with only his nose and eyes visible from his oilskins, there was no thought of attempting to get drowned that day. So stormy was it that the usual Wednesday prayer meeting for the natives could not be held. We wondered what God was detaining us for, as nothing of the kind exactly had occurred before, but it was all explained in the evening. As we were sitting at tea, a native came overland with a mail from the other side, where Mrs Goodwill and her two children had been left with Mrs Murray. The letter was from Mrs Goodwill to Mrs Inglis, telling her that little Tommy was dying and bewailing her husband's absence, little dreaming he was still on the same island and would himself read her sorrowful epistle. We had a silent perusal of it round the table, as it entered so much into the detail of the darling child's sufferings that it could not be read aloud. How clearly then we saw the guiding Hand in the storm! Mr Inglis at once looked out a crew for next morning, as it was impracticable to go that night, and proposed that instead of the sermon usually read on Wednesday evenings there should be a meeting for prayer on behalf of the dear child. He conducted it, and each of the missionaries except Mr Goodwill, and Dr Steele made earnest supplication that the child might be spared. (I am happy to be able to say that the little fellow is alive and kicking!) I don't believe there was a dry eye in the room, and poor Goodwill seemed prostrate, his tears dropping the whole evening. It was really, 'the strong man bowed down'; and he quite took our hearts by storm, as I believe we did his (for once!), for after the closing prayer he said, in as steady a voice as he could command, 'I thank all you dear brethren for your kind sympathy and prayers,' and bidding us goodnight he walked off to his room.

The vessel merely showed herself in the distance, not being able to send in a boat; but next day, Friday, when Mrs Inglis was assuring us that we would have another Sabbath at Anamé, in came the boat with a message from the captain, to the effect that he could not keep dodging about any longer (there is no anchorage at Anamé), and must make for Tanna now without us if we could not come. The missionaries thoroughly sympathized with the captain, and also with the other mission families, who might be in sickness or starvation while waiting so long for the vessel; so we had to bundle and go, in the drenching rain and high wind, with the sky all black and the waves all white. It was a dreadful sail. A squall came up and we lost sight of the vessel, while the tremendous waves threatened every moment to swamp us, and we were literally soaked with sea and rain. I never felt so faint with terror, except once at Efaté, when we lost our rudder just as we got in among the boiling reefs; and I made the most solemn resolutions to end my days on Aniwa (should I be fortunate enough to get there!) rather than risk my nervous system in a boat again.

When we got on board, however, we found that others had been in more imminent peril than ourselves, for one of the sailors, a young boy, had been pitched overboard in the storm that morning, while the vessel was tearing along at full speed, so that she was three miles away ere they could pull her up. A boat was of course lowered and sent in pursuit, though with but slender hope of success; but the poor boy battled bravely with the waves, and being a good swimmer kept up till he was rescued, feeling none the worse after a short sleep for his prolonged bath.

We anticipated, however, more serious consequences for

John with his rheumatism, and for Dr Steele, who is subject to fever; but one and all of us jumped out of our wet clothes and went right off to bed, leaving Hutshi and the steward to wring and dry them as best they might. The next day was a lovely one, and we lay off Kwamera, Mr Watt's station, before dinner, which we were all determined to have on shore, notwithstanding the previous day's experience. So, when the boat was lowered, we were all ready to jump into it, not one whit the worse, except our hats, which were rather in a battered condition! The sail was really pleasant, all but the narrow passage through the reef, when one has to hold one's breath for a minute, and we had a most hearty welcome from our dear friends Mr and Mrs Watt. I can never forget their intense loving-kindness, when they came over to Aniwa in the time of our distress last year.

The notorious 'Ross Lewin' has met with his long-predicted fate at last, having been shot by the Tannese after a quarrel about land. His widow and brother had to make their escape in a little boat, taking the dead body with them, and were picked up at sea next day by a trading vessel. The body had to be buried at sea, along with Mrs Lewin's dead baby, still-born in the vessel. How many of these traders die by violence, and yet they will not take warning!

We had finished up at Fotuna soon after breakfast, and how intensely delighted we were to hear the captain's cheery voice shouting out that we would be able to have a drink of milk at Aniwa tomorrow morning, as the wind was fair. We had all packed up in the afternoon, and the first sight which greeted me, on looking out at my porthole next morning, was the trees and rocks of dear old Aniwa! The first boat was sent ashore with eight or nine Fotunese and their cumbrous baggage, who had insisted on coming to visit our island, rather to the disgust of the captain. Meantime we were having our breakfast, and Mr Arthur, the mate, brought back word that our natives were in a state of great delight and excitement—dear Yawaci making the younger girls fly round their work—also that our six cows had increased to ten, and that our goats no man could number! He had also heard that a number of our natives had died, and some had been taken away by traders.

When we neared the shore, we could see that the great majority of the people had turned out, and even the very cattle and goats had been brought to meet us! There were my girls, standing in a group, in bright pink dresses sewed and shaped by themselves, and turkey-red turbans; and, in short, by one and another of the natives, the colours of the rainbow were well represented. Not one person, I am thankful to say, was *without clothing.* True, some of their garments were ragged and scanty enough; still, they had them, and it was almost more than we expected from some of them, after being away from them so long. They do *so* love to run naked!

What a shaking of hands and *alofa-ing* there was! Two or three little groups were sitting apart sobbing for their dead; indeed, they firmly believed that if we had been on the island to attend to them they would not have died. When we reached the house, everything looked beautiful and the ground so well kept, new coral on the walks, a fine new mat on the diningroom floor and another in the lobby, and last, but not least, in the estimation of weary sea voyagers, a great jug of new goats' milk! When Dr Steele and Mr Robertson made playful speeches about our homecoming before drinking it, I could most truly say, even after all the enjoyment and kindness of the Colonies, and delightful Christian fellowship with kindred spirits there, *home, sweet home, no place like home.* There was great lamentation among the natives over the absence of our dear Bob and Fred, and John had not got further with his dinner than the first mouthful when he began to think of them. 'Why didn't you bring them back?'

was the first question we were greeted with on landing; but I had no time just then to indulge in sentiment, having to rush about and see after the dinner. Masitaia, my cook and little Litsi's intended husband (a very fine fellow), had, most thoughtfully, the kettle boiling, the yams cooked, and a couple of fowls plucked when we arrived; but, native-like, he waited for me to give him things to stuff them—as if I were going to manufacture stuffing the moment I arrived! We had a jolly dinner, however, for we had only one spoon at large, and I had seized a bedsheet for a tablecloth, not being able in my excitement to remember where the right articles were packed away.

Amidst all my hurry, however, I had five minutes alone by my little Lena's grave. The beautiful white coral was blackened, but the grass and shrubs had grown, and the lemon branches with their bright fruit were bending over and shading it beautifully. How naturally one looks up to the blue sky above, and wonders where the spirit is, or if she can see the mourning hearts below. She would have been running on her own little feet now, had she been on earth but though my heart aches for her still, I would not have it otherwise, for she was not sent in vain, and oh, what a little *teacher* she has been! When John took Dr Steele to see the grave, he said, 'You have thus taken possession'; and I felt we had taken possession of more through her than that little spot of ground on Aniwa.

Our visitors and vessel left us in the afternoon, and on my return from seeing them off (John was too exhausted to go), I met a very nice man, one of the church members, who stopped me and said, *Missi, I've give my boy up to you and Missi the man, and you're to feed and clothe and teach him, as you do the other children.* I could hardly believe my ears, and you would need to know how boys are prized here to appreciate as we did the sacrifice made; at least, as John did, for I must confess that the thought of their bodily sustenance comes between me and the fervent thanksgiving of my earnest little man for 'another soul being added to our care!' We've got ten of these souls, with bodies attached, at the present time, besides several outsiders who come during the day, and it taxes all my ingenuity to keep them in work and 'Kai-kai'—their capacity for the latter being of no mean order. Their clothes are no concern beyond the making of them, and that they soon learn to do for themselves for we have always been abundantly supplied from kind mission friends.

Our Victorian Committee too offered some years ago to be at the expense of their support, but John would not hear of it; for he said it would only keep me worrying to run up numbers and so forth, when really there are but few children to educate, and I would require to make out what they call an 'encouraging' report to please subscribers and all that sort of nonsense. Now we are thoroughly independent to work for our Lord and for our fellow-creatures, as he himself leads us; and John very cheerfully puts his donation to the mission and other good causes (which we have little chance of giving to here) in the form of casks of biscuit and bags of rice for our natives. Although I *do* sometimes think how nice it would be to be in civilization with a small house of our own and with the care of only one or two servants at most, yet we are more than repaid for all our love to these dear darkies. They are just like our very children, and such we always call them, and they are so confiding and loving with us, and tell us everything—especially the three elder girls, who have lived with us now for more than five years.

By the way, we have just had an *affair de coeur* amongst them, and as Hutshi is the young lady you will be interested to hear. You know she was given away, when an infant, by her parents, to Nelwang, another infant about the same age, but who is now one of the best and most intelligent boys on the island—the only drawback being that his limbs are rather diseased, and he is so fearfully timid that he won't let John apply anything to cure them. Well, when we were in Sydney, a middle-aged man, a returned labourer, whose betrothed wife is yet a baby, came trying to curry favour with Hutshi's guardians (her parents are dead long ago) by bringing them large presents, and finally got them talked over to give him Hutshi when she returned with us—so it was settled, only awaiting her and our consent. Now, her guardian has always been most honourable with us. He gave up Hutshi to us, when she was of the greatest use in his village (but I took care to let her go and help them pretty often), and when we asked if she might go with us to the Colonies, he and his wife said, 'She is more your child than ours, Missi; do as you like.' So, when they explained matters to John one evening in the study, and said that both Hutshi and Nelwang were agreeable to the change, he felt he could not interfere much, but warned them not to be too rash, and to ask God about it.

Hutshi, the mischief, flirted with her new admirer when she could get a chance, and I felt it would be a great relief to have her married; but we could see, from Nelwang's looks (he is one of our boys), that there was a pain at his heart. I set him a piece of work in the dining room one day, and, sitting down to help him, got all his confidence. The poor boy's heart was breaking, and he wound up by saying, 'I can't tell *them* my heart, Missi, for they would but laugh, and I am only one; but if my father had been alive, they would not have *dared* to give Hutshi away before my eyes.' Seeing his lady-love, however, who at that moment came in at the open window and evidently comprehended matters, he tossed his head proudly and said, *It's very good that she takes him!*

John and I espoused Nelwang's cause from that moment, and he soon found an opportunity for saying a word on his behalf. I also got Hutshi alone, and told her what Nelwang had said. She replied that she did not know what to do, as they were all urging her to take Sarra (the new lover), but she said, 'I would cry more to give up Nelwang than that old fellow!'

She came to me the other day, and said she had finally made up her mind to keep by Nelwang. I answered, 'But I thought, Hutshi, you seemed for the while to prefer the other?' 'Yes, Missi,' she replied, 'when everybody was praising him and telling me to take him, I thought it would be nice but Nelwang and I have had a talk. We told each other what our dead parents said about our being married when we were big, and then we both cried, and we are going to be true to each other!' So you see there is sentiment in blacks as well as whites!

We had such a nice quiet month, after landing, to put things straight and to hear all the natives had to tell us. One man came grinning from ear to ear to tell us that his wife had twins; and as that is of the rarest occurrence here, we had to make a great *waho-ing* over it, and get out a nursing bottle, which the devoted father carried backwards and forwards to our house for fresh goats' milk daily till he got tired of it!

Then we had, I think, about fourteen deathbeds to hear of. Kalangi, little Litsi's father, a strong, middle-aged man and earnest Christian, died after a few days' illness, and has been very much lamented by the natives around. They have testified their respect to his memory by stuffing one of our young bulls, which Kalangi had *named* for himself, with sugar cane and all sorts of niceties, till the animal's sides stuck out! So devoted were they, and especially his widow, to this creature that John felt he must ask their leave before giving it to another missionary. They gave a reluctant consent; but begged John to make Mr Milne promise *not* to change the name—and oh, what a scene there was at the parting!

Here I am at the end of my fourth sheet, and have not even begun to tell you of the nice ladies' meeting we had at

Aniwa, or the lively time we have had with visitors ever since the vessel returned with the missionaries on board for the Annual Synod. We are all so well ourselves too, and the effect of our delightful Colonial visit has told wonderfully upon us, now that we are clear of the seasickness and excitement of travelling and got quietly nestled down among our darkies. John, but for that vicious rheumatism, would be his old self again; and as for me, I was never better in all my life, or ever stouter; and that day the Annands and Milnes were left here, we were overpowered with compliments upon our healthy looks from Dr Steele and the other gentlemen who came off to dinner. After enjoying the week's refreshing intercourse with all these dear friends, the vessel came again from Tanna, picked up all our husbands for the Synod, but left dear Mrs Watt with us. We four wives had then a most delightful time; and there was no gossip, no small scandal talk, which our lords and masters ungallantly predicted there would be when our four heads got close together!

Seriously, it was an improving time, for we had precious Christian fellowship, and we divided the day methodically, thus:—In the morning, when I looked after my many household duties, the others generally wrote letters, but sometimes helped me. In the afternoon, we all gathered to the study, to which Mrs Watt and Mrs Milne had given quite the air of a *studio*, with their drawing boards and paintboxes, for they were copying one of my paintings. Mrs Annand and I brought our workbaskets, and one or other of us read aloud. After tea, we generally devoted the whole evening to music, all being so fond of it; so the little harmonium was brought in from the church and made to do duty. We invariably began with *There is a Name*, to the music dear Mrs Macdonald gave me; and nearly always wound up with the *Te Deum*, at Mrs Annand's request, as she said it reminded her of old times—she having been brought up in the English Church. *Ruth and*

Naomi, and other nice pieces, we took in parts. I did so enjoy those evenings, for I seldom get in the harmonium unless we have visitors, for the natives suddenly take pains in their backs the moment I propose it!

If we got too tired singing we would continue our reading or chat, and the books we read were well worth talking about. Mrs Milne brought us all the accounts about 'Moody and Sankey,' and we were stirred up to long and pray for a revival here. We read also *The Higher Christian Life*, with preface by Miss Marsh, *Jones*, and some of *Goulbourn*, and that precious old book, Traill on *The Lord's Prayer*. A kind friend in Sydney gave me the loan of it, but I had to skip the latter part for want of time; so, when I got to Aneityum, Mr Inglis hunted for it in his library and lent it to me. There seems to be less philosophizing, and splitting up of the Trinity, with these old Divines than in more modern writers. He (Traill) presents the Lord Jesus Christ to his readers in all his majesty and glory, not only as the Saviour of the world and the second Person of the Trinity, but as the great Triune Jehovah, in whom dwelleth all the fullness of the Godhead bodily. He says we can never find God till we are content to see him in Christ. I cannot forbear from quoting one *wee* paragraph, exactly as he has it in his fifth sermon:—

'By virtue of this interest in Christ, believers have all Christ's fullness for their supply. He is all in all to them (Col. 3:11). "It pleased the Father that in him should all fullness dwell" (Col. 1:19). And surely, this longing of all *fullness* should please, and doth highly please, all believers. John 1:16: "And of (or out of) his fullness have all we received, and grace for grace." Eph. 4:7: "Unto every one of us is given grace according to the measure of the gift of Christ." Whence had Paul and John all their grace, but of Christ's fullness? Whence was it that they received so much grace beyond others? It was according to the measure of the gift of Christ. But the stock and treasure is common to all believers. They are partakers of Christ (Heb. 3:14), and called to the fellowship of his Son Jesus Christ our Lord (1 Cor. 1:9). The apostle (Col. 2:8-10) giveth a needful warning, "Beware lest any man spoil you through philosophy and vain deceit." But how shall we know and discern the snare? It is after the tradition of man, after the rudiments (or elements or principles) of the world, and not after Christ. His argument to enforce this warning is deep and strong. Verse 9: "For in him dwelleth all the fullness of the Godhead bodily." It dwelleth really, substantially in this one man Jesus Christ. So that they do deceive you, that direct you to any for supply but to him. If ye would be filled with all the fullness of God (Eph. 3:19), ye must seek it and find it in him in whom dwelleth all the fullness of the Godhead bodily. And this shall not be in vain, for "ye are complete in him" (verse 10). Never did, never could, a believer use this fullness, suitably to all its worth in itself and to the gracious right he hath to use it.'

I was telling Mr Inglis, when they all called here after the Synod, that I went to *Traill* next to my Bible, when I wanted 'the finest of the wheat,' and he said I was to keep it to myself and wrote my name on it.

That was a refreshing visit, on the return of the vessel from the Synod; and we had a cheery houseful, for in addition to our four husbands, whom, as canny Scots say, 'we were *not sorry*' to see after a three weeks' absence, Mr and Mrs Inglis and Dr Steele (the latter to remain with us) came and stayed from the Saturday till the Monday, the vessel going out to sea with the rest of the missionaries, who declared it would kill me outright to have any more! Those who came tried to make me promise just to give them a pillow and a blanket on the floor, but we got them snugly stowed away in beds and on sofas, and we so enjoyed their society. It is especially delightful to hear their voices mingling in the psalm at family worship. It makes one think of the great company of the redeemed, singing the 'new song.'

The Sabbath was such a blessed day too, and it was quite an event in the church history of Aniwa to see six missionaries on the platform, and five ladies in the missionary's pew. Mr Inglis preached at the first service, Mr Annand at the second (John of course translating), good gospel truth; and Dr Steele gave us a *white* sermon in the evening in the drawing room, upon the *Prayer of Jabez*. The language was very beautiful, and the doctor suited himself to his audience, leaving out his appeal to *unconverted sinners*!

I had nearly forgotten to tell you that the Synod were unanimous in sanctioning John's return to Australia, at the end of the year, in accordance with the Victorian invitation. He is bound to keep his mouth shut for six months; then, if he is able, to visit the churches, and not come back to the islands till after the next hot season. The mission vessel is not to be sent to Victoria till then to tempt him to speechify, so it goes to Sydney this year as usual, and next to Melbourne, Adelaide, and Tasmania. Our hearts beat at the prospect of seeing our boys again; but still I would prefer to remain here for many reasons. I believe in the inclination of *people*, as well as things, to *rest*; for I shrank from leaving Australia when we were there, and now it seems such a pity to turn out of our home again. If John feels much better, he says he will remain; but our God will lead and guide us as he would have us go.

Everyone in the house is asleep, and my eyes will hardly keep open; so I must say goodnight to you all.

With heart's love from
your ever loving daughter and sister,
MAGGIE WHITECROSS PATON.

13

The Mission Forces at Work

ANIWA, NEW HEBRIDES,
2 NOVEMBER, 1874.

MY DEAREST SISTERS AND BROTHERS,[1]

About half an hour ago, we decided finally, after much earnest prayer, that it was our duty to remain on Aniwa, instead of going to the Colonies a fortnight hence in the *Dayspring* (the *Paragon* rechristened), as we had fondly anticipated. So John and I are both in the study, setting to work vigorously with our pens, instead of packing boxes.

I felt strongly tempted not to write the family epistle this time. It does seem so hard to leave out my precious mother's name! But, in one way, she is nearer us than ever; indeed, I cannot divest myself of the feeling that she sees and knows all about us, with joy, instead of the anxiety she used to feel on our account while here on earth.

You are waiting patiently, I suppose, to hear the reasons for our non-appearance; and, oh, how I wish I could make you see them as we do! The path of duty to us both now seems so plain, for we have asked the Lord for direction, and conferred not with flesh and blood (there isn't any flesh and blood of our own kind here to confer with!), but gave our wills to him. Certainly, we do not follow our own inclinations, which would lead us to Australia, and right on to our

[1] To the family circle.

boys—and God only knows the gnawing at our hearts sometimes for one sight of them! But they could not be better cared for, or have more privileges, than where they are; and, were we to leave our darkies, they would have literally no one to care for their souls. Of course, I know, God cares for them; but we could not ask him to work a special miracle on their behalf, when he has removed to a great extent the one grand objection to our remaining here—I mean John's ill health. He is not, indeed, in perfect health, as the children and I are; but his rheumatism is in abeyance, owing, we believe, under God, to the acetic acid; and the faint, breathless fits now seldom come. Every other way he is strong and well, and, as usual, going through a vast amount of work.

Ever since the *Dayspring* left, with Dr Steele and our mail for Sydney, four months ago, mission work has been going on like steam here; and we are both as busy and as happy as the day is long, having almost more teaching than we can manage, as the natives are turning out better than they have ever done since we came to Aniwa. The young men too, whom we might reasonably have expected to be our pests, have now become the most eager to learn, to John's immense delight!

Besides the little village schools, we have school three times a day at the mission station. The first is at daybreak, which one of the teachers conducts, specially for *reading*, which the natives are awfully slow to learn. Then, after breakfast, comes my sewing class, twice a week, which continues for about three hours, and the average attendance is thirty, which is good for this time of the year, when they are busy yam-planting. Our fine broad veranda has been my schoolroom now for years, as I used to get so faint, when we crowded inside. I carry it on in the old way, and give each woman or girl a dress, or print to make one, who has attended three months without missing a day; and this, for a long time, they firmly believed to be payment for helping me to sew! John's school comes on after dinner, and continues about two hours. He commenced it for the improvement of teachers and their wives and those who could already read fluently. It has increased to forty-seven scholars; so that he is glad to let me take the writing class entirely off his hands, which are full enough with reading, ciphering, and giving out next day's lessons.

By far the most interesting, as well as laborious part of the work, however, is with our own native boys and girls, who live with us. They now number fourteen. I think we had only ten or eleven when I wrote last. Besides all their other duties, they each bring an essay, twice a week, neatly written on a sheet of paper with a lead pencil. They give them in, after evening native worship, which we have in the dining room; and John reads them aloud, corrects the spelling, etc., and furnishes them with fresh paper, and pencils if need be. The little ones, and some big ones too, who are not the length of writing essays, fill theirs with small words or rows of letters. I don't know that I am right in calling them essays, for there are no particular subjects given out as yet. But they certainly are compositions after a sort, and their own too; for, the literature of Aniwa being so very circumscribed, they can't cheat us by copying out of books! They are never at any loss, however, except sometimes to get all crushed into one sheet; and it is, of all others, the exercise they like best, and are most careful to prepare.

We thoroughly enjoy those essay evenings; for some of them are really racy, and supply in a small degree the want of a local newspaper. They catch at any little exciting incident which happens, and if there is *bad talk* going on, we are sure to get it, with their decidedly-expressed opinions about it and the authors thereof. We were greatly amused, one evening, by the subject of one of those effusions walking in at rather an awkward moment. He was a decent man, too, one of our church members, who happened to be staying over the night at the next village, and looked in upon us. I gathered from little Litsi's (cousin of Litsi the greater) alarmed looks, and the suppressed merriment of the other girls, that she had been making free with his name in her essay, which John was just beginning to read. So we telegraphed that it would be necessary to look before reading and to skip personal allusions. These were that 'Simonia (the gentleman in question) had scolded some of the women for not dressing properly; while Nabowsi, his own wife, had been seen with a mere apology for a garment thrown across her shoulders.' And Litsi was strongly of opinion that 'Simonia should have seen to his own wife, before attacking other people's!'

John occasionally gives out the subject. Once he told them to write all they knew of the stars; and it was wonderful how many of them they could name—native names, of course—far more than I ever knew. But you will form a better idea of their style by my enclosing an ordinary specimen; and, if time permit, a translation. This has been a means of improvement to us all, as well as to the natives; for it is wonderful how many new words we have got, especially little ones, as well as prefixes and affixes, which in their rapid utterance, as to us it seems, we had never observed.

I dare say this earnest fit will wear off them by-and-bye; but, meanwhile, they are hardly ever to be seen on Tuesdays and Fridays without paper and pencil, to which every spare moment is devoted. They allow almost nothing to interfere with that duty, ingenious as they are sometimes in finding excuses for others. For instance, when the *Dayspring* returned from her last Colonial trip, we got a sight of her well-known sail the afternoon before she arrived; and, immediately after tea, the whole fourteen of them were squeezed round the dining-room table, hard at work writing. I asked what in the world they meant, as the essays were not to be given in till tomorrow, and they could write them in the daylight. They replied, 'O Missi, just let us sit here with the lamp till the worship, for there will be no time tomorrow when the vessel is here, and we must have our books written.'

I truly envied them, that they could compose themselves at all; for our hearts were beating at the thought of the *Dayspring* lying so near, with mails from home on board! No one, in your civilization, can ever realize what a thing of hope and life the sight of a vessel is to us away here. To admire, with the feelings we had that evening, from the veranda, and through the opening made in the trees by the hurricane, our beautiful new *Dayspring*—the one visible link between us and the Christian world—lying almost becalmed in the distance, with her sails spread, and a gorgeous sunset behind her, you would need to have gone through our experience in this lonely island. We stood and watched her till it was dark, little dreaming she contained the sad tidings of my beloved mother's death.

Next morning, we were up with the earliest daybreak to receive our visitors, who, however, did not arrive till the afternoon—there was so little wind. We had such a refreshing visit from the Watts and Murrays—the former on their return from their fortnight's visit to Sydney, and the latter going round the islands on deputation work; also from our old friend Mr McArthur, the mate of the vessel. But, by far the most important visitors, in Minn and Frank's estimations, were little Georgie Murray and two cats, brought for them all the way from Sydney by one of the sailors!

After tea, the captain made his appearance, and was besieged with entreaties to allow his passengers a quiet night on shore, but he only laughed at the idea. It was our turn, however, to laugh, when we stood at the boat wharf an hour afterwards, among the flaming torches of the natives (we had a torchlight procession, for it was pitch dark, no moon), gazing out into the darkness for the vessel's lights, which were nowhere to be seen; nothing visible but the glare of torches, lighting up the dark faces of the natives and reflected on the black water at our feet, with the grand old volcano over at Tanna—a magnificent sight, in the blackness of darkness, through its bright red smoke, and every few minutes bursts of flame and great fiery sparks shooting far into the heavens.

One of the sailors ashore, an old man-o'-war's man and the donor of the pussies, seemed to think it rather a wild-goose chase, not to say a dangerous one, to set out in search of a vessel in the dark; so we had our way after all, and were not sorry to have had the walk, which we all so thoroughly enjoyed. The captain, of course, was fidgety about his ship; but McArthur had gone on board, in whom he had the fullest confidence; and we did so enjoy the evening's conversation with our dear friends—not going, you may be sure, to rest any earlier than usual!

My girls did splendidly, and got beds made up for our guests, nine in all, with not very much help from me. Next morning dawned so bright; the vessel sailed close in; and all got comfortably off after breakfast, with half a cow, killed in honour of the visit, and which they got more good of, on board, than the whole cow which John gave them at the Synod, for it jumped overboard and was drowned!

We had three days' hard reading at our mail, for it was a large one; the great Adelaide packets being speedily devoured first, and those precious pages from Mother, forty-six in all, telling about our boys and their cousins, her gaol-visiting, the revival work, etc. I little knew of the sad telegram that John had hidden away so carefully; for people had been very thoughtful about us—at least, about me—and Dr Steele's letter of sympathy, which contained it, was kept separate from the rest of our mail; and McArthur was instructed to give it to John, when he saw him alone, which he did at the boat wharf on landing. Poor John's thoughts flew to Bob and Fred, when he was told the letter contained bad news, and he began to show signs of fainting. But dear Mr Watt, divining his thoughts, assured him of their welfare, and told him what had happened. All the news that reached my ears when we met at the gate, where I was waiting to welcome my visitors, was the hearty *Peggy, your boys are well!* and it was a glad heart I lifted silently to God, dreaming not that anything else sorrowful could have happened, when they were all right.

I felt, however, through it all, that mute sympathy was being shown to me by our visitors, and there was no mistaking its drift and presence in the family prayers. And, at length, the truth came upon me suddenly enough, two days later, notwithstanding all dear John's thoughtful care. Mrs Neilson had written me a note of sympathy, and that had been overlooked, till I fell upon it unawares. The natives, poor things, were so kind; and when John told some women who wanted me that I could not be seen, and explained the reason, one of our little girls slipped into the bedroom and said, with the tears in her eyes, 'Missi, was it the mother who gave you birth?' A real native question! Mother has such a wide meaning here, and may include an aunt, or other near friend.

How we long for the particulars of our dear mother's last days! We can hardly realize, even yet, that she is now with her Lord, to whom her whole soul was so devoted. It is so hard to part with such a mother; but my first thought, dear Helen, was for you, with your beloved husband so far away. Litsi and Hutshi cried sorely; and even some of the natives who never saw her, for they heard the others speak of her so often. We both feel thankful that our boys were privileged to be with her all these months.

I must not, however, fill this paper with my own feelings alone, when I have so many things to write to you. I think the next event of importance, after the visit of the *Dayspring*, was Hutshi's marriage, a few weeks after, with Nelwang, her first love. It was quite an exciting time, as it is years since any of my girls were married before; or, to use the native description, *Got up in church.* Both bride and bridegroom were dressed out of the Adelaide mission box, which came safely in the *Dayspring*, along with our mail, and another box from Miss Glen in Scotland, so that we felt quite prepared for any number of weddings!

Hutshi chose one of those bright purple skirts and jackets, and one of the little white hats I trimmed with purple and yellow silk, mixed with white tulle, which Fanny sent in Miss Glen's box. Nelwang chose a very nice, quiet, grey suit. My other girls all got new hats and dresses for the occasion, so the church was quite merry, that Wednesday afternoon, when they were married at the close of the prayer meeting; and they behaved very well during the ceremony, which was a terrible ordeal to the bridegroom. He had been living in terror of it for weeks before, afraid, as he told me confidentially, that the people would laugh at him!

We feared, rather, that some of the young men would do more than laugh; for a marriage on these islands, even on Aneityum, where women are so very scarce, creates a deal of rage and ill-feeling. We killed a large cow, however, to be divided over the whole island, and ostensibly in honour of one of our girls being married, but really to sweeten the hearts of some of the disappointed suitors, who, we hoped, would hardly feel inclined for deeds of revenge upon the fortunate bridegroom, while smacking their lips over roast beef, which they are quite as fond of as any Englishman.

For many days before, poor Hutshi's heart was full, and she could hardly keep back the tears when we spoke to her. She protested that she could not leave us. We reminded her that it was only three minutes' walk from our gate to her future home; and I provided her with a few things 'to set up house with,' such as a tin washing-basin, bar of soap, looking-glass, couple of tin plates, spoons, jugs, saucepan, etc., with which she was much delighted. But she cried bitterly, the day before the wedding, when one of the neighbours came to carry away her box and things from the girls' house; and, the same evening, she brought me a nicely written and most touching little letter, thanking us for all we had done and for taking her to Australia; and, after saying how sad she was to leave us, she gave her love to each one of us by name, and said *her heart remembered* Bob and Fred this night and loved them and cried about them, and also that she remembered Captain Jenkins' kindness to her onboard. John and I were so touched and gratified, that our eyes were rather misty by the time we came to the last lines. Hutshi has been with us about six years now; and we told her that our fondest wishes for her would be realized if she would but begin her married life with God.

My other girls are all doing well; and two more have been added to our care, since I last wrote. I can't say, though, that they always come from the purest motives. Nagitshi, one of the two little girls, came to us suffering greatly from a loathsome disease, which I must not name, and I instantly shrunk back from having her near us. But, after a few moments' reflection, we took her as from God, though I was in perfect terror of infection, for my own children's sake, as well as for the natives. John at once set to work anointing her carefully; and the elder girls and I made warm clothing, as the cold then was intense for Aniwa, and she was shivering. I gave her a warm blanket to sleep in, and plenty of nourishing food, managing to keep her from touching things about the house or the children, without hurting her feelings, as in that case she would have bolted. So, after a few weeks of great care, she perfectly recovered; about which time, her worthy father, a returned Queensland labourer, came and demanded payment for the use we had had of his little daughter! He was made thoroughly to comprehend how matters stood, however, and has made no more demands since, while the little girl is getting on fast, though only about seven years of age, being naturally quick.

It is these dear girls and boys, under our own especial charge, to whom our hearts cling the most. They regard us with such true affection, the elder ones especially, and how could we turn them adrift? People may say of natives what they will; but, give them a proper chance, and they'll show they've got hearts. I could wish, though, they had a more judicious way of showing it just at present; for, every time they think of the parting with our children, my girls take them away and stuff them with cocoa-nuts and native puddings, till they are sick! Bob and Fred are fondly remembered too; and, the other day, an old woman, who brought two finely plaited baskets to be sent to Fred, just managed to steady her voice to say who they were for, and then burst into tears. As we have only now decided, ourselves, about staying, the natives do not yet know, and I so long to tell them; but John thinks it will be nicer to announce it after the Communion, which we are to have on Sabbath, first.

Oh, how we long to be able to tell you of a still deeper work among our natives, a thirsting, not after knowledge only, but after the Lord Jesus Christ! There is none of that very apparent yet; and I was writing dear Mrs Inglis lately, that it was perhaps only the prospect of our leaving that drew the natives out, but she answers me that it is nothing of the sort, but the Lord Jesus himself working in them, and drawing them to us first and then to himself through us. And Mr Inglis writes to John that he believes we are already feeling the effects of the blessed work at home and the prayers of God's people; for they are much encouraged on Aneityum just now, having admitted fifty-six new members to the church, a few weeks ago. We confidently look to the Lord to manifest himself to the hearts of these benighted ones, as he has done to so many in the old country.

Oh, how intensely we are interested in all accounts of the blessed work going on at home! Dear Mrs Milne was writing me, that it seems to her that a great deal of the revival has been in the hearts of God's own people, getting a more exalted view of the Lord Jesus Christ, and seeing everything in him—all the fullness of the Godhead, all their salvation and all their desire. We are both so delighted with Philip Phillips's *Song Life*, and indignant enough to see it sneered at in one of the home papers, because it gives the worship to Christ instead of God! As if Christ were not very God, *God Manifest*; or as if there were any other God to worship, but the God who is 'in' Christ reconciling the world unto himself. Oh, if people would but take the Lord's own words, since they won't take the other parts of the Bible—'He that receiveth me receiveth him that sent me.'

It is pitiable to read of 'a tendency to that Unitarianism which virtually excludes the Father and the Holy Spirit.' It has been the joy of my life, since I found that it was impossible to have Christ without having the Father and the Spirit, for 'in him dwelleth all the fullness of the Godhead bodily.' A sinner can't even come to Christ without the Father and the Spirit being engaged in it: "No man can come to me, except the Father which hath sent me draw him.' … 'No man can say Jesus Christ is Lord but by the Holy Ghost.' How I wish I had known, or felt, all this years ago; for it is just in proportion as I *dig in Christ*, as Traill puts it, that I can know anything of God; and it is only when I speak of that name which is above every name that my lips are unsealed to the natives.

John and I were reading such a precious sermon lately, showing that it is only when the glory of God is revealed 'in the face of Christ Jesus' that Satan is up in arms. He'll let you alone as long as you talk vaguely about God or good works; he'll even let you denounce 'sin,' and talk about 'the church' or the 'Bible'—anything but the Lord Jesus Christ, for therein lies danger!

It is getting very late, and I have been so often interrupted today that I fear this can't be very coherent; but I well know you would rather have anything than nothing; so I send it as it is, with all heart's love,

From your loving sister,
MAGGIE WHITECROSS PATON.

P.S.—Forgot to say that we have got up a fine new Aniwa Printing Office, and John has printed a new edition of our Aniwan *Catechism.* Also a 'Smiddy,' or Smith's Shop!!—M. W. P.

14

The Year of the Hurricane

EMERALD HILL, MELBOURNE,
3 NOVEMBER, 1875.

MY DEAREST SISTERS AND BROTHERS,[1]

If I could only put one of the earthquakes we've had into this journal it would produce a sensation—descriptions seem so very tame after one has experienced the awful feelings they produce! But I must begin and go forward as best I can, there being no possibility of gratifying you in that direction.

You know, it was not till very near the time of the vessel's sailing that we decided last year to remain; and I sent my last 'journal' on board with an aching heart. We had been so nearly going to see our precious boys, and till I saw the *Dayspring* slowly disappear in the distance I did not know how intensely my heart had been set upon seeing them! And instead, we were left with the tidings of their illness, which reached us in the letters left behind for us on that day. Our work too that evening was rather sad, for not being able to purchase nearly enough biscuits and rice from the vessel for our natives (some three or four casks was all the captain could spare), we had to dismiss a lot of our boys. They offered to stay without food, but we knew that could not be, and, not having the heart to say who were to go, we left it to themselves to settle, saying we could only keep three. So, after

[1] To the family circle.

some consultation, they told us that the *newest* comers had the best right and the most need to remain.

To crown all, John got very ill and sank so low that we feared he might not live to see the return of the *Dayspring*. But all the time I had an inward conviction that God had not kept him on Aniwa just to die, after giving us such encouragement to remain, and we had waited so confidingly upon him just to show us the way. And he did not keep us long in suspense, for one event transpired after another to show how wisely we had been guided.

The first of these happened about a month after the vessel left and as John was slowly recovering from his illness. We heard, one lovely day, as I was setting the copies for afternoon school (I managed to keep it going all the time), a cry of *Sail ho!* which set us all into a fine pitch of excitement. School was the last thing to be thought of, and the natives scampered off towards the other end of the island, where the vessel lay. John was unable to walk so far; but you may be sure we were quite on the *qui vive* for news, and I waylaid the first returning native, who shouted to me in Aniwan: 'Missi, what *do* you think has happened? A whole shipload of Tannese, men, women, and children, have been driven off their own island by war, and have come over to live on this little island, because the worship is strong and they know they are safe. They are many in number for the people of Aniwa; and where are we to get food for them, Missi, for they had to escape at night with what little baggage they could bring in the vessel?'

Another native soon after arrived with letters from Mr and Mrs Neilson, confirming the report, and we were rather dumfounded at this turn of events; but, like most of the other missionaries, when they heard of it, we were also deeply impressed with God's mysterious ways. Tanna was the island upon which John's whole heart was set; and it was one of the bitterest disappointments of his life when the Mission Synod would not allow him to return there, instead of coming to Aniwa, nine years ago; but we both felt we were following God here, and now he had brought the Tannese to Aniwa, for those who had come were from around Port Resolution, and some of them were John's old friends!

Some of the islanders themselves were as much struck with the event as we were. And at last Mission Synod, Mr Neilson amused all the missionaries by giving the outline of a speech made upon the occasion by one of the Aneityumese teachers on Tanna, apt as all natives are in drawing illustrations from daily life to point their addresses on Sabbath. He took the story of Joseph for his subject, and made out Missi Paton to be *Joseph driven from Tanna by his wicked brethren*, the Tanna men; but that God had gone with him to Egypt, *alias* Aniwa, and prospered him and the land for his sake, and prepared it for them to go and live upon and thus save much people alive!

Our natives behaved admirably. The chiefs and church members came to consult John about it that evening, and they agreed to meet next morning and go in a body and offer among their different villages homes and lands for the refugees. They just pled with John to accompany them, offering to carry him on their backs (no cabs, you know); but he doesn't care for that mode of conveyance, and being unable to walk so far, he sent me in his place. I did not like the business, and tried hard to get out of it; but John and the natives insisted—they were so anxious to let the poor things see that they were welcome. I got through the performance, grinning and shaking hands with all the women, and patting every child on the head, some of whom set up frightened screams at sight of a white woman, which made me feel rather awkward, though my heart *did* go out to those bonnie little curly brown pates and their poor mothers sitting nursing their babies in a strange land. Most of the *men* I skipped (there were exactly a hundred of them altogether, men, women, and children, a big proportion of the population of Aniwa)—they looked so thoroughly bold and impudent, and, what John has so often described the New Hebrideans in heathenism to be, 'naked painted savages,' whom I never do pretend to admire. I must except two or three of the men, however, and dear old Nowar at their head, who looked like a gentleman, with his short hair—so grey now—no earrings, and respectable clothing. His fine old face just *beamed* when he saw me, and he told me to tell John *that he had come to live and die with his own dear Missi.*

Nowar applied vigorously for baptism, which John however would not consent to without first consulting his missionary, Mr Neilson; and besides, the rule on Aniwa is that candidates for baptism first attend the communicants' class for twelve months. His conduct on Aniwa has been that of a Christian; but as for the others, instead of getting good themselves, their influence upon our natives has been *down-dragging*, especially upon some of our wilder rogues, who have only given in to the changed state of Aniwa because they are obliged to, Christianity having become the law of the land. You can easily understand how a lot of vigorous fellows, with nothing to do, away from their own island and their own missionary's influence, and full of heathen superstition, never having attempted to learn either reading or writing, could influence those whose hearts are not changed and who are impatient of the outward restraints imposed by Christianity upon their heathen practices.

John immediately set to work revising his Tannese, which he had well-nigh forgotten, so that when the Tanna gentry declined to come to church he was soon able to go to them and first read his addresses and then preach to them in Tannese. How it did remind us of the early Aniwan days, when our worthy parishioners used to enjoy a pipe or a nap, as they lay on their backs listening to the sermon!

Their curiosity led them to make a fine turn out, the first Sabbath after they came. I was touched to see the marks of care and pains bestowed upon the women by Mrs Neilson, for some of them had dresses put on so neatly. I know from experience how much has to be done ere one can get them to wear clothing even to church; and it must have been so trying to have them run off just when labour and instruction were beginning to tell.

We took good care to make work for them—weeding waste ground, getting reeds for fences, etc.—so that they might earn clothing; and several of them took advantage of it. John also urged the men to make banana plantations, as it was past the yam-planting season and they were likely to remain awhile. He gave them all the young bananas that he could spare, for them to plant. And, meanwhile, all the Aniwans contributed to their support, which was no light matter for this barren little island. But it is wonderful how they have all managed to subsist, for a month after they came we had the most terrific hurricane that ever swept over Aniwa.

The hurricane began in earnest about noon on January 14th, after a heavy thunderstorm which had blackened the air all the morning. As we sat at dinner the wind suddenly became furious; we had to jump up and make preparations, as the house was shaking and creaking, the thatch standing on end, and the rain pouring in. Immediately trees, fences, etc, began to occupy a horizontal position; so the children and I took refuge in the study, which seemed to stand firmer than the rest of the house, and from the windows watched the progress of the storm—a magnificent sight, tall trees bending and falling before the awful force of the wind. John came in greatly dejected, saying that if it continued much longer the church would go, as it was already bending, notwithstanding its being so strongly propped. There was a lull just then in the storm, which cheered me; but his more experienced eye led him to pronounce it the stillness that precedes a great storm, it was still so black and ominous. And sure enough, just before dark, a terrific blast sent us flying down to the cellar, our usual place of refuge.

John and a couple of the girls made a final attempt to get into the house for one or two loaves and whatever else they could grab—we were now awfully hungry, having been so unceremoniously interrupted at our dinner. My faithful little cook was precipitated into the cellar before a great blast, puffing and panting and holding on to a kettle of boiling water, which was an unexpected luxury in the circumstances. So we managed to make a very jolly meal off the top of a box; and all our stores being in the cellar, we got hold of a tin of salmon—the girls had thoughtfully brought a great basin of milk for the children and when Frank found we were all to eat the salmon out of one plate, his joy knew no bounds, and he stuck his fork into the biggest bit in the dish—which proved too large for his wee mouth, causing great merriment.

The storm raged till midnight, when we were thankful to get up to our beds, and found our own room, fortunately, the only habitable part of the house. But oh, what utter desolation the morning light revealed! Our fine large church a mass of ruins, with one great pillar standing solitary and upright through the rubbish, against the clear blue sky. The schoolhouse in the same condition, at the other side of the *Imrai* (= public meeting ground). With the exception of our cookhouse and printing office, not an outhouse was left standing on the mission premises; but oh, how thankful we felt that our dwelling house stood secure, as John was in no condition to have attempted building another. Not even a pane of glass was broken, though, of course, the roof could not escape, and consequently everything was soaked. The day proved fortunately very hot, and we got all the mats lifted, and mattresses, blankets, etc., washed and dried. The pigs were in their glory, running riot over all the plantations, and I am sure if they could have spoken they would have said in Scotch, 'It's an ill wind that blaws naebody guid!'

Almost every native on the island was at work before daylight at his fences—dwelling-houses (and there were not a dozen standing uninjured on the island) being left till the plantations were secured. School duties were not even thought of. It was so sad to see the destruction of food—fine large breadfruit and cocoa-nut trees torn up by the roots, and bananas with the fruit half-formed lying useless on the ground. But the greatest lamentation seemed to be about the *Tafari Moré* (= House of Worship), though the general public were complacently viewing it as a judgment from *Tiapolo* (= His Satanic Majesty, in Aniwan), for their being so *strong for the worship*. This is a popular error; and John guarded them against it next Sabbath, preaching an impressive sermon from the text, 'Labour not for the meat *which perisheth*'—rather *apropos* to the occasion!

We worshipped under a very widespreading banyan tree—which however was no shade, the hurricane having left the trees leafless—with the ruins of the church on the one side, and of the school on the other. John told them at the close that we would not speak of a new church for a week or two, till they had got their own plantations, etc., in order; but after that they did set to work with a will; and oh, I wish you could have seen sometimes forty or fifty of them bending under the weight of a huge tree, which they had carried two or three miles over a precipitous path, and drenched in perspiration. We could hear the joyous noise a long way off, and it ended in a triumphant shout as they laid it down at the church. I could not settle to anything for running out to watch the progress; and as for John, he had to be everywhere at once, directing and working as hard as any of them. The villages all took it in turns to provide a feast for the workers at the close of each day; and as the food was brought in the morning, the women came to cook it, and those who could be spared were busy plaiting sugar-cane leaf to thatch the roof. So you may imagine what a bee-hive appearance the *Imrai*, or public square, presented; and how sometimes great roars of laughter burst forth, at some woman indignantly pitching a cocoa-nut shell at a man who was slily running off with a choice morsel! My girls used to get through their work in the morning, and run to help; and I often contributed to the entertainment with an enormous bucket of tea. One day, when a lot of Tannese were helping, they had as many as fourteen pigs cooked and eaten.

They wrought so hard that, after five Sabbaths in the open air, we again assembled in a new building where the old one had been; and, though by no means finished, it was rendered sufficiently comfortable to worship in—the roof nicely thatched, and the framework of the walls covered in with plaited cocoa-nut leaves, until they could make lime, as they resolved to have a wood and plaster building, this time. Of course the whole of the work and material was given *gratis*; but John promised them a large cow for a feast when all was finished—an inducement to the lazy ones to work!

After a week's rest, they began again to collect coral to burn for lime, which is heavy labour, as the coral has all to be dug out of the sea with crowbars, three miles off at Tiara, and boated round. Tiara is a lovely little island, adjoining Aniwa, where the children and I took advantage of the boat to do a little picnicking, their Papa being always with us, as he had to superintend a good deal, and see that they did not smash his boat right up amongst the reefs.

All were getting on with great glee, when a sudden stop was put to everything and the whole island thrown into a ferment by two wilful and cold-blooded murders, which took place on the morning of March 2nd. No one had any suspicion of what was going to happen, and the murdered man was one of the most active on the day before, diving for coral for the church. He was the son of such good, respectable church members, though not one himself—a fine fellow, attending church regularly with his children and young Tannese wife, whom he had lately married, and who was murdered along with him. It is supposed that she was the ground of jealousy that led to these awful deeds.

Poor Patesa and his wife went to bed as usual; and, just as the day began to dawn, the two murderers, an Aniwan and a Tanna man, crept quietly to their house and removed the cocoa-nut leaves at the door. Patesa stirred in his sleep at the sound, but he was shot through the heart before he awoke to consciousness. His poor wife tried to hide, but was shot down by the other villain, and hardly spoke during the few moments she lived. Patesa called to his brother and mother, and told who the murderers were, while the blood was spouting out at his heart, and then died; and both were buried in the grave before the breakfast hour. The news spread like wildfire, but not correctly at first, and we were in hopes the wounds were not mortal; so John hurried off to the village with bandages and everything he could need, but was met half-way by a native teacher, who told him they had just been buried.

The chiefs and people assembled in the *Imrai*, full of consternation, to consider what was to be done. The scoundrels were hidden, of course, and the punishment they got (the destruction of all their property, except food, which was divided among the people) was no more than they could afford to laugh at, as anyone can pick up a living of some sort, either in the bush or in the sea. Oh, how an event of this kind teaches one to prize and admire British law! The injured party were afraid to stay in their own village, not knowing what might happen next, and one of the murderers being a

Tanna man, the whole of the Tannese were ready to back him up. I sent for the friends and collected every scrap of black I could find for mourning, for which they were very anxious; and John, in consideration of his speedy return to the Colonies, parted with his scuffy blacks. The old mother looked twenty years older; her hair had turned quite grey with the shock, and she was perfectly outworn with grief.

It was altogether a sad time, that, for we had been so tried with Hutshi, the girl I had last time with me in Australia, and who has turned out a complete *vixen*—the first of my girls, I am thankful to say, who has not turned out well. She was married to one of our best young lads, and went quite gracefully through the whole affair—I think I wrote you all about it before—but all the while she was dying for my handsome young cook, who is engaged to the little tablemaid. She began, soon after the marriage, to persecute her husband and flirt with the other, going from bad to worse, notwithstanding all we could say to her and one day she behaved so frightfully, that, when we were told of her guilt, John and I sank down on the nearest seats, perfectly overpowered with disappointment and horror. I could hardly have believed that any woman, either black or white, could have so deliberately planned to lead others so young and innocent into sin.

The young chief came to ask John how she ought to be punished, as something would have to be done; but he hesitated to give advice, never having been called upon to legislate in a similar case, being indeed too vexed to collect his thoughts; only he strongly forbade them to shoot her, as one or two of the enraged fathers proposed, and advised them to be guided by the Aneityumese teachers, two wise Christian men from Mr Inglis's station. They said that the punishment inflicted on Aneityum by the chiefs was to tie up the guilty parties, collect all the goods of those most deeply involved, and distribute them among the people at the other side of the island—so as not to tempt those around to bring false accusations against neighbours for the sake of their property.

This was accordingly done in the case of Hutshi; and we had an invitation to be present at the ceremony, which we declined, as John told them it was better he should not be too much mixed up in these things. The only way in which he did interfere was to shorten the time to *three* hours, instead of the twenty-four they were determined to keep her tied—and which, in my opinion, she richly deserved! Two or three Tannese happened to arrive at her village before she was unloosed, and expressed their disgust at the consequences entailed by the worship, saying they could have as much 'fun' on Tanna as they liked without being punished for it. But one of our Aniwans answered, with a sly wink at his neighbours, that, bad as the worship might be, it had at least not driven them from their own land!

We were awfully vexed about this happening with one of our girls, as everything connected with the mission station is so talked about, and the worst characters are generally the most censorious. The father of one of my little girls, a wild and greedy fellow who wanted to be *paid* for letting me attend and nurse her through an illness (!), came with a grand face, expressing his horror of Hutshi's conduct, and saying he must take away his little girl, as he could not think of letting her remain to follow such an example. I was both amused and indignant, but took care to show neither feeling, and jumped up pleasantly, saying I would let her go at once and give her one or two of her dresses home with her (I took care to make no mention of her blanket-box, which they most value), as she had been an attentive girl. The man looked rather dismayed at being taken so sharply at his word, and muttered something to the effect that his daughter might not wish to leave, whereupon I expressed my horror at allowing the girl to disobey her father for a single moment! The fact is, that it suited me to make an example of her, for I knew that owing to her mother's health she would soon have been taken away at any rate, and besides she was the boldest and least grateful of all my girls. My heart smote me, however, when she looked up at me with the big tears in her eyes, as I was taking her hand in mine to say goodbye after giving her the little bundle. Yet I felt I could not rightly do anything else; and I comforted the little woman by telling her I would always look upon her as one of my own girls, and that she was not to hesitate to ask me for anything she wanted—a piece of advice which I have since found to be quite unnecessary!

I did not take time to consult John, as I had them off in less than ten minutes; but he said afterwards that I had acted perfectly right. We heard the natives tease the poor man most unmercifully as he crossed the *Imrai* on his way home, shouting out they were glad to see he was able to set up his village as a pattern even to the Missi's (it never before was distinguished for morality), and that if he would inform them when the change took place they would send their children to him! A few minutes afterwards, the guardian of my next youngest girl appeared at the window with a rueful face, and asked if his child might be allowed to remain? I told him I was too glad to keep them all, and had not asked the other girl to go; and reminded him, besides, that so long as Hutshi lived on the mission station her conduct was irreproachable.

I wish I could say that was the last of the trouble we had with Mistress Hutshi; for she professed great repentance, and sent one of the girls two or three weeks afterwards to say she wanted to tell me all her badness, as that would make her feel better. She had not been allowed to come near the mission premises, nor had we since taken any notice of her. We had very little faith in the young lady's repentance, but feared to crush any yearning after amendment, if it *did* exist, and I thought that God might give me a word for her. So we had a long interview; but I felt, all the time, there was no change in her, as was immediately proved, for she went back tossing her head and telling the others they might talk as much as they liked, she didn't care, for the Missi was quite satisfied with her now!

She did not improve, but the church members round kept such a watch upon her that she did not do anything very flagrant. She did, however, lead her husband a miserable life, and I never believed that a native could have borne with patience what he did; at last, being able to stand it no longer, he came to bid me goodbye, saying he was going to live about three miles distant (it was as far away almost as he could get on Aniwa, either in one direction or the other, as his lady-love lived close to us in the centre of the island), and that he freely bestowed her upon any man who might be fool enough to take her, as henceforth he would have nothing to do with her.

She had, out of pure bravado, professed to elude their vigilance and implicated a Tanna man, as well as Rangi (the wildest man on Aniwa), who both proved their innocence. Perhaps Rangi agreed with me that he had enough sins of his own to account for without being blamed for what he really did not do; and being an out-and-out savage in his disposition, we feared trouble when he came with all the Tanna men at his heels to inquire about it one morning after her husband had left her. We little expected, however, the scene there really was, right outside our gate too, for it was there Rangi caught hold of her. She gave one spring to John for protection, but the gate was between them, and Rangi wrenched her from it, and the savage yells that got up nearly sent me frantic with terror.

John stood leaning carelessly against the gate, viewing it all—the calmest person there! He felt that his presence would be a sufficient check, though it would have been folly to interfere. My girls were groaning and crying; and Yawaci (the girl I have here) was unconsciously doing her best to wrench the handles off the dining-room door in her despair, groaning out, 'Missi, blood will be spilt!' while I was on my knees in the middle of the floor calling upon God to interfere. But my little Frank stopped me, saying, 'Mamma, Mamma, I don't like to see you look up and talk like that! Are you ill?' So I tried to be myself again to the wee man, and felt comforted in having left the case with the Lord. Only I *must* see Rangi, though I had very slender hope of influencing him; and I put my careful husband into a fine consternation, as he would rather have seen an apparition than me coming on such a scene. I had only a very dim notion, then, of his gestures and entreaties, being deaf and blind to everything except Rangi, who came nearest my idea of a *demon* of anything I had ever seen!

The poor girl was tied, with her arms backward, to a cocoa-nut tree, pale with terror, and a hundred muskets bristling round her. The Tannese were in full *heathen* costume, which means paint instead of clothing; and the church members stood calmly like John, looking on, except two or three of them who kept guard around her with loaded muskets for her defence from murder if necessary. Her life was all they or we wished to see spared, for she richly deserved any punishment short of death. I caught Rangi's eye at last. At a sign he came quietly forward, and I began to tell him he should not dare to shoot my girl, but being too excited I ended in sobs and was marched off—but not before Rangi earnestly assured me that he would not touch a hair of her head or let anyone else do it, only he said she deserved to be tied and ought to be well beaten for blackening his character! We could not keep from smiling, even in the excitement, at Rangi's care for his reputation, which was truly as black as it well could be.

Well, here was Mistress Hutshi practically put up for public sale; for, according to native law, whoever dared to unloose her from that tree had to take her for his wife, her husband having renounced all claim to her. Rangi reminded them of this when he tied her up, saying that the Missi only could alter that law if he wished. The Missi did not feel inclined to do any such thing, having devoutly wished her at Jericho ever since she commenced her pranks, as she was proving a curse to the place, and now only hoped that the most tyrannical unmarried man on the island would take her off bodily as far away as the limited circumference of Aniwa would permit (so did the church members); but for John to *say* so would only be the beginning of mischief. He was so anxious they would not appeal to him for advice, for we both felt that for her native law was the best. But though a score of younger men would have gone down on their knees for her before she was married, there she stood for about three hours without a single bidder!

John had got the whole crowd dispersed to go and cut wood for the lime-pits (you know he is of a rather practical turn of mind and likes to utilize the most unlikely occasions), which they did with great energy, having the steam up; so she was left alone, as the women had all to run and cook food. I had a grand donation for the labourers besides the tea, that day, as we had a calf killed the evening before, and I was giving orders about it when I saw John waving me to the study with such an amused face. It seems that Hutshi's *old* sweetheart had rushed to him in eager haste, saying, 'Missi, I never will have such a chance for a wife! Will you marry me to Hutshi, if I untie her?' John said he certainly could not, and that if he took her it must be *à la native*, and that he would have to discontinue his attendance at the candidates' class, of which he was a member. He explained, at the same time, that it was not like running away with another man's wife, as her behaviour (which in Britain would have divorced her) had led her husband to give her up; only that for the sake of example, he could not countenance such proceedings on the part of intending communicants. Sarra said in that case he would have nothing to do with her. But, alas, female influence prevailed, and he unloosed her an hour or two after amid the hurrahs of the passers-by and our intense though secret delight; for though Sarra is obliged to confess he has 'caught a tartar,' yet he manages to keep her in tolerable check, being a determined fellow.

We heartily re-echoed the sentiments of one of our church members, when speaking of Hutshi—viz., that 'it was awful what a *woman* could do, when she was bent upon mischief!' Indeed, according to the natives, we have her along with the two murderers to thank for those awful earthquakes which nearly frightened us out of our senses, though on Aniwa very little damage accrued from them.

The first, at least the first to speak of, occurred near midnight on March 28th (the second anniversary of our Lena's birth), and woke us up with a vengeance, being the worst we ever had, the earth heaving so awfully that we expected every moment to be swallowed up, and were almost paralyzed with terror, but Minn and Frank slept through it all. After it a *tremendous* rush of the sea seemed to take place, from the noise it made, and which we found next morning was the case, carrying our boat from where it lay high and dry about one hundred yards inland, also canoes, two of which were smashed.

I lay in awful terror after the earthquake till three o'clock, and was dropping off to sleep, when another terrible one sent us flying out of the house in our nightgowns—John dragging the children out of their beds, and the girls rushing out of their house. There was not a breath of wind, and it was awful to see in the bright moonlight the great trunks of the trees swaying back and forward, and to feel the ground going to and fro with such force. We had one or two slight ones after that, and then just at daybreak an awful repetition—every one of us simultaneously rushing out of doors! This was number *five*; and before breakfast we went to see the damage done to the boat (but it was uninjured); and we had two more violent shocks ere we got home, making *seven* in all before breakfast, after which we had a commotion of another kind.

John felt so exhausted, and had just got fast asleep on the study sofa (a most unusual occurrence with him), when I heard high words between Taia, one of our church members, and Nalihi, an Erromangan. I knew not what to do, for natives never waste time on high words—they at once rush to arms; and I was unwilling to wake John to more excitement, as it was exactly that day two years since he had been seized with that awful fever, and I had been in fear of its return, as people predicted it would, about the same time of the year. Well, I actually made up my mind to show my wifely devotion—and it was a good test for me, I beg leave to say; I always had such a foolish terror of a loaded musket anywhere, and infinitely more so in the hands of an enraged savage—by going between the combatants myself. To make matters worse, all the men about had gone that morning to bring lime-coral, and only a few women had collected, and one or two timid fellows who stood a safe distance.

Nalihi was flourishing his musket in Taia's face, as an accompaniment to an eloquent harangue he was delivering in Erromangan, not being able to speak Aniwan; and Taia, who understood and could speak seemed to be paying him back with interest. They subsided for a few moments, when it was whispered the Missi was there; but on finding that it was only the *Missi-finé*, they went at it with renewed vigour. I took no notice of the Erromangan, knowing my only chance was with Taia; so I went over to him and implored him not to utter another word, whatever provocation he might receive; and though reluctant at first, he behaved nobly and stood what I think few white men would have done in the circumstances. I kept close beside him all the time; and though for three-quarters of an hour that villain stood heaping insults upon him, and at last in his rage cut down his bananas and fences before his eyes, he never spoke, though his muscles twitched and he clutched at his great club sometimes—one that I knew had done good (?) service in heathen days under the great brawny arms that wielded it, for Taia is a perfect Hercules, and such a contrast to the little treacherous sharp-nosed Erromangan who was dying for an excuse to get a shot at him. When I thought Taia was going to give way I put my cold white paw (it *did* feel so cold) on his black arm, and every time I did so he turned and looked down at me with a grim smile, saying, *Don't fear, Missi; I'll not speak.*

Now I maintain that though John sometimes fears Taia's Christianity is not of the highest type, yet he is undoubtedly *a perfect gentleman*, or he would not have stood there, the greatest living orator on Aniwa, silent at the bidding of any woman! When I saw the good food being destroyed, and so little left from the hurricane, indignation mastered every other feeling, and I felt it was high time for John to interfere with Nalihi; as no one else dared to speak to him, except Master Frank, who had by the way found us out just then and proceeded without hesitation to deal with him in plain terms. His little figure heaved with indignation, and he drew such a long breath before calling out, *You naughty, naughty man! You're a wicked man! Jehovah so angry at you!* Everyone was so amused, and a general titter went round, while Nalihi, with whom Frank had been a favourite, began vigorously to defend himself to the child in broken English, at the same time wielding his axe to some purpose amongst Taia's bananas. So, feeling my own strength would not hold out much longer, I sped off and brought John, who quietly went up to Nalihi, and relieved him of his musket and axe (oh, I was glad to see that musket in dear old John's trusty paws, for Nalihi held it in a horizontal position, and it always *would* point at me the whole time I stood there!), clapped him on the shoulder, and had him sobbing like a child in a minute and offering payment to Taia for the damage done—which, however, Taia was too seriously offended, to receive, and I do not wonder at it.

The crowd began to disperse, and John was taking Nalihi off for a day's work under his own eye, in case of him coming in contact with Taia again, when I put a graceful finish to the proceedings by going off into a fainting fit under the cocoa-nut trees! John said I managed bravely, all except that; but I do think that after *seven* earthquakes and such a scene I had a good right to get up some demonstration, and it was the first I ever perpetrated for the public benefit!

We had three more earthquakes that day, but slight, making *ten* in all; and I took care at night to provide for emergencies by putting a supply of blankets on the veranda, as there is not a moment to snatch clothes when they come and we had felt chilly the night before. I got laughed at for what was termed my needless precaution; but we had hardly got into our first sleep, when another violent earthquake turned us out and we were thankful for them. It was not so bad as some, however, and we got asleep till morning without further disturbance, as the grand performance did not come off till next evening at nine o'clock.

John was busy in the bathroom, with the girls, damping paper for next day's printing, and I was in the diningroom, jotting in my journal the events of the day, when we all had to rush out with the most frightful earthquake that had yet taken place. The house danced, the windows rattled awfully, and Frank woke up with the first of it screaming in terror, but

Minn took it more gently, telling him it was *nice.* It might have been nice to feel ourselves rocked on the bosom of Mother Earth (we lay down on the ground at a safe distance from the house, which we expected to fall every moment), could we have been sure she would not open up and receive us into a closer embrace!

The heaving must, I think, have continued nearly five minutes, and we had just got into the house again, still trembling with agitation, when a terrible gust of wind and roar of the sea half prepared us for the shouting of the natives, who called to us that the sea had actually come close to our gate! We went out and found natives up to the waist in water, where it had been bush two or three minutes before. We heard something flapping, and Yawaci picked up a large fish about twelve feet from our gate; and as the tidal wave receded they were left in hundreds, which the natives spent most of that night and next day in gathering. An enormous turtle was found too amongst a lot of debris—*Jehovah's turtle*, the natives called it, owing to the way in which it was found.

No serious accident occurred from the wave on our island, as in most of the others, though some natives fishing at Tiara were nearly carried away, and our boat, which lay at anchor there, was lifted, anchor and all, and carried a long way inland, but to a sandy place, where it got no damage; yet not a canoe, if I remember rightly, was left whole.

From that time we had a constant succession of earthquakes and were kept in continual dread, though none of them so violent as those I have mentioned. We had to sleep with our doors open, and at last John went to bed in his clothes to be ready to run! I suppose you have heard that the tidal wave swept right through Mr Inglis's, doing terrible damage and half drowning them, and the earthquakes kept knocking down his walls and chimneys as fast as he could rebuild them. Dr Geddie's fine church too is all but destroyed. But I think the greatest damage done is to the nerves of the poor missionaries' wives (the missionaries themselves would be indignant if you accused them of having any!). It is such an awful sensation to feel the very earth trembling and heaving beneath one, and such an *eerie* feeling comes on at night.

I was thankful to bid goodbye to Aniwa for a while, though vexed to part with the natives, poor things. I am so proud of their progress (the women and girls) in hat-making, which has been quite a success this year; and now they are entirely independent in this respect of the outer world, and begin to take them on board the *Dayspring* and trading vessels for sale. They are just simple round straw hats, with narrow brims for the men and broader for the women, neatly plaited all in one, like leghorns, with the pandanas leaf, which grows plentifully on the islands. Minn and Frank are wearing them to school in fashionable Melbourne, and don't look a bit outlandish; indeed the islands are not so far behind the age after all, for neither the children nor I have needed to go near a dress-maker or get a single new garment since we came (John hasn't either), and we look just like our neighbours, and a great deal better than some I have seen! Nearly two hundred hats were plaited at school, and I trimmed them—for the women with bright calico, and the men's with a narrow band of Turkey red. While they plaited, we got through the singing of thirteen new hymns which John printed and added to the little hymn-book, two or three of them being translations from *Sankey's Collection*, which the natives sing so heartily, often attracting a poor Tanna invalid we had, who would come slipping round the veranda to listen.

Nisei's was a sad history, poor man. He was out one day fishing in his canoe, about five years ago, and was run down by a trader's boat (he had no idea they were chasing him, or he could have escaped), dragged out of his canoe, which was sent adrift, taken on board and put in irons till he became 'reasonable,' and soon found himself in a Fiji plantation; there he was not badly treated and had plenty of food, till he got ill (he was brought to us in the last stage of consumption), and then they kicked him to make him work, but as he could not, and neither would he die—which was so inconsiderate of him!—they were obliged to bring him home, at least as near home as suited their convenience. They landed him on Tanna at Port Resolution, thirty miles or so from his own village, and amongst the most deadly enemies of his tribe, who began to smack their lips over the prospect of a cannibal feast the moment he was landed. But our old friend Nowar came to the rescue, and showed them how very little picking they could get off his bones, and offered them a fine fat pig in his stead—which they were gracious enough to accept! Curiously, this was the means of saving Nowar's life afterwards, for the poor man gave him his box as a little return for his kindness, being all he had, and it was this box which received the bullet intended for Nowar during the late war which sent them to Aniwa, when he happened to be carrying it on his shoulder from his own house.

Nisei, the sick man, came over with the refugees in December, and was brought to us one day for medicine, and we kept him altogether as he was unable to walk back. He was evidently dying, reduced to a perfect skeleton, and in agony sometimes from his breathing. It made our hearts ache to see him, and he clung so to John, telling him all his story at intervals as his cough would allow. His tears fell thick when he saw Minn and Frank playing and tumbling over their Papa, for his own two were about the same age when he left them. He said if the white men had only let him say goodbye to them before he left, he would not have felt it so much; and he was very anxious to be kept alive till the *Dayspring* came, John having promised to try and get her to land him at his own village, about ten minutes from Mr

Watt's station. I gave him the most nourishing food I could think of, but it was so little he either could or would take that it was a difficult matter to sustain him. He was very fond of sponge-cake, and I charged John and the natives not to let him know it was made of eggs, but he found it out one day and would eat no more.

He felt that the natives were tired of him, and he was so grateful to us, for we always took care, either John or I, to take his meals to him ourselves. His mind was so dark, but he was yearning to know something of that world to which he was hastening, and I felt it so hard to be tongue-tied, for I can't speak a word of Tannese, and it was impossible, with all the multiplicity of work which John had to attend to, that he could be much with him. I could do little more than mention that blessed name which is above every name, and point upward; and oh, how eagerly he would look up with his great wistful eyes, and then at me, as if he would fain drink in more! He had a violent attack of haemorrhage one evening, and after that was afraid he might die in the night, and wanted John to go and sleep in his house, which was rather awkward; but we decided to give him the study—a great privation for John—but he was not put to the test, as Nisei could not think of dwelling in a *big house*, though he was told that John would sleep in the same room on the sofa; but he *insisted* on lying on the veranda (I had given him warm blankets and clothing) outside our bedroom window, which opened on to it, and John went to him two or three times every night. We were amused at his calling him *Cap'ain*, evidently intending it as a great compliment to John, who would scorn to put even the title of *King* on a par with that of Missionary!

Nisei was still alive when we were ready to go to the Mission Synod, and was put ashore at Mr Watt's, who promised to have him sent round in his boat to his own village. He heard, when he got there, however, that his wife was married to another man and his children either dead or stolen away; so he lost heart, and said he would die where he was, as he had friends in a village five minutes' walk from Mr Watt's. I stayed to keep Mrs Watt company, when our husbands went on to the Mission Synod, and we visited him to the end, Mrs Watt speaking and praying with him every time. (John always managed to have a little worship with him once a day, and he used to cling so to that poor man, and he, on the other hand, would send for John when late in going.) The last day he was in life, Mrs Watt asked him if he knew the Lord Jesus, and he said so sadly and earnestly, *I don't know him, Missi*, and then listened so intently as she spake of the Saviour's love. When we went back next day with more little comforts in the shape of tea, etc., Nisei was in his grave.

I must pass over everything else that happened until we turned up in civilization, as it is close upon mail time. I would have liked to tell you about our pretty new church with its snow-white walls, which was finished just before our beloved friends Mr and Mrs Inglis paid us their farewell visit—which was like to break our hearts, for they have been a father and mother to us and to the mission. Our parting too with our darkies was intensely trying, as we are to be away from them a longer visit than the last; but the society of our dear friends the Murrays was an unexpected treat, and made the voyage so pleasant, notwithstanding the seasickness.

And now I have our *grand* joy to tell you of, and which I often feared was too good to be realized. Our precious sons Bob and Fred have been given back to us again after an absence of nearly two years. From the time we got the telegram saying they had left Adelaide, till we folded them in our arms, our hearts thumped most unmercifully, and all was fever and preparation. Even Yawaci, who always goes on in the even tenor of her way however others may be burning with impatience, got so excited when the lightning 'message' came that she kept tramping up and down stairs without in the least knowing what she was going for! The shipping office people must have come to the conclusion that people of note were in their vessel, from the many inquiries made regarding it! The three days *did* pass, however; and on Saturday night, after seeing the children's room as pretty as flowers, books, and their little home-box presents could make it, I went through the ceremony of going to bed myself, though not to sleep; for our boys were to arrive on Sabbath morning, and long before daybreak I was up and dressed with such fastidious care that John came to the sage conclusion that a mother's love was the most intense feeling human nature was capable of, as he had never known me get up in the night and spend as much time over my own and the bairns' appearance for any living being! He had to submit to a thorough inspection himself before I sent him off at daybreak, for I didn't see why our little men should not see us looking our best.

He steadily refused to let me go with him, fearing the result of over-excitement; but was glad to change his mind on finding that the steamer would not be at the wharf till after ten o'clock, and that he could not bring them here and be back at East Melbourne to preach at eleven; so he came tearing back in a cab for me, and we got to the wharf a quarter of an hour before the steamer. As it came in sight I learned, if I did not know it before, that grief can be more calmly borne sometimes than joy; for I parted from them without a tear, feeling as sensible of God's presence carrying us through it as if I had seen his glorious person in the room. I can't say that about the meeting. The dear boys broke down at the sight of their Papa (he had to cross another steamer to get to theirs), and sprang into his arms sobbing, unable to utter a word. They were a great deal taller and much the better for their stay in Adelaide, but the same dear old fellows still. Their Papa came a bit in the cab with us, and then turned off to his pulpit duties (he must have given the people a grand sermon!), leaving us to encounter the meeting with Minn and Frank, who were as excited as two little mortals could be, but Yawaci's black face was decidedly the best of the whole affair. It was perfectly radiant with joy; and with what a loving voice she said *Fareddy* and kissed him—a *tremendous* demonstration of affection for a native! They have been with us over a fortnight now, and how delightful it is to tuck them all under the clothes with my own hand at night! All four are at school, and *like it*. The home mail closes in the morning; and I must close, with fondest love,

From your loving sister,
Maggie Whitecross Paton.

15

The Madness of Mungaw

Aniwa, New Hebrides,
8 July, 1878.

My Dearest Sisters and Brothers,[1]

Sons and Daughter, I should almost have added, as the biggest half of our little flock are separated from Aniwa, and will as eagerly look for the family *billet* (letter) now as the rest of you.

Now that I have sat down to write, so much comes crowding upon me that I hardly know where to begin; but I cannot put down a word of news before testifying of the Lord's goodness to us, which has just been vouchsafed during this last hot season. He has encompassed us round as with a shield, and preserved us safe and well, though from the day after the *Dayspring* left for the Colonies on November 14th last until March 30th we have lived in daily—I might almost say *hourly*—terror of our lives. We have seen—especially John has—the rage of the heathen, and passed through earthquake and hurricane; but all seems as nothing compared with coming into constant contact with an unrestrained *madman*; and this we have had to do with poor Mungaw, who from the time he was with us in Melbourne began to show symptoms of insanity, which increased until he was a terror to the whole island, and attempted so many lives that at last he was shot

[1] To the family circle.

down himself on March 30th, almost at our very gate, close to which was his house. We deplored the murder, but when I tell you of some of his ongoings you will wonder with us that he was spared so long. It is amazing what an amount of mischief one man can do; otherwise everything would have prospered so far as we could see.

The natives were all so thankful to have us back, and so willing to be taught; and we got a welcome worth coming for from those of the missionaries we saw on our way home. We were both in better health than we could have expected, after the first prostration on a return to the tropics. Frank declared there was no place in the world half so good as Aniwa; and little Jay took quite naturally to the black faces, being so accustomed to Yawaci's. There was abundance of work to do, and we were able to get through a great amount—John as usual doing the lion's share. Indeed I feared it was going to kill him at first—there was so much that no one else but he could do. It takes so much manual labour here just to live, besides the multifarious duties falling to the lot of a missionary. I'll give you just one day as a specimen; and though, of course, the same incidents did not occur daily, yet other things demanding as instant attention seemed always starting up.

After our usual breakfast at half-past six, he went off to visit the little schools conducted by the teachers at the other end of the island, and did some visiting at the same time; then home and to work (I think, roofing an outhouse with zinc, as we were anxiously looking for rain to fill the tanks); then dinner, and off to a distance to settle some native quarrel he had just heard of, and returned pale and trembling with weakness. He threw himself on the sofa, declaring he must give in, and asked if I could manage the afternoon school myself. I strongly urged him to go right off to bed, when a messenger came to say that one of my scholars, a fine young woman, had been bled too deeply in her leg to ease some pain (bleeding is the panacea for all aches and pains here, and a broken bottle is the favourite instrument), and that she was fast dying, as they could not get it to stop. I flew to get bandages, etc., and John had to set off to a distance of three miles as fast as he was able to run, and found the poor woman in the last stage of exhaustion. He bound up the wound tightly; gave her a little brandy and water, which revived her so that she opened her eyes, saying, 'That puts life into me,' and in less than a week she was going about her ordinary work. How natives *do* get over a thing of that kind! The women just shout with laughter when I warn against bathing in the sea, the day after their babies are born. They pay for their recklessness some time or other, though, for they don't as a rule live nearly so long as white people; and they give as much heed to warnings as does your venerable brother, who declares he has been threatened with death from overwork ever since he was the age of sixteen, and as he's not dead yet he thinks he has abundantly proved to all concerned that they have been false prophets, and he's 'not going to change his tactics now!'

He was forced to take a week's rest, sorely against his will, after the *Dayspring* left us for the Colonies. … He was much fevered all the time, and we had serious apprehensions. … I felt myself a very important member of society—keeping schools going, giving out medicine to the natives, etc., besides housekeeping—and I asked John rather triumphantly what he would have done without his nurse, had I stayed in Melbourne, as he insisted? To which he rather profanely retorted, that he would just have died and got a far better rest in heaven, while I would have been comforted among kind friends and had my bairns around me! That would have been rather too great a price to pay even for my children, though how terribly we miss them God only knows!

A more beautiful spot than we have here, it would be difficult to get; a pretty commodious house (for, you know, it's 'the house that Jack built'!), with large grounds tastefully laid out, and the smooth grass dotted with choicest shrubs. But 'Ichabod' seems written on everything; and when I pass the day-nursery, with its bright prints on the walls, and Minn's old stumps of dolls, now converted into most precious relics, my heart fills and yearns so for just one sight of them; and I envy the people in Melbourne who will be passing every day with unconcern the dear faces we would give so much to see! How precious the most trivial incidents connected with them become when they are absent, and even things that were an annoyance at the time, treasured up and viewed so lovingly when they are gone. I remember, when we first left Bob and Fred in Adelaide, we found on coming home a large grotesque picture drawn in pencil on the study wall, which we knew to be theirs, as it was the only room in the house locked up from the natives—John not wishing his books and papers disturbed. Now I am perfectly certain they would get a thorough scolding for it at the time; but now not a picture in the house was lingered over with the peculiar fascination of that one, and it was actually a question with us at the next annual cleaning whether we would have that part of the wall washed at all!

It has always been a poser to me, since parting with my own, how *for any earthly consideration whatever* people can live away from their little ones; for instance, those in the civil service in India and elsewhere, whose children must be sent away at such an early age. Only in the most direct way, *for the Lord Jesus*, does it seem to me justifiable—or indeed possible—and only his strength could have carried us through the trial; for we firmly believe he will be true to his word and watch over those so left with special care. Even with it all, the separation is hard, *hard*, to bear; and I dare not speak of the absent ones at meals, for not another bite can their Papa swallow.

You will be apt to say, it serves him right, after all your repeated advice to him about leaving the mission and doing a parent's duty to his children; but I must vindicate my old man even to his relatives, and most emphatically deny that it is mere obstinacy that makes him stick to mission life. You know, his whole spirit is saturated with it; and it's just as impossible to take the missionary spirit out of a man, as it is to put it into him. Besides, he does not feel that God has given him a direct call to leave it; and until that is the case, you may be sure *he* will not make the first move! Even I, who have never indulged in missionary sentiment (believing that John had enough for the pair of us!), would not leave one hour sooner, even for my children, than God would have us; but if *he* does give the call, won't I spring with alacrity to obey!

You must not think of us as pining in solitude, however. Indeed poor Mungaw took care to keep us all in lively exercise, and acted his first scene the day after the *Dayspring* left for Sydney with our mails. You know that he married Litsi, one of my best girls (and how delighted we were at the time that she was getting such a good young man!), who was with me on my first visit to Australia from Aniwa, and you remember how pleased you all were with her. Well, he spent the night beating that gentle girl (who was near her confinement) and their little boy about two years of age; and when John met him in the *Imrai* and quietly remonstrated with him, he stalked off in high dudgeon; and in two minutes more, a tremendous crackling and roar of fire made us rush to the windows where we saw his nice house and all that was in it one mass of flame. Not content with setting it on fire, he tore off Litsi's jacket and flung it in too. We quite expected that our own house would go, as there were only two light fences betwixt some of our outhouses and his, but providentially the wind carried everything the other way.

He then took Litsi and Namakei, their little boy, to a distant village, and oh! how we hoped he would remain, as Litsi had friends there; but back he dragged them, terror-stricken and breathless from having to keep pace with his tremendous strides. I sent Litsi an old jacket (she begged me not to send a good one, as it might go the same way), and a blanket to sleep or rather to roll herself in—for there was no sleep for anyone near that night. He had threatened to murder some of the villagers, and was stalking round and round our premises with his loaded musket, but an Aneityumese teacher kept watch over our house all the night.

It so happened that next day had been appointed for a 'Members' Meeting.' These meetings are held monthly, for John to appoint them their work and change it from one to another, so that it might not always devolve upon a few. You know there is no paid doorkeeper or paid service of any kind connected with the church, so the women take it in turns, two by two, every Saturday morning, to clean the church and enclosure. One man is appointed bell ringer, another to take off and on the pulpit coverings and carry in the Bible, etc., two to stand at the doors and see there are no loiterers outside, and so forth. Cases of sickness or wickedness are also reported, and church matters generally talked over. At this meeting one woman was scored off for absconding from her lawful husband and living with another; and Mungaw, who came in with the greatest boldness, as if nothing had happened, got a thorough 'talking to,' and was suspended till it should be proved whether he was more rogue or fool—for at that time we could scarcely tell. That he had become decidedly cracked, and his mind to a certain extent unhinged, no one who saw and heard him could doubt—especially knowing what a dear good fellow he was before; still he seemed sane enough at times; and when he did break out, it was more like being possessed with evil spirits. All his madness took the form of wickedness, and when he saw people afraid of him he was the more emboldened. It was very difficult to know how to treat him. He was rather cowed at the meeting, though, and kept pretty quiet till the full moon, while meantime we had peace to get all our machinery into working order again.

I was most anxious to have as few natives living with us as possible, there having been no rain here for many months, and not a particle of native food procurable to feed them with. We had brought several casks of biscuit and bags of rice, and Mr Robertson had kindly exerted himself to buy two casks of beans for us from the Erromangans. *We* were all secure in that way, having laid in a large stock of comforts, our bills as well as our full-stored cellar testifying to the fact! Kind friends, too, seemed to have made it their study to furnish us with choicest luxuries. Dear Yawaci was married and out of my care; but my three small girls came back, the day we landed. I hardly expected to get them, as their intended husbands are waiting impatiently for them—girls marry so very young here. Then we managed to engage four boys—two as cooks (I require two where the cook has to be butcher, baker, and wood cutter as well), and two as herds. Along with four washerwomen, and my married girls to come about twice a week to do the harder work, I felt well enough supplied; but three little boys, one a deaf-mute, the only one on the island and a dear wee fellow, and two little girls applied to be taken in, one after another. We could not refuse, though the idea of feeding twelve natives during the whole hot season was rather appalling; but we took them as from God, firmly believing that in some way or other he would send food for them, and he did!

Notwithstanding the want of rain, we never had such a fine crop of breadfruit, and it extended over two months (we never knew it to last more than one before), so that for that time I had more brought for sale than the whole of them could devour, which saved our foreign food. It was a great boon for the natives generally, as they have a way of preserving it, soaking it so long in the sea in baskets, and then burying it in the ground. How they can eat it I can't imagine, for the smell is frightful; but they insist it is no worse than our *cheese*, which they abominate. When biscuits, etc., were done, I fed them on bread (the cooks growled a little at having so many loaves to fire every day); and we had still a quarter of a cask of flour left when the *Dayspring*, always punctual in leaving Sydney, arrived with fresh stores for the season.

These girls and boys are the hardest part of our missionary work, there is such a responsibility and care connected with them. One girl, the latest comer, I had to pack off—she made such mischief among the older ones, who threatened to leave if she stayed. Her friends have since applied to have her taken back, as they can't do with her, and I have promised to let her return in a couple of months, if spared. I suppose you can guess what is the prevailing sin on these islands, and it is this which keeps us in such constant anxiety with our flock. John has often to be up in the night to see that all is propriety. He has had great comfort with his big boys, however, especially the one we were most averse to take in—a great ugly-looking fellow of about eighteen, couldn't speak without a growl, and scowled at everybody from under his black wool, which hung down over his eyebrows. To crown all, he had been with the *slavers*—and that is no recommendation!

After keeping with our boys a day or two and coming to evening class, on the third evening he sent in for a blanket, as he was 'going to stay.' We looked aghast. John was for receiving him; but I was at the crying point, and declared I could not feed more natives or make food go further than other people. John said, 'Then am I to send him away?' Well, no! I was hardly prepared to do that either; so, after talking over it a few minutes, we felt sure the Lord had sent him; and though I did not feel particularly grateful at the time, I have often thanked him since. We went to the blanket box, got a nice warm blanket (the natives feel chilly at night), called him in, and John had a talk with him about certain rules, after which he took his gift with a very pleasant grin. He looked like a different creature with his hair cut; and a more faithful, helpful, warm-hearted native lad we never had. In times of danger from Mungaw, he stuck by John like his shadow—no ostentation with it, but quietly getting some pretext for keeping close to him when there was any fear. A capital worker too—for John does not approve of keeping his boys idle, and they help him with whatever he is at, fencing, roofing, gardening, house building, etc.

One day he and another big boy (a great wag—keeps the others in roars of laughter, and himself the picture of solemnity) had been planing wood very nicely, and John praised them, calling them his *carpenter* and *joiner*. In the afternoon a slate full of writing was sent in, informing us that they wished from henceforth to drop their old names and be called 'Carpenter' and 'Joiner.' Nor would they answer to any other. We often forgot, at first, but were reminded by their paying not the slightest attention, till we came out with the new name—when they would instantly wheel round with a smile and be at our service.

Besides their food, and £4 each yearly which we give our cooks, herds, and any lad really doing hard work, we have no other expense, as we clothe them entirely out of the missionary boxes with which kind friends have always kept us well supplied; and we keep to the old rule of making the natives generally do something for every bit of clothing they get—except the old and the sick. Always abundance of work about a mission station; if not we make some, by setting them to weed a piece of waste ground, or the like. I keep twelve or thirteen women clothed for keeping all our grounds clear of weeds, etc.; and school prizes are given in clothing.

Their progress is most provokingly slow for the amount of teaching expended on them. There are morning schools for reading, all over the island, at daybreak, conducted by native teachers. Then I have my sewing class, twice a week, after breakfast. They last about two and a half hours altogether, with reading and singing. Some of them sew beautifully, and the attendance averages thirty. John has his afternoon school daily, from three till five o'clock, for the more advanced, for writing and figures; but it takes us both hard work to get over them, our own boys and girls attending as well. After tea and worship (English), all on the premises and any of the villagers who choose to come assemble for native worship and evening class in the dining room. They have reading and spelling, and twice a week they bring neatly written essays on given subjects, and those unable for essays write letters or words. This is about the most interesting class John has, but I'm too exhausted to remain up, and as soon as the girl has bathed Frank and Jay I slip off to have my wee while with them, and then to bed.

I give Frank his reading lesson, etc., during the day, and also teach English to a half-caste 'Johnnie,' son of an Aniwan woman, his father some white slaver. He made great progress and could read the Bible a little before going in the *Dayspring*, and John got one of the sailors to promise to help him while on board. He has led a wandering life among slavers, and this is the first opportunity he has had of learning. He is coming back here, when the *Dayspring* goes to Sydney again, being anxious for further instruction. He attended John's afternoon school, and made progress far beyond the Aniwans, though he did not know how to hold the pen a few months ago. He sat next to Mungaw, and they were a contrast! Johnnie perseveringly trying to imitate every letter, and Mungaw, though a capital penman, writing the greatest nonsense.

One day, before John was quite recovered, Mungaw put a lot of impudence on his copy for my special benefit. I took no notice—he looked so wild—but pointed out a misspelled word, wrote a fresh line, and telling him to follow it closely passed quickly on to the next writer. I told John, when I went in, I was sure he would do some mischief ere long; and just an evening or two after, we heard him shouting and scolding from his house in an awful voice. John limped off, in spite of my entreaties to let them fight it out, and found Mungaw flourishing an axe over a poor woman, whose husband was from home and who had been helping Litsi to cook his fish, but had been unfortunate enough not to divine that on that particular evening he wanted it wrapped in a different kind of leaf from what was usual. He had brought the axe within a few inches of her shoulder, when two or three natives, attracted to the spot just before John, stayed his arm and wrenched it from him. He got his musket next, but poor Sibo and Litsi both ran to our house for protection, while John and the natives tried to calm him down. They got his musket from him, and I saw a teacher slip it behind a tree in our lawn; but Mungaw was sharp enough to notice, and got it away again when the affray was over, and ordered poor Litsi back to her cooking. Sibo went to a distant village to be out of his way, declaring she was half-dead with fright; and I would very much have liked to get away from the island altogether! John's spirit always rises equal to the emergency, but I get perfectly faint with terror, and the longer the worse. This was merely a little prelude, however, to what followed.

Next morning, he had the audacity to appear at one of the dining-room windows, as the girls were clearing away the breakfast things, and he demanded the keys from John, as he wanted to sharpen his axe at the grindstone. John said, 'No,

Mungaw, you'll learn to put your axe to a better use first; and I want you to return the two you have of mine.' He looked the picture of innocent wonder, and replied, *What do you mean, Missi?* John replied, 'I just mean that I want you to give up your bad conduct.' '*My bad conduct! What have I done?*' protested Mungaw. John said pointedly, 'Do you not *know*, Mungaw?' That was all the provocation he got; but he went off for his musket, muttering, 'I'll let you know who you're talking to!'

When he was gone, John went out to his printing office for something, and on leaving it saw Mungaw just inside our fence taking deliberate aim at him with his musket. John turned round to lock the door, showing no signs of fear, but feeling that all was over, and that he was to be shot down so near us all, and yet none near enough to save; but God was watching! The next instant he heard a rush of feet, a scuffle, and looked round to see the musket pointed high in the air and four strong arms grappling with the intended murderer. Two men had been accidentally (?) coming up the path, took in the scene at a glance, and my husband was saved.

I knew nothing of what was passing, but feeling restless after Mungaw's parting look, went out to hurry John in for worship. I met him coming in, and stopped short at sight of his pale face to ask if he were ill, and he told me all. We had just begun to sing at worship, when Mungaw reappeared flourishing his musket, trying the doors and windows (you may believe, I had them securely fastened by this time), and demanding entrance. We went on, taking no notice, but the *celestial quaver* was plentifully introduced into the music, and the girls rushed into the dining room in great fear. Meanwhile, the news had spread like wildfire, and the church members near came running to order him out of the premises, which only made him wilder; so they seized him, took him to the *Imrai*, and bound him hand and foot with ropes. It was a terrible noise and scuffle, for he had the strength of ten men, and yelled like a demon.

Two of his brothers so-called (not real ones) arriving on the spot, he thought to get up some sympathy, changed his voice to a whine, and bewailed his hard fate—*bound and persecuted for doing nothing at all*! Litsi, gentle Litsi, took her boy in her arms, and walked up to him before the crowd, saying in a loud voice, 'Look at the marks of your brutality on me and my helpless child, and say whether you deserve to be tied or not!' It was an imprudent speech for her to make, poor girl, for which he did not forget to repay her. It was a terrible day for us all—poor little Frank white to the lips with fear, I lying in a fainting state, and John walking up and down the room, trying to keep up our spirits, and wee Jay—oh! how we envied him—running about, playing 'Peep-bo' in happy unconsciousness of all. The church members feared that some of the wilder young fellows, whom he had been favouring of late would come to his aid; but when it was known he had attacked the Missi, not a finger was lifted in his defence.

They did not know what to do with him, now they had him bound—nothing in the shape of a prison or secure place on all the island! They proposed our cellar, but we didn't want him quite so near as that so they let him off at the end of four hours, and Litsi and little Namakei took refuge with us. Mungaw got a little boy to tell him where they hid his musket; and, once more possessed of it, he flew all round the island till towards sunset, when he divested himself entirely of his clothing, stuck on paint, and with musket shouldered walked sentry before our front gate for more than an hour. He seemed to be imitating the sentinels he had seen before Government House in Melbourne—a slight difference in the circumstances! But it was thought necessary to have a counter-guard over our premises that night. The only good thing he did was to send his gracious permission to Litsi to stay in our house for the night, which she thankfully accepted.

Next morning (Sunday) he met her pleasantly, called her to speak to him (our fence was between them), and threw a large stone at her head, informing her that was the price of her yesterday's speech. We bound up the deep wound and advised her to lie quiet, but she preferred going to church with us as the safest plan, for he had been caught several times during the night stealthily approaching our house to burn it, as they thought. None of the villagers slept, two of their lives being in danger. It was a most anxious Sabbath, and we had worship under difficulties—guards being placed at our house and the principal approaches to the church. Oh, how regretfully I thought of the peaceful Sabbaths and quiet walks to church in Melbourne, none making us afraid! But we tried to realize that the Lord Jesus was encompassing us around, and that he stood between us and Mungaw. The people begged John to be short, as they were in terror, so we had only one service in church, and, instead of Sunday School, a prayer meeting on the *Imrai*. Mungaw employed the time during church service in ransacking the villagers' boxes for ammunition, but they had it hid away; and at the prayer meeting he was reclining, with folded arms, eyeing us from our back veranda! After the prayer meeting, John urged the different villagers to take it in turns to sleep near Mungaw's house for the protection of Litsi, who was being killed by inches, and at last they agreed; but as soon as we were in the house, he went and patched up a sort of peace—a sham to get the people away—and then abused the people near for tying him, and dragged Litsi home. We were half the night praying for the helpless girl, so completely at the mercy of that madman.

Next morning, he came into the *Imrai* in grand style—musket in hand, of course—and scolded the people, working himself up into a frenzy and keeping us all on the rack, for *we* could see from one of the study windows—when, to our great joy, *Sail ho!* rang out, and it was comical to see how quickly he had to subside before this counter-excitement and slink away! We felt it was in answer to prayer, more especially when a little afterwards he stood before our gate painted frightfully, and told our herd boys that he was going in the vessel if she called here. How earnestly we asked the Lord to let him go, if it were his will, but prayed above all for submission to bear what was appointed us, for we had the feeling he would stay. Poor fellow, he drove us closer into the Saviour's arms than all Dr Somerville's meetings in Australia, for we had him alone to look to. Natives were kind, but not capable of giving much help—they rather look to us for it—and, poor things, we did pity them, when it was known he had bought a large stock of ammunition, including balls, and that he stayed behind!

It turned out to be the schooner *Daphne* for Fiji; and the government agent sent half a sovereign in a note, begging for opium, as he had seventy-five people on board, and one case of 'assured sickness.' John, of course, returned the money, but sent opium pills, laudanum, and chlorodyne, having no opium. We were glad of the opportunity of sending a few hurried notes, bearing a month's later date than the *Dayspring*, which left on November 14th. This is the only other vessel that has called at our island, since we returned, except the *Dayspring*.

A few days after this we had a wedding excitement, the fifth since we returned. The bride—I can't say 'fair, fat, and forty,' she being black, of course—but I can vouch for the two latter qualifications; a comely dame, withal, with a pair of brilliant eyes and an evener little set of ivory than ever came out of the dentist's. She was the widow of one of our best church members—just suddenly dead—and she had the whole fraternity of bachelors (of whom I think there are about thirty without the slightest hope of getting wives, women being so scarce here) at her feet. She discarded them all but the two most determined, and came to us in desperation to decide which she was to take. We told her she alone was the judge of that, asking, Which did she like best? She could not say, and did not know what to do, for whichever she took the other would be in a towering rage and inclined to take her life! We told her to ask direction about it, and think she has chosen the better husband of the two, though he had to carry off his lady-love, musket in hand, for fear of an attack from some of the disappointed suitors! Indeed, several of his friends were keeping watch round the church, while the ceremony was being performed. It struck me as being rather comical, to see her arrayed in her wedding attire, while the mourning dress of black print she had been making for her late husband was not quite finished!

Christmas came next in order. The little stockings had been duly filled the night before, as Frank took care to have Jay's and his hung up, with dim eyes at the thought of the other three, which had been filled the year before. It turned out to be a bright day; the bairns were jubilant over their gifts; and there was a general rejoicing over dear Litsi's reappearance at the evening class—her lord and master having gone out in a canoe with some boys for a night's fishing by torchlight. Litsi's face beamed at having an hour or two with us all, for Mungaw did not allow her over her own fence or anyone to go near her; and, as all the women were frightened, his commands were obeyed to the letter, except by us, and for her sake even I had to go stealthily with food (he starved her), as he beat her when he found it out. Our girls did not require two biddings to put a plentiful supper before her, and were cheering her under breath with the hope that his canoe might turn bottom up and he get eaten with a shark, when the most unearthly yells from the shore turned us all pale with terror, and 'Mungaw!' was gasped from every lip. Litsi flew home, in terror he should find her *out*. The villagers seized their muskets and ran to protect their boys, and John and I to our knees in the study.

But the whole turned out to be a hoax! The boys' canoe had upset among the reefs, and though they could swim like corks and were in no danger, it was their pleasure thus to exercise their lungs while splashing about. They got paid out a day or two after. John had given our boys leave to go for a day's fishing with the others, and they were about half a mile from the shore when they saw a great smoke issuing from the direction of our house, and, concluding Mungaw had at last carried out his threat of burning it, they paddled back with all their might and rushed panting to the mission station, to find the old women who had charge of the banana plantation quietly burning some rubbish in the corner of it. The poor fellow kept our nerves so constantly on the strain, that all was put down in the first instance to his account whether he was guilty or not.

Mungaw made rather a sad New Year for us, though. The natives had been looking forward to it with such pleasure, as John had promised them the large bull to be killed and divided over the island; but at the early morning meeting, with which we always commence the year, only about forty were present; and they looked so suspiciously at each other, that we felt sure there was something underneath it. After worship, one or two of the men told John that they would rather not kill the animal that day, and all the explanation he could get out of them was that they 'were frightened.'

While we were at breakfast, more people assembled in the *Imrai*, and high words ensued. John went out to them, determined to sift the matter to the bottom; and at last it came out that Mungaw had gone the day before to the village of Towleka, and said that the people of Inahutshi were going to shoot them on the morrow, and then he deliberately walked to

Inahutshi and told them the same thing about the people of Towleka. He was bent upon war; wanted, in his own words, 'to see blood run.' Burning houses, and he had burnt several, was becoming rather tame work; and he wanted something more exciting. He boastfully acknowledged the part he had acted the day before, declaring that if they had not *said* they were going to fight they *meant* it, which was worse—better to have it out and done with—why else were they carrying their muskets? This was a little too much for their patience, and they did lay about him with their tongues, saying it was he and he alone who had introduced this carrying of muskets by flying about with his own and threatening to kill everybody. He then said, that if they were not going to fight they ought to come out boldly for the worship (he certainly did not approve of doing things by halves), singling out by name those whom he knew to have little differences with each other, and ordering them to shake hands and exchange pigs there and then!

When John thought they'd had enough of it, for Mungaw was getting excited with his nonsense, he suggested that one of them should engage in prayer, and let them then get home. A fine old chief stood up under the banyan tree, and, waving his hand with a majesty a native can assume at times, offered a simple, earnest prayer, and the people quietly dispersed. But Mungaw tried hard to get them together again, and insisted upon everybody being converted on the spot. He kept on this religious tack for about a fortnight, which was very pleasant, as it allowed us to sit with open windows and doors and get fresh air and freedom.

One day, when he was unusually gushing and had presented a pig and food to the very men he had sought to murder—his speech indicating that the Millennial Reign was about to commence on Aniwa under his auspices—a church member said, 'I think, Mungaw, the people will understand us better, if we burn our muskets and show that we'll not fight, whatever they may do; here goes mine!' And suiting the action to the word, he broke and flung his musket into the flames. Mungaw immediately followed suit, with a grand flourish, to the intense relief of all around, for he was a much less formidable personage without the musket, though he still fancied himself a great king. He sent in for a black suit, and permission to conduct the worship next Sunday, which of course he did not get.

John sent for him and had long talks with him, but saw it was little use—he was so crazed, and thought everyone in the wrong but himself. His standing grievance against John was, that he kept all the collections (!) taken at the close of mission addresses (he insisted they went into his private pocket), and did not halve them with him, though he helped him to speak.

He never forgot the scenes he saw in that den of drink and iniquity, to which some wretches took him in Melbourne under pretence of kindness, when John was unable from my sudden illness in the country to take him home.[2] It bamboozled his then simple mind, how in a land of gospel light such appliances could be deliberately and systematically set on foot for the on-carrying of evil. I do think, that for their light—mind, I say *for their light*—our *black* Christianity is superior to the *white*. The natives often said, 'How is it, Missi, that he was so good and strong for the worship before he went to your good land, and has been nothing but a plague since he returned?' John, of course, emphatically cleared the 'good land' from all blame, adding that he would take care not to give any of the rest of them a chance of going daft by a trip to Australia! They don't pursue the argument after that, as all are eager to go, and perfectly willing, they say, to accept the risk.

[2] See *John G. Paton: Autobiography* (Popular Edition, p. 408; Banner of Truth Trust, 2024, pp. 412-13).

It was a blessing the natives were so kind, and oh, how truly we experienced that 'God stayeth his rough wind in the day of his east wind'; for, except the trouble with Mungaw, we had no other serious ones to contend with, and he gave us to realize, as I at least never did in the same way, how entirely the work was his. It looked so mysterious, that after we had come down at such a sacrifice to health and family ties to devote our whole time to the work, it should be so retarded by one individual; for often, at his worst, only eight or ten had courage to come to school, and we could as well have taught fifty. But we could leave it trustingly to the Lord, feeling that all we had to do was the work he laid to our hands from day to day. What a restful feeling it gives one to be 'only an instrument in his hand'!

Even the great hurricane, which swept these islands and did such damage on January 10th, was comparatively little felt here. It certainly was a great storm, and we lay awake the whole night expecting every moment to have to fly; and next morning, we prepared for a hurricane, taking down pictures and curtains, lifting mats, etc., as it still looked dark. Fences, etc., were lying flat; but, towards afternoon, the wind died off, leaving us with the refreshing rain so earnestly desired. We were soon in a mass of greenery again, but didn't the weeds grow too! My women had to make up now for the easy times they had had with their bits of ground; and the people set to work planting their yams two months later than usual. Our tanks began to fill, and we had refreshing cups of tea, though John had actually to put a little salt in his, it tasted so strange after the brackish water of the well!

We found that it had been a very different story upon Tanna. Mr Watt's boat came over with letters. It was a delightful break in the dull season to get news from our next neighbours, and our chicks appreciated the fine oranges sent them. Their account of January 10th was frightful. Along with the hurricane they had an awful earthquake, causing the land to fall and the mouth of the harbour to be blocked up. A heavy tidal wave also rushed in, rising forty feet above highest tide mark, while both at Kwamera and here, each only fourteen miles distant, the earthquake was not felt.

The month of February was furiously ushered in here, with a great thunderstorm—wind and rain all night, and at early morning the most magnificent tidal wave I ever saw came rolling over land and bush, smashing canoes and everything in its course up to near our gate. I never saw the sea in such majestic grandeur—those great mountain waves going into deep shadow as they arched round, and then breaking in one huge mass of whitest foam. No life was lost, but every canoe, save one, on the island was broken to pieces, and a few plantations were destroyed. We were kept anxious for a while, having two very dear invalids, who could not have exerted themselves, had escape been necessary; but oh how precious these words in our circumstances,—'Hitherto shalt thou come and no further, and here shall thy proud waves be stayed.'

We *felt* them indeed that morning. Litsi was the most in danger, her house standing a little below ours, and having been roused at three o'clock to attend her only the morning before. John was very averse to my going, in the circumstances; and I would fain have contented myself with sending her comforts, but could not think to leave her with her mad husband, who had still sternly refused to let anyone go near her; so I hurriedly dressed, roused the cook to boil the kettle, and took one of my girls with a lamp. We found to my intense relief the baby already born, and Mungaw so delighted at having another *son* that he was inclined to be tolerably kind. I took advantage of his mood—as it was only through him I could reach Litsi—praised him for being such a clever doctor (by the way, I believe I'll write a book some day upon 'Midwifery in the South Seas,' just to horrify the Faculty!), and advised him to get her into the house out of the raw cold air, and offered him the services of my girl to light a fire, which he graciously condescended to accept! When I went back in a few minutes with some tea and things for the baby, they looked much more comfortable, Litsi sitting in the house by a bright fire, with the lamp beside her. Urging her to lie down, I returned home and looked into the girls' house to see how it was faring with my other invalid—for dear Yawaci had been carried to us at her own request the evening before in a dying state.

About six weeks after her marriage Yawaci had a serious illness, from which she did not rally sufficiently, and she gradually got weaker, though we did everything we could, and I sent her food from our own table at every meal, as she did not care for native things. It was such comfort when she was brought here, and I could be constantly near her and have her properly nursed; but I had no idea she was so near her end, though John suspected it. It was her breathing alone that troubled her now, and for the last six days she could not lie down for a moment's rest. When I told her about Litsi's baby she smiled and sent her congratulations, saying she wished she could go and see it. She had no rest the whole night, but said she felt so much more comfortable in the nice airy room, propped up with pillows, and having a light all night.

All that day was spent running betwixt the invalids. Dangerous symptoms ensued with Litsi. Mungaw got fearfully excited at a lot of women coming to see her, and stood over her with his loaded musket (he had stolen another, as the pious fit didn't last long), appealing to me whether his word as chief should be obeyed or not. I seconded his efforts, as they were doing no good, and got them cleared to a little distance—at hand if they were needed—and by deferential behaviour got him to let me come and go with food, etc. He attributed her illness to an absurd crotchet of his own, and held to it that she would be better at sundown. Meanwhile, the time was being wasted, and we had so many anxious thoughts. Was it right that her life should be sacrificed to a madman's freaks? Was it right to give in to him, or how far was it right to risk his wrath?' We took it all to our ever-present Counsellor; and then John decided that if I found her no better he would go himself, whatever the consequences.

On my way I met Mungaw coming in at the gate with the empty dishes, and he said quite humbly that he was wrong in his supposition, and would like exceedingly if the *Missi-tané* (= man Missi) would go and see her, for he did not know what to do. John soon put matters all right, telling them there was no cause for alarm, gave directions about one or two things that had been neglected, and ordered fomentations. She had no more relapses, and he really seemed grateful the next morning when he came for her breakfast, as I could not go to her very early on account of the tidal wave.

Poor Yawaci was our chief care after that. It seemed strange that Litsi, who so longed for death, should survive so much ill usage, for I could not pen a fiftieth part of the cruelty—the refinement of cruelty—with which he treated her. One instance will suffice. We missed him from church one Sabbath, and found that he had spent the time *skinning* the lower part of her face and *pinching* little bits of flesh out of her chest from shoulder to shoulder, threatening her with his club if she dared to cry out. You will wonder that the natives did not interfere. We began to lose all patience with them. I remember Mr Inglis once saying, 'It was worth living twenty years on the islands just to know what we owed to Christianity,' and how I thought they were stupid who did not find out all that in six months or less! I myself have had to live twelve years on Aniwa, however, to know what we owe to lunatic asylums, and also to learn how *exclusively* a man's wife is regarded as his own peculiar property—that is to be used exactly as he likes. They would as soon think of interfering with a man's conduct to his wife, as we would if in civilization a man chose to burn his own carpet or smash his own timepiece. They would break out into the most amused smile, when John was begging them to protect her, and say, '*But, Missi, it's his own wife!*' Of course, they were mad enough at him, Litsi being a general favourite, but could not well see their right to interfere.

Yawaci, on the other hand, was devotedly loved by her husband and his friends, and she clung to life. She said, '*Say* I'll get better soon, Missi.' She cried for Dr McMillan, saying she was sure he could do her good, adding, 'I would not mind a broken arm or pain of any kind, Missi, but this breathlessness is awful.' A ship appeared in the distance that evening (how it lived in the morning's sea we could not imagine), and I cheered her with the hope that Dr McMillan might be on board, as he had often spoken of taking a trip to the islands. She did not take much comfort from that, but said, 'If it should be a man-of-war, there will be a doctor of some kind on board, and perhaps he'll have a new kind of medicine that will make me well.' I felt so disheartened when she said, 'I've been ill so long, Missi, and I have not done very bad conduct.' I replied that, first of all, if our hearts had not been desperately wicked the Lord of glory would not have left his throne above to suffer and save us from our sins; and then further, I spoke of his love in sending trouble for high and holy uses even to those he loved best, however hard to bear. She acquiesced in all, and seemed cheered when I added that it was the gold—not the common—stone that was tried in the fire. The vessel, though still seen in the horizon next morning, faded quickly out of sight, and she was not so disappointed as we expected.

One of our Aneityumese teachers, a godly man, breathed his last that morning, while John, who had been constantly attending him during his illness, was praying by his bedside; and his poor widow, after following his remains to the grave, lay down prostrate with grief. I trimmed a hat with black for her—next day being Sunday—and put some on my own as well, to show my respect for him, little dreaming that Yawaci also would be in her grave ere we entered church. She kept stout, but on sponging her I noticed her chest rather spent. I did everything for her, as she preferred me, and hardly left her that day. Her friends were kind in helping, and sat up with her every night. Yawaci's breathing was rather easier, and about eight o'clock, after getting all she could want for the night, we were so thankful to see her lie down for the first time, and fondly hoped she was beginning to recover. She called the girls round her, telling them to sing; and, after beginning the translation of 'Nearer, My God, to Thee,' I slipped away leaving them singing it, and got to my bed thoroughly exhausted.

During the night, her husband knocked at our bedroom window, saying she was dying. John sprang up and went to her side, offering a short prayer, but her spirit fled before he had done, and she was buried amid heartfelt lamentations before church service on Sabbath, February 3rd. Our hearts were like to break, for she had been a faithful attached servant—*daughter*, rather—to us for ten years; a sweet little thing about eight or nine when she first came, and every year we liked her better. She had a great lump of *heart*, and I can never forget her devoted care of us all at that time when we were both laid up and our precious baby died. It was she I trusted to put the little form in its last resting-place, myself too weak to move! It was so sad to see her friends going about the next few days, their eyes red and swollen with weeping. Weeks after, on putting her photo into the hands of one of the sewing women, her head sank lower over it till the heavy sobs welled up; and as it was passed from one to another, there was hardly a dry eye—so generally was she beloved. You have all the same likeness, a true one, taken in Melbourne. Mungaw's was not so good—at least it did not do him justice in his best days; but it is charming to what he looked like in his last few months—his face was so wild and ghastly.

Poor fellow, I would fain pass over his sad end; but I must hasten on and have done with him, as I daresay you are as tired of the subject as I. The last open break-out with his wife was on the day that her baby was three weeks old. He was in a very excited state in the morning, threw off his clothing, stuck on paint (he supplied himself with balls of blue from our washing-house!), and seizing his musket said he was going to shoot someone ere he returned. The alarm spread, and John came to me at the sewing class to warn the women; but Mungaw soon came back and I dismissed the school, feeling anxious to get the children into the house (John would not budge from his usual work, but he had always natives with him), and get doors and windows shut. They had hardly gone when terrible screams came from his house, and I flew to implore our cooks to protect Litsi. Just then John rushed past me, telling me I must not hinder him, as he could not hear that poor girl being killed. Our boys ran with him, and they met Litsi running from her house covered with blood streaming from the back of her head. John caught her as she fell forward in a fainting fit, and a woman caught up her baby; they were carried to the *Imrai*, where John bound up her head and revived her with brandy and water. I sent her some fresh clothes, as John would not let me see her till she was revived and doctored, and I followed with some dinner. Her tormentor was coming too, but John gave him a look which made him disappear into the bush in quick style. He reappeared with the utmost coolness in a nice clean shirt about half an hour afterwards, and walked right into the mission premises, helping about a score of men to carry a huge log of wood which John had asked them to bring for some purpose—I forget what. During the afternoon school he sat eyeing Litsi and grinning from the opposite side of the *Imrai*, and chatting with the passers-by as if he had done no wrong.

Poor Litsi sat leaning against the church fence, too weak to notice anything, but thought she was safer there when John had to be in school. He told the natives that she must not be left to her husband's tender mercies any longer, but that they must take her to one of their distant villages, and if need be protect her with their muskets. Our house was too near; and besides, if he burnt it to get her, it would simply mean death to us all—our food was in it, and neither of us being extra strong we could not exist on roots and leaves like natives—whereas any of their houses could be replaced in a few days. He said also that it would never do for him to use arms—his work was to teach, theirs to protect each other when necessary. They all saw the force of his words, and heartily agreed with him, but all managed to back out of it one after another, Litsi being too high-spirited to ask protection from any of them.

When we heard that she was left with only a few women we both felt it our duty to shelter her, regardless of consequences, and ran out to fetch her; but the poor girl had fled with her two little ones to hide for the night in a plantation, one or two women keeping her company.

Amid all her own danger, she was mindful of us, and sent a messenger to warn us that Mungaw would be sure to burn the house that night if he could. We had a few necessaries selected, a cask of flour, hops for yeast, changes of clothing, etc., to put into the printing office, which would not burn so easily with its zinc roof; but when our Aneityumese teacher came after dark for their quiet removal, Mungaw accompanied him as far as the door! We all laughed. It was no use, with such a vigilant spy upon all our movements. But we were specially reminded of Someone watching over us.

It began to pour torrents of rain, as it so often did when there was imminent danger, and I sent coverings for the wanderers, hot tea, etc., by a circuitous path—with orders to take them to another invalid should Mungaw meet them. Our girls entered eagerly into it, and poor Litsi was made tolerably comfortable in body for the night, there being an old deserted hut in the plantation. Next morning, her cousin whispered to me that two men had taken her under protection to Touleka, a village a mile off, and that Mungaw had no idea of her whereabouts, supposing her to be with us, as he had sent word the evening before that he would kill her if she went anywhere else.

He got fearfully roused at not finding her by the afternoon, and sprang up after writing a line or two of his copy (he insisted on attending school) to go in search, beginning at the nearest villages, armed with club and killing stone, and nearly frightening the life out of a dumpy little virago who was in the habit of henpecking her own husband. It was capital to see her thoroughly cowed for once! His wrath grew with his want of success; and, returning after school, he told our boys in a voice of suppressed rage that he was now going to Touleka to kill Litsi if he found her there. One of them flew through the bush to warn her of his approach, and John and I went to the study to commit her to God. I think I should have gone mad myself, if we had not had our never-failing Refuge in these troublous times!

We heard after retiring for the night an infant's piteous wail, and found that, failing to get the mother (for the natives would not let him finish her quite, though he dragged her out of the house by her hair, *wool* rather), he had torn the baby from her and rushed home with it, knowing that she would follow it at any risk. It was *awfully* hard to keep John in the house, but I felt there was not the slightest use in going. We heard other voices remonstrating, and by the cries ceasing we knew that Litsi had come. About midnight, what seemed to be the death-wail in Litsi's voice made us think he had murdered the baby. It continued for about three hours, and rose to a perfect agony of distress before stopping. On inquiry at daybreak, for which we anxiously waited, it turned out that he had tied her arms and legs in the most savage manner, only loosing her when two or three natives went to the rescue. It was at the risk of their lives they did it, and all warned us not to go to their house that morning, as he was raving mad and would not hesitate to kill anyone coming near.

We just felt that poor Litsi had all the more right to our sympathy, when no one else would go. They insisted she was dead, and the baby too; there was such silence round all the place. John would not let me go alone, and I would not let him go alone, so we compromised the matter by going together, and took a plentiful breakfast as an excuse for intruding on his lordship's privacy, the natives looking after with wistful eyes, but not one offering to accompany us to the lion's den! I trembled violently, though I felt that the Lord was with us, and was almost relieved when we found the house deserted; but John called aloud for Litsi several times, and at last she came staggering from an enclosure opposite, from which the occupant had fled when Mungaw first went mad. She was trembling with pain and weakness, and when we were going over the stile she looked back alarmed and said, *You'd better not, Missi*; so we spoke a few cheering words as we stood, and told her again that our house was open to her, night or day, whenever she needed shelter.

Some of the church members came to ask what was to be done with him. Tying only made him worse; confining and shooting were the only other alternatives. To confine him was impossible. Were they to shoot him? John, of course, would not hear of that, and they asked if there was no sort of medicine to cure madness! A near friend got him away to his village, where they had a long talk, and warned him of the consequences. The moment he went, I ran off to sit awhile with Litsi. We feared she would sink under her trials, and wished she had access to the rich consolations with which we were upheld every day in our little readings both of the Bible and other books. It seemed as if the words were printed for our express circumstances and comfort. My own morning reading was in the Psalms, and I never felt them so suitable. The very ones I used to think David had written in a fit of indigestion were fraught with the deepest comfort and meaning, and favourite passages were more precious than ever. I never noticed before that the passage, 'Lead me to the rock that is higher than I,' begins with 'From *the end of the earth* will I cry unto thee'—so applicable to us! John and I have often remarked to each other that we had to come all the way to the South Seas to understand some bits of the Bible; and I see Bowen in his *Daily Meditations* says the same in reference to India, where he laboured so devotedly as a missionary. We had another precious book which we were reading aloud and enjoyed next to the Bible—Boardman's *In the Power of the Spirit*, given us also before leaving Australia.

How we wished poor Litsi could share all these privileges, and wondered if her faith were keeping alive at all; but her spirit was beautifully submissive. When I told her that, however difficult it might be for her to believe it, her Saviour God was tenderly caring for her every moment and would not let her have one more trial than she could bear, and that it would relieve her to take all her sorrows to him, she replied, 'Oh, I know it, Missi; my whole words now are prayer; for I have no one else to speak to, and would have gone mad if

I could not have told my Saviour! I tell him everything, and know that it's all right even if Mungaw should kill me, *for he can't harm me beyond the grave*.' I told her not a single night passed that we were not engaging in prayer for her, and she said, 'These prayers have been answered; for he has had the wish to kill me and burn your house, and he could easily have done both had not God prevented.'

The whole provocation (I forgot to say) he had for laying her head open at this time was her saying, *Oh, don't do that!* when he got up to burn the fine new house he had recently completed. She learned never again to contradict him, even when he made the wildest proposals. The next house he burnt, a neighbour's, he told her with a diabolical grin (he had such a beautiful smile in his sane days!) of his purpose, and she merely said, *Are you?* and slipped round to take everything valuable out of it, as the owners were living a week or two on a lovely little islet adjoining this, where the natives often go for a change and fishing. Of course, they said nothing about it on their return; no one in the island was prepared to tackle such a character, and he presumed accordingly, turning his attentions more to the general public after this, and dividing his favours pretty equally over the whole island. He plundered the plantations in rotation, and shot all the pigs which came in his way, bringing Litsi part of the spoil; but she suddenly seemed possessed of the spirit of half a dozen, sternly refused to touch one morsel of stolen food, and took their eldest little boy to the farthest village, begging the people to keep him, as he was too young to refuse what was stolen.

She then came to beg of me for a dose of poison—she thought the stuff we killed the rats with would do—as he was too wicked to live and would bring a judgment on the whole island. She had such a chance through the night when he fell into a deep sleep (the first time he was known to sleep for many weeks), and she had a great wish to take his life, but was afraid God would not like it.

I confirmed her fears, and counselled patience a little longer, as the Missi was getting the boat repaired to go to Tanna, and it was well known Mungaw wanted to go there and stay a while. This was the last hope of the whole island, and all were eager to see the boat finished—none more so than I, having an additional reason, viz., that it took John away to a distance nearly the whole day, and though he always left me with a bodyguard, he was not so careful of himself. I must say, the natives were very thoughtful about him, however, and would not let him continue to take his nightly turns in watching our house. They begged him to arm himself, but that of course he would not do. He and our Aneityumese teacher were the only ones who would not carry a weapon of any kind, or give in to him when it was right to be firm, and they were the only two Mungaw had the slightest fear of; but he kept prowling about our premises day and night, for what intent he best knew. When he used to set off on his peregrinations, it was such a relief to throw windows and doors open for air; but back he would come, with the rapidity of a racehorse. Many a fainting fit he gave me; and Frank used to get white to the lips when he appeared. Even little Jay began to lisp, *I frightened Mungaw!*

About the only time I was thankful to see him come was after he had been tracking John's footsteps closer than I liked. I was watching him from our front veranda as he went off to his boat, the two lads a little before, when Mungaw suddenly appeared close behind him—axe in hand. I could see a long way, and when John stooped to examine a bush or fern Mungaw stopped too, always keeping right at his back. Visions of the murdered Gordons rose vividly before me, and I felt distracted. I knew that John and the boys were on their guard, and plenty of natives were about, but a blow could be so easily struck! I went indoors and told my God and then our Aneityumese teacher (we showed as little fear as possible before our natives), so that if he thought there was real danger he would go to him. He looked anxious and questioned me minutely, but went on quietly with his work, and I tried to follow his example; but my feet *would* carry me to the veranda, till the welcome sight of that usually dreaded form, tossing his axe in the air and catching it by the handle, allayed all fears, for I knew that had he done any harm he would have rushed into hiding.

His last days were spent pulling up the people's bananas and sugar-cane, destroying what he could not devour. He took our boys' blankets and boxes, and walked off with the looking glass from the girls' house. Just the Sunday morning before he was shot, he turned out all the girls' boxes while we were at breakfast, and pranced up and down our front veranda. We had just finished our own family worship and John was going off for a little quiet to his study, when we heard the church bell being furiously rung a full hour before the time! The natives already gathered stood staring at each other in consternation, others hurried forward thinking they were late, and the usual bell-ringer came panting to know why the work was so unceremoniously taken out of his hands! The more they begged Mungaw to leave off, the quicker he rang, till John ran out and ordered him to stop instantly, which he did.

He did not trouble us another Sunday, poor fellow; but he gave me two or three thorough frights through the week—once surprising me suddenly on the veranda, when mounted on a high box and oil-painting the woodwork of the house. On the following Saturday morning, as we were in the garden, Litsi passed the fence, and I ran to her. She said, 'When will the boat be ready, Missi?' I told her that there was just a little painting to finish today, and it would sail on Monday, so she would only have two days more of endurance. She jumped and clapped her hands, saying, *My heart sings, for he's sure to go!*

But that same evening, as we sat at a late tea, our spirits brighter than usual, feeling that relief was near (though it came not in the way we expected), for the *Dayspring* was to leave Sydney on Monday, and would be getting nearer us every day, we heard the fatal shot go off close beside us! We have heard as loud reports and even nearer, when they were killing flying foxes or birds, which caused us nothing more than a start and a laugh; but there was something in that which made us spring simultaneously from our seats and stand in awe. John said, 'Someone is shot! Either Mungaw, or someone by his hand.' He had barely uttered the words, when the awful death wail in Litsi's voice confirmed our fears. Our girls rushed in from the bathroom, where they had been filling baths and getting all ready for Sunday, and said, 'That's Mungaw, Missi, for the Inahutshi people told us not to be alarmed if we heard a shot after dark, as we would know it was Mungaw killed.'

It had all been deliberately arranged, and we knew not a word about it. John said, 'Then I must run and see what I can do for the poor fellow,' and was off; but another loud report made me implore him to come back, till we ascertained certainly what the matter was, as he might be shot in the dark without anyone meaning it, and Frank decided the matter by saying in a faint voice, 'Papa, will you stay and take care of us?' His Papa put his arm round him and said, 'Yes, my boy, I'll not leave the room again.'

Two or three natives came to tell us that Mungaw was shot dead, and that John's going would be no use now. He engaged in prayer, and oh, how our hearts bled for the poor fellow! Now that his sad end had come, we could only think of him as he once was; as, for instance, we saw him one evening years before stand calm and tranquil, with three enraged men pointing their muskets at him for spoiling some heathen performance, and telling them he would not fight and that the worst they could do would only send him to heaven. Or again, as he used to go about pleading with the young boys (a mere boy himself) not to follow the footsteps of their fathers but come out decidedly for the Lord Jesus. Or again, we thought of the time when he was John's right-hand man, and would almost have laid down his life to serve him. His two nearest friends, on coming to ask if they should bury him at once, laid down their heads and sobbed aloud, though like all the Aniwans they had wished for his death. It was a sad, sad night; the hurried midnight burial, the suppressed excitement, the fear and uncertainty about the real murderers and what would follow next, and, last of all, that young and once noble fellow cut down in the midst of his days.

He had just left our premises and gone home for supper, and then had worship (!) with Litsi—after which she told him not to go outside, as two or three men had been watching for three nights to get a good aim at him. He courted death, and *would* go out, saying to Litsi, *You come with me.* She went out first and thought she saw a man standing; but next moment the attention of both was suddenly directed to a meteor in its transit, and while gazing at it the musket went off, going through Mungaw's body from arm to arm. He fell down by his own door crying, *Awai!* (Alas!), and died immediately, the murderers making their escape as they shot the other musket into the air.

It has at last been traced to a Tanna man, who some years ago along with his adopted brother murdered a nice man and his wife in cold blood; so it may stand hard with him yet, as *their* friends seem to be egging on Mungaw's to revenge.

You may be sure, after these trying times and seven months' utter silence regarding our absent ones, we were intensely delighted to welcome the dear old *Dayspring* once more. But, strange as it may seem, this is our most trying time; for all the anxiety of the past months seems to accumulate into an agony of suspense, from the time her sails are discovered till we have opened the most-desired-for letters of our mail and found all well. She arrived at Aniwa just two days after we calculated upon seeing her, April 24th. The first announcement of her approach came as we were assembled in church at three o'clock for the prayer meeting; and I'm afraid the services had not their usual interest for me! How John could proceed quietly with the address, under the excitement, was a puzzle; for I saw him start, and we exchanged earnest looks, as the well-known cry greeted our ears, and then two natives came panting in with beaming faces, darting intelligent looks all around.

The service *did* come to an end at last, and then everyone's tongue was loosed. It *was* the *Dayspring* without doubt; but was there wind enough to bring her in that day? I made an agreement with the herd who went for the goats to shout again if it were very near, and soon a dozen voices yelled back the answer. I flew to give orders for all sorts of preparations, but not a girl was to be found—all having rushed up the hill to see for themselves; and when they came they were so mad with joyful excitement, that instead of their usual respectful demeanour they tumbled heels over head on the veranda two or three times before they could compose themselves to work—and so many little things waiting to be done. There was the veranda mat to put down, a substantial tea to be laid out, the drawing-room dusted, fresh flowers cut, and the children dressed to go to the boat landing with their Papa. We were going on like steam at high pressure, when the *Dayspring* came slowly into view at the opening in the trees, and we all rushed out to wave handkerchiefs (the girls waved towels and dusters!) at a furious rate till she passed out of sight, and we were again at liberty to go on with our work.

My cook had stuck to his post; and, all being satisfactorily arranged, at last I had a little time to let gloomy thoughts get the better of me, and to make up my mind that one of the children would be dead at any rate!

It began to grow dusk, and the girls had set the house in a blaze with lamps to give as cheery a welcome as possible, when white faces were seen among the trees. My teeth really chattered with apprehension, but trying to hide it I ran down to the gate and welcomed my visitors. There were the Robertsons and McDonalds, and a new missionary was introduced whose looks I liked—but oh! if someone would only tell me about my children. I inquired of Mrs Robertson, as we walked slowly up to the house; and she, naturally supposing I meant hers, told me all about their leaving Gordon behind till next trip of the *Dayspring.* I listened patiently, and then asked when she saw mine. She quietly replied, 'Oh, we did not go on to Melbourne, but the McDonalds were there all the time,' and then went on to praise our premises! *Just as I thought*, I bitterly commented within myself, and she's changing the subject to hide the bad news. I heard her admire this shrub and that, as if her voice were a long way off, while the little bits of coral at our feet were photographing themselves on my mind with the greatest minuteness. Isn't it strange that such little things should occupy one's observation, when the mind is strung to the highest pitch about something momentous?

Faintness coming on, I turned abruptly to Mr McDonald close behind, and said, 'What about the children?' 'Well, we had rather an anxious time with little Alexander in Melbourne' (their own children again!); 'he had a slight attack of inflammation on the lungs, and has not been well since.' I tried to stammer out some expression of sympathy, before saying, 'Did you see *our* children, Mr McDonald?' 'Oh yes!' he answered in a hearty voice; 'we met them all three at Mrs Beattie's, before we left, looking so well and happy!' How the whole scene in a moment was changed! I was quite ready to admit now that the premises *did* look lovely, and to sympathize heartily with my neighbours' bairns!

We gathered round such a happy tea table; for it is the most exquisite treat to have intercourse with kindred spirits in our own tongue, after jabbering so many months to the darkies, and to get all the news from the civilized world. Such a mail too! Over one hundred letters, and no end of papers. We simply looked at all your different handwritings, but devoured our bairns' monthly budgets that night after our visitors had retired to their rooms. Fancy us having ten, including the babies, but not their nurses, after not seeing a single white face for such an age!

The vessel was five weeks away among the islands, and during that time we had the pleasure of Mrs Captain Braithwaite's company, which was a delightful change for me. We had one or two little excursions, and she was quite delighted with our little island—especially with one romantic glen, abounding in ferns. I gave my school a holiday, and enjoying the rest tried to persuade John to do likewise; but he said there was time enough for rest when he went to the Synod.

The second Communion since our return also took place at this time, and was a season of great refreshing and comfort; but the sight of that little group of communicants is always too much for me, especially when they stand up to sing so heartily! I could fain lay down my head and sob, were it not that I have the harmonium to attend to and must crush my heart down as best I can. All our trials and privations, looked at in the light of that little *sable band* (glancing back at what they once were) now sitting at their Lord's Table, seem as nothing—as less than nothing.

A stranger might simply have his *risibles* excited by the somewhat grotesque costume of the congregation. Indeed I had to turn away my own head, as our two worthy elders came in for the 'elements' before the service, with the most imposing gravity, with manifest devotion in their looks, but in all the dignity of their office and with special hats to grace the occasion. The one had his white shirt done up round his hat so as to represent a puggaree, and, as it hung a long way behind, he had to keep his head well balanced for fear of it falling back. As for the other, who or what his hat had been originally intended for, we were at a loss to divine! It has always been our difficulty to get them large enough to include their *wool* but this, a light grey chimney-pot, overtopped wool and all, till it rested on the tip of his nose, which fortunately being a very large one prevented his face from disappearing altogether.

It being the weather side of the island, the *Dayspring* couldn't stand in close to Tanna (*en route* for Synod meeting on Aneityum), so we had a seven miles' pull in the boat before breakfast, sick to the last and thankful beyond measure to get into dear Mrs Watt's bright little paradise of a house, ourselves and bairns bathed, and then to sit down with such an appetite and feel we had no further voyaging meantime. How intensely pleasant was the time passed with these two beloved friends, Mrs Milne and Mrs Watt! There were no untoward circumstances to mar the enjoyment, though the Tannese did get up a slight demonstration, next morning, on the beach in front of the mission house, but no one was shot, only a few broken arms and heads, and Mrs Milne and I did not know till all was over. Mrs Watt has the sweetest wee harmonium, so we had music in abundance—all the best of *Sankey's Hymns*—and very sweet fellowship; but it came to an end all too soon, for the *Dayspring* returned in a fortnight, and I did so want three weeks of a holiday.

It was announced on Saturday morning at daybreak, and we had our husbands and the other missionaries on shore to breakfast. They were in fine spirits, enjoying the little while on shore; and we all gathered round the harmonium ere setting off, and sang 'Pass Me Not, O Gentle Saviour,' and 'Waiting and Watching.' The weather was again beautifully calm in going as it had been in coming, which was so pleasant. On remarking this to the captain, after getting comfortably onboard, he said, 'Ah, you see the weather was bespoke!' They had been praying earnestly for a favourable day.

There were thousands of oranges on board (and John had two huge boxes for us) from Aneityum, where the missionaries had been luxuriating on them during the Synod. This time they had only one long sitting daily, leaving the afternoon and evening free for botanizing and enjoyment. They all declare that they got through as much work, as when they used to have three sittings, and went back to their stations jaded instead of refreshed by the change. John, along with Mr Watt and two or three others, were the Annands' guests on shore, and enjoyed the visit so much. They all had the Communion together (a *white* service, not with the natives), and were refreshed in soul as well as body.

John missed Mr Inglis sadly, however, at the Synod; and more when they went round to his old station, where the natives mourn his and Mrs Inglis's absence daily, and are keeping everything in apple-pie order. When Mr Robertson asked Esther (Mrs Inglis's head servant) if she still missed Mrs Inglis, she burst into tears and replied, *Just don't speak about her, Missi!* They all say they are left *orphans*, and were bitterly disappointed at Mr Watt not being appointed their missionary. We are sorry too, for they richly deserve our best missionary, having given ample proof of their true Christianity by themselves going forth as teachers to heathen islands, and freely shedding their blood for Christ's sake and the gospel's.

The captain's plan was to land us on Sunday morning, lie off and on till Monday to land our luggage and some wood John had bought on Aneityum, and then return for the

McDonalds at Port Resolution on his way northward. Mrs Milne and I lay pillowed on deck, enjoying the moonlight till quite late, and having such a musical treat from Mr Michelsen, who sings and accompanies himself on the guitar with such taste. He had been playing it on deck in the afternoon, and we begged him to bring it up again after tea. The moon was brilliantly reflected on the water, and the ship lying so still, when he began with exquisite guitar accompaniment to sing 'Jesus, Lover of My Soul'—the missionaries standing round and joining softly in parts, while we were quietly crying. I have heard oratorios in the old country rendered so that they almost took one out of the body, but never anything that went to my heart like this! You would need to take in the whole circumstances to know how we felt it. The vessel, with her little band of missionaries so far from kindred and country, and about to separate for their lonely homes, and we knew not how much trial awaiting them!

Ours met us, as we put foot on shore next day, and found that instead of the usual Sabbath services there had been almost a fight. We saw the house and garden looking so pretty as we sailed past the opening, but no one about; so we gave them credit for being in Sunday School, as it was afternoon, till we reached the boat landing and found only a few women and our Aneityumese teacher, and then two or three men emerged from the bush with muskets, which made John exclaim, 'War must have broken out on Aniwa.' The men apologized for carrying them on Sunday by telling us that while the church bell was ringing for morning service, and most of the people had assembled, three of Mungaw's relations tried to shoot his murderers as they were hurrying on to church, but missed fire. The people in church were alarmed at hearing shots on Sunday, and the church members rushed in that direction, and succeeded in putting a stop to further fighting. But high words were bandied about, until the vessel was announced, which the people declared that God had sent just at the right time; so I felt he had his own all-wise purposes in cutting short our holiday.

Our earnest prayers have been answered so far, for there has been no more fighting, though most of the people carry their muskets, feeling still a little alarmed. They have been kept as busy as bees ever since, making arrowroot to pay for their own Gospels being printed in Melbourne, and are trying which village will make the most—better work than fighting! The want of suitable water is the great drawback here, and I have to let them draw upon my precious tanks for the last watering, to make it white. We have already 600 lb. put up, mostly in 10 lb. bags; and as there is a good deal of work connected with it, from beginning to end, I hope it will realize at least 1*s* *6d.* per lb. I know, when I was in Melbourne, a chemist in Ballarat was selling our arrowroot (Aneityumese) at 3*s.* *6d.* per lb. Now, though I have no ill-will to the worthy man, seeing I don't even know him, I would rather see the mission get the 3*s.* *6d.*, if the arrowroot should rise so high again!

The natives are still making more, and the demands upon me for calico have been endless. After ransacking boxes for every inch that could be got to dry it upon and to make bags, I had to sacrifice all my common sheets and tablecloths; and, while trying to bear up under this calamity with Christian fortitude, John roused all the old Adam in me, by coolly bidding me be quick and get out my *linen* ones and best tablecloths, as it was a splendid day for drying! I emphatically declared that my few best things should remain untouched, though the natives should never get their books; and, by a little management in making the others do, I have kept to my *wicked* vow.

This is the first donation from our natives in money, or what can be converted into money; and John thinks that in a very few years the mission may be self-supporting. For my part, I think that our natives have done pretty well so far, it never having cost the church one penny either for the erection or upkeep of church and school buildings, which is more than can be said of most missions. But it will be grand, if this little island with its limited resources and inhabitants, can learn to support its own missionary.

It is now the first of August, though I see that I began this on the eighth of July, and I have not begun to write a single *private* letter, and so many to answer; and the huge piles which made our eyes dance with joy on receiving them, are regarded rather ruefully now that we have got to reply to them! I must leave out, therefore, all other items of interest which I intended writing, as this is already far too long—and close with warmest love from

Your ever loving sister,
MAGGIE WHITECROSS PATON.

P.S.—September 5th.—As I've kept my grand item of family news till now, I'll verify the saying that a woman puts what most interests her into the postscript, in here introducing by far the most important personage in the house—viz., 'Walter Watt Paton'—the finest little fellow that ever was, and a fortnight old yesterday! He introduced himself on August 21st, was exhibited to his admiring fellow-islanders in the dining room on the 25th, between the services, and the 'Wahaws!' and 'Kai Missis!' that resounded through the room as Mr Watt lifted the shawl to let each one take a peep would have convinced you that the boy is something beyond the common! He was baptized last Sabbath by our dear brother-missionary Mr Watt, Mrs Watt taking him into church, as I was unable to go. We can never forget all their kindness, in coming over to be with us at this time, when it was anything but convenient for them to leave Tanna; and we don't know what could have been done without their thoughtful care and help, for John has been going about with his left arm in a sling, having smashed two of his fingers.

I think I have got over the disappointment of its not being a *girl*, as I wished; and John is in the seventh heaven of gratification at having another 'little missionary' to devote to 'the noblest work on earth!' He tried hard to bring me up to the scratch, and said that surely I would not withhold my *fifth* son from the mission field; but I maintain that I take higher ground still, in dedicating this little lamb like all the others to my Lord, and letting him choose their life-work. He shall have them all for the mission field, if he calls them to it, for I know that in that case he will give me the necessary—well, I hardly like to come out with it, *resignation*!

That word makes John groan in spirit; but I find that those very noble women whom he holds up as examples to me, in devoting all their sons from infancy to be missionaries, and whose only regret is that they have not another dozen to dedicate, *have never been in the mission field themselves.* I once met a lady, whose only son, she told me with kindling eyes, had been dedicated to the mission field, and her greatest earthly wish was to see him ready to go. I looked at the woman with a respect amounting to awe; but the bump of reverence not being too largely developed, it soon gave way to curiosity as to what her ideas of the mission field really were. I found that she laboured under the impression that her boy had only to get on to a heathen island, and hold up the Bible amongst an interesting group of Ethiopians, who with outstretched arms had been crying in vain, 'Come over and help us!' Now, having been behind the scenes, and knowing what it actually costs, my dedication of them will be worth something when it comes!

M. W. P.

16

Slavers and Friends

ANIWA, NEW HEBRIDES,
19 JULY, 1879.

MY DEAREST SISTERS AND BROTHERS, [1]

As Bob thought my last journal too much of a murder story, I promise that nothing of that kind shall occur here, and I begin with something more in his and Fred's line—what they would call rather a 'sell' that we had, and on Minn's birthday too, so it will interest all the three.

It was a few days after the *Dayspring* left us for Sydney last December, and we were feeling the loneliness that always comes over us for a little, when we are left for the season by our only link to the outer world. Papa was late in the evening finishing some outdoor work with the natives, and I was sitting alone with an intense yearning to know what our 'wee wifie' was doing on her birthday. Being unable to battle with the fevered longing for one sight of them all, I took Baby up and began to pace the veranda in the quiet starlight, giving a passing glance down the opening to the sea. The vision of a great ship seemed to rise before my eyes, as I withdrew them, and I stared again, when to my amazement there loomed out in the dim light a large schooner in full sail, close in to the land, and framed like a picture by the trees on either side. Not a soul had seen her approach, and I eagerly shouted 'Sail

[1] To the family circle.

ho!' which set the whole place ablaze with excitement in a twinkling. John and his blackies came rushing to the side gate, and the girls tumbled out on the veranda from different windows—howling that it might be the French!

We thought it might be one of the English 'gunboats,' and feared they might have landed with no one to receive them; so John flew to his room, made a spring into his clerical suit, and dashed out at the front gate, with all his black 'gentlemen-in-waiting' flying helter-skelter at his heels, and they did not slacken speed till they went full tilt into their visitors about half-way from the house, and nearly succeeded in knocking them over! I had delivered little Walter into his nurse's charge, and making a dive into the drawing room had barely got it lighted up and the antimacassars arranged, when the girls rushed in to announce that the Missi was bringing in a lot of 'great chiefs as tall as trees!' So I whisked into the diningroom, fast filling with excited blackies, eager to know if it was a man-of-war. I was as eager to be informed as they, and waited impatiently for John to come out and tell me who our visitors were; but never a foot did he stir in my direction (perhaps too tired with his race), and I was left in a most distressing state of perplexity in regard to my costume!

I considered myself perfectly well-dressed for a trader, having on a pretty clean print, but then it was slightly old-fashioned and hardly the thing for Her Majesty's representatives! For *them*, I wouldn't grudge to wear my best muslin, with black velvet bows, though the hot night might fit it for the washtub. Then I had not a moment to lose, in case they thought I was getting myself 'up' for them, and that would be the worst calamity of all! Just fancy what conflicting emotions were rending my bosom. I dispatched a girl to 'keek' [peep] and tell me if she saw *uniforms*, but as she began to smother a laugh, I pulled her, and down she fell on the lobby oil-cloth like a clap of thunder! She told us afterwards that she expected the men-of-war would be out on her, and she made such violent efforts to regain her footing, that she brought down a shower of hats, sticks, and umbrellas clattering on the top of her, while the rest of us were gasping with suppressed merriment. When that 'to-do' subsided, I slipped along myself, and, concluding from their speech that they were gentlemen, I determined to be genteel at all risks. So, on went the muslin and bows, and after giving strict directions to the two best-looking girls to follow in five minutes with the salver and cake-basket (nothing on the salver but milk!), I gave the last pull to the dress, straightened myself up, and entered the drawing-room with a pleasant smile, to behold—two villainous slavers, with nothing on but old nether garments and woollen shirts!

Our next bit of excitement was on New Year's Day, when the usual shooting match came off, and prizes were awarded to the winners. The most amusing part to us was the racing amongst younger boys and girls. The chief, whom John had placed in charge of the prizes, would put a belt, necktie, or bit of red calico on a post at a certain distance off, and then the word of command was given to the eager little monkeys, and they made such a scramble as they neared it! The grand entertainment, however, the Magic Lantern, was reserved for the evening, and was quite a success. Everybody on the island that was able to crawl at all put in an appearance, including two old bedridden women, who set out in the early morning and managed a journey of two miles by the time it got dark! John had all Mr Watt's slides, as well as his own, and the natives were in perfect ecstasies of delight the whole evening; but when he finished off with 'the revolving light,' they fairly yelled with delight and amazement, declaring it must be 'Tetovas' (= gods) who made that!

We had even a more exciting time that night week, though by no means so pleasant, as it came in the shape of a violent hurricane, which has certainly left John a ticket of remembrance, for he has never been well since. It began on the evening of January 8th, and raged till next morning. I was never so little able to battle with an event of that kind, being ill at the time, and when we had to turn out of bed (John never went to his) to face the blast I was too weak to stand. But out we must go; the house was creaking and shaking as if it would fall any moment, the thatch was standing on end, and the rain coming down in bucketfuls. The *lamp* was the occupant of Walter's little bed, protected round with curtains from the wind. Frank was woke up to get dressed; and John rushed out with Jay rolled in blankets to leave him in charge of the girls at a safe distance, but not one was to be found on the premises. They had fled into some cave for shelter, so he had to lay the child down asleep and fly back to hurry out the rest of us. He got Baby and me enveloped in a pair of thick blankets, but the moment we reached the door they flew into space! Frank was got out, and Jay found again with difficulty in the pitchy darkness, still uninjured—though trees were flying like hailstones—but frantic with terror, poor wee man. We were all soaked to the skin, ere we had gone two steps—all except Baby, as I bent nearly double over him, remembering poor Baby McKenzie in the Efaté hurricane—and glad we were to reach the cellar door in safety.

You've had hurricanes described often enough, and this one proceeded in the usual style; only I vowed to put down a pair of speaking-trumpets in our next Colonial order, the wind made such a deafening roar. Worse than the storm, and night refuge in the cellar is the return to the desolate, miserable-looking house, picking our way over fallen trees, branches, bits of thatch, etc.—walks that were trim and neat the day before nowhere to be seen. When we got into the house, our clothes still wet and clinging around us, the first thing John did was to shovel out the water! Broken windows greeted us on every hand—blankets, mattresses, curtains, mats, everything soaking and all covered inches thick with nasty black debris from the thatch—boxes, drawers, and their contents, all managing to come in for a share of the rain. No houses were blown down, at least not at the mission premises, and it was not the most violent hurricane we've had; but owing to the week of incessant rain which followed, when we could get nothing dried, and, I suppose, our being less able to endure it, it told more upon us than any previous storm.

I managed to keep up for an hour that weary morning, making a desperate effort to get things a little tidy; and then, yielding to John's entreaties, I sank into bed. He had got mattresses brought to a dry corner in one of the rooms, putting dry things over all, and there I lay for a week between death and life. Rain, rain, incessant rain, the whole time; and John at last left without a dry change! Splendid for his rheumatism! But fortunately he did not feel it at the time; it is bad enough for the mistress of a house to be laid aside at such a season. It was a great blessing that Baby had such a splendid nurse, but all the other girls had been married off, except little 'smitchets' who were too young to be useful. They were adepts in mischief though. The two newest comers distinguished themselves by emptying sugar basins, etc., as fast as they were filled, spiriting away whatever took their fancy, and cheating poor John right and left almost under his very nose, helping him to look for the missing articles with the most innocent faces imaginable! They danced out in the rain to their hearts' content, lay down at night in their wet clothes, and took midnight rambles on the beach. Altogether, they managed to make the time pass most agreeably, till I got an inkling of things from one of the washerwomen, and dispatched them home instantly with a message to their parents to take charge of them till I was able.

After that dismal week, things grew brighter; the sun burst forth, and the house was turned inside out to get dried, but some of the matting was ruined. What tremendous washings we had! The tanks had been filled, and the whole island now shone verdant after the long-continued drought. There was a 'needs be' for all the dark rainy days we had gone through. The whole house was rethatched; and then I determined to inaugurate the great annual cleaning to save another turn up, though two months before the usual time.

Just as we were in the middle of it, however, and had set all hands to work so as to whitewash the whole house in one day, there was a cry of *Sail ho!* A man-of-war, they declared, even to the very smoke. I sank down panic-struck. Not a hole ready for their reception! Our own room and the dining room were nearest completion, but would not be habitable till evening; and there were all the old sticks, exposed to view in the midday blazing sun, a very different thing from seeing them in cool shady rooms dressed up in bright chintz and fancy work! John had no such concern, and only grudged having to leave his precious study to our tender mercies while he went off to the boat landing.

The vessel turned out to be a *slaver*, and sent in a boat with native crew and two white men in search of natives. The boat kept in deep water just outside the reef, and some Aniwans waded out and were shouted to in *sandalwood English.* They wanted men or boys, and would give a musket for every one they got. Our natives shouted back that they were *Missi's worshipping people*, and did not want to go with traders. One of the white men stupidly (it must have been in fun) levelled a musket at one of our natives, when the cap snapped and set the natives in a great rage, believing that he tried to kill some of them. The man levelled at, a fiery fellow, a returned labourer, flew for his musket, and would have made short work with the white man, had not John and the church members interfered, John actually standing right between him and the boat to prevent shots being fired. He waved the boat off with his hat, pointing to the armed man, which they seemed to comprehend, and after returning hats, they made for the ship which soon disappeared in the horizon.

I was annoyed enough at John exposing himself, not that a person on Aniwa now would harm him, for I often wish that they loved their Saviour as much as they do their missionary, but it is seldom one's duty to stand in the way of loaded muskets! You would hardly believe, though, the kind of thanks he got from the wretches he tried to save. They went to Efaté, and wrote out a paper to the effect that they 'had called at Aniwa for labourers, but that the missionary, Mr Paton, had come out to attack them at the head of an armed party. The man in charge of the boat, however, had Mr Paton covered with his rifle, so that had a single shot been fired into it he would have fallen in revenge.' And the paper has been posted up on the door of the principal store in Havannah Harbour! Those are the sort of men authorized by our British Government to scour these islands. We were perfectly thunderstruck when Mr McDonald happened to mention it to John, after he had decided to go north, in case he should see it himself. Mr McDonald sees enough of the traders and their doings, and treated it with amused contempt, as it deserved.

It is nearly as bad as the Nguna case, where the chief mate of the *Jason* swore in a Queensland lawcourt that the Rev. P. Milne caused the natives to fire into his boat. A man-of-war was dispatched to inquire into the proceedings of this dreadful missionary, and it was proved that poor Mr Milne was sound asleep in his bed (it was early morning), and did not even know of the affray till months after it happened. It was the two husbands of two native women, that this honest mate was trying to make off with (and did make off with), that owned to having fired the shots! It is not the first time that John has interfered to save the worthless lives of these slavers; but the whole fraternity may be riddled with bullets before I consent to his stirring his finger again in their miserable quarrels.

Notwithstanding the hurricane, this last hot season was a most charming one compared to the previous, when poor, poor Mungaw kept us in such constant terror. It was strange that the anniversary of his murder should be ushered in with the most tremendous thunderbolt conceivable, causing everybody on the island to spring out of bed in terror, supposing in the first moments of consciousness that someone had fired a cannon right into their ears. The loudness of the report, however, and the roars of thunder, proclaimed it to be heaven's artillery. It occurred a few seconds after midnight, and we thought the island must have been split in two, but no real damage was done. The natives were greatly impressed with the coincidence, and did not fail to inform Mungaw's murderer of it in the deafest side of his head—adding that Jehovah was showing his strength now, and letting him see what he would get if he did not repent of his conduct, both he and his accomplice!

Litsi has since consoled herself with another husband, related to poor Mungaw, and a real love-match, as they both freely confessed. Litsi was as playful and coy over it as a young lassie; though, when she stood up for the ceremony, she whisperingly informed the bystanders with a giggle that she didn't want to get married! I suppose she thought some pretence of an apology necessary for her third appearance in that church as a bride. We felt thankful when the marriage was past, for there had been the usual scramble to get her, and consequent bitterness of feeling by the rejected ones—some of them far handsomer and better men than the prizewinner. But then Noopooraw had shown the depth of his affection by threatening *to kill her* if she did not have him, which according to native ideas is the strongest expression of devotion, and is precisely the same as a wildly enthusiastic admirer threatening to *kill himself* in similar circumstances amongst you. The despairing lover in these Seas never dreams of taking his own life, but hers instead, finding that probably the more powerful argument of the two!

We had another marriage among my girls, some time before this, which made us very sad. It was dear little Kawiwi, who used to be Bob's playmate when he was a baby. She has the softest and most gazelle-like eyes I ever saw in a native, and has been with us since she was quite a little thing, so her wedding was a great affair. There was no 'bad talk' about it, as she had been promised by her parents some years previously—only our herd, *Joiner*, a handsome boy, decidedly objected to her being given away to a man who had two *dead* wives already, and opened his heart to John one evening upon the subject, pleading with him to get the match broken off more than a year ago. John referred him to her father, but he seemed to lack courage, so the old engagement was adhered to and the wedding finery finished.

The evening before the ceremony, Kawiwi slipped into the study and sat down on the floor—rather an unusual proceeding—with the great tears dropping from her eyes. That drew forth John's whole sympathies; and, finding that it was about her wedding, he sent for her father at once, and we had a long talk with him. In his first surprise and indignation, he spluttered out that he would shoot her if she dared to say a word against it; but, being really a tender-hearted father (and in the presence of the Missi moreover!), he calmed down quickly and apologized for his rough words, saying they came *from his mouth only, not his heart*. We begged her to speak out her mind freely, if she would rather have 'Joiner' (John was secretly attached to 'Joiner's' cause), but all that could be got out of her was, 'Let the wedding be delayed for awhile.' Her father alluded pathetically to the *pigs* that had been killed for them by the bridegroom, and showed how awkwardly it placed him after receiving them—she should have spoken out sooner, etc., etc. But we persuaded him to do as the poor girl wished. He got her away for a while next morning, however, and reappeared triumphant, declaring she was perfectly reconciled to the wedding, and that it was sorrow about leaving us which caused her tears! They had just talked her into it, and perhaps frightened her too, for she returned with red eyes, only crying bitterly when we asked if she were willing.

John sent again for her father, and before her dared him to risk the girl's happiness for life; so they got her outside again and had another long talk with her. The principal argument would have caused great amusement in a white community, for I overheard her step-mother saying very earnestly 'I can assure you, there's not a chief, or a creature on the island, has any objection to this wedding except yourself, and how can *you* object when *everybody else* is pleased!' We had our turn at her after that, though privately (poor lassie, how her ears were dinned that day!), and besought her to be true to her own heart ere it was too late, and we would protect and care for her as our own girl and she could still live with us. She seemed by this time determined to go through with it, and said it was good she should marry Kafoi; so she was brought up to the stake, a sweet young lassie of sixteen! Not that Kafoi was a Bluebeard by any means; for a kinder, nicer-looking little man, there is not on Aniwa; but then she did not at all love him—and John said, as he stamped indignantly along to church, that he would sooner follow her to her grave. To crown all, she turned round and gave John such an imploring look at the church door as sent him nearly frantic, and he looked pale during the service. I had a lump in my throat, but it changed to palpitation and alarm when it came to Kawiwi's turn (there were also two other couples being married), and

John would not take the muffled sound she gave for answer to the momentous question as to whether or not she would have the fellow at her right in his new white vest to be her lawful spouse, etc., etc. He repeated the question very gently (as if to encourage her to say *No*), but out came the affirmative low and clear, and she was done for.

Her revenge, however, was now to be taken. She came to bid us goodbye in the evening, sobbing bitterly. She then went to her father's village, where Kafoi had made a nice new house for them both; but into it she never has entered, and we firmly believe she never will. She is gentle and sweet to them all as ever, but just meekly *dour*. Kafoi bore most patiently, thinking she might change in a few months, but by that time the young lady had brighter prospects. Her old flame, 'Joiner,' had gone a voyage in the *Dayspring* as one of the boat's crew, when his year's engagement with us was up, and had learnt to sing *In the Sweet By-and-Bye* from the sailors. He came back full of it, and begged John to translate it—which he did, chorus and all—and we had a fine large singing class every evening, with the piano wheeled into the dining room. I took the bass with the boys, as the girls, who have decidedly the best voices, needed no help with the air. I never saw them enter so heartily into any hymn, and they manage the parts well. They would have sung the whole night if they might, and would go into the cookhouse after I dismissed them and have a rehearsal there.

We now fear, however, that it was at these meetings that 'Joiner' and Kawiwi resumed their former intimacy; at any rate, not very long afterwards she eloped with her 'true true love,' in broad daylight, under cover of attending a little Bible reading which I have with my girls every Sunday afternoon! It was an awful blow to us all, and there was little sleep that night. Next morning, the islanders rose to a man—except, of course, the offenders—and came to ask John what was to be done, as some course must be taken to punish the desperadoes in that village, who had long kept the whole island in disquiet by their wicked deeds from time to time and were only getting the more emboldened by forbearance. They said that 'Joiner' would never have dared to act thus, if he were not thoroughly backed up. John frankly told them that it was easier for him to say what was right, than to advise them as to what was expedient, as the two villains (Mungaw's murderers) in that village would think no more of shooting a few of them than of breathing, in fact would enjoy the excitement, and he told them to pray for and expect guidance before deciding.

They did so—I think, with their minds made up beforehand to go in a body and demand them to deliver up Kawiwi or take the consequences. Poor 'Joiner' and his friends didn't wait for consequences, but made clean heels into the bush, the moment they caught sight of the two armed chiefs heading the large party, and left poor Kawiwi to entertain her visitors alone. She was soon marched back to her village by a guard of honour; and then the business of the day commenced, and the ringleaders were rewarded for all their evil deeds. Houses were burnt, plantations demolished, and the food divided among the warriors. Their next effort was to secure the pigs; but they, like their owners, took to their heels and hid in the bush—so they contented themselves with what they had done, and left a message for the delinquents to the effect that they had only attacked their property this time, but if they ever again tried to set the worship at defiance they would attack themselves. The chief of that village, himself a good man, stood by and concurred in all that was done, saying, as he had often done before, that he was broken-hearted with them. John also approved of all that was done, and was relieved beyond measure that it was accomplished without bloodshed. The chiefs finished up to him the recital of the day's work, triumphantly declaring, *And, Missi, they'll never dare call us Women after this.* That village has certainly kept a 'calm sough' [*Scoticé*, 'kept quiet'] ever since, and 'Joiner' has found it convenient to pay a visit to Aneityum.

It is getting very late, and I must pass over all else and tell you what a charming time we had at Erromanga, where the Mission Synod was held this year. Mrs McDonald and I were the only ladies to keep Mrs Robertson company; and I was complimented upon now being the 'mother' of the mission, and carrying my honours quite becomingly—having become plump and vigorous since the hurricane. It seemed like fairy-land to enter dear Mrs Robertson's pretty, shady, cool house after enduring two days' suffocation with the horrid bilge water on board the *Dayspring.* Every day brought us fresh pleasure, afternoon rambles on the mountains and walks by the river-course up that beautiful valley, when 'the brethren' were at liberty to dance attendance on us, having all their Synod business over before dinner. How pleasantly those days flew past, only they can understand who have been shut off from kindred spirits as we are! We three ladies were, of course, all that could be wished for; and every one of the missionaries was kinder than another. Even in Synod, where ministers are apt to indulge in the grace of *candour* to an uncalled-for degree, there was not a jarring word—owing perhaps to that bilge water having taken all the bile out of them on the voyage!

The house is charmingly situated on terraced ground at the foot of a high mountain near the centre of the bay, with that lovely river to the right flowing past within a few yards of the enclosure. Our eyes were constantly wandering off to the lovely scene before us—and one with a history too! That very river was once reddened with the blood of Williams and of Harris, and the grass-covered mountain towering up from it was the scene of the Gordon tragedy—while their gravestones gleam white through the greenery on its opposite banks. Dear Mr McNair's grave is close beside them. All looked so peaceful now, with the *Dayspring* lying quietly at anchor in the bay, and canoes manned by *Christian* natives paddling about in its blue waters!

What a contrast to those former days of blood; and even a contrast, as the Robertsons told us, to what they had to suffer only in January last. The heathen chiefs were getting fierce at the rapid strides Christianity was making all round the island, and laid a deep plot to take the missionaries' lives. They chose their time well, when nearly all Mr Robertson's young men were away at Cook's Bay; and you may imagine his and Mrs Robertson's feelings, when the alarm got up one night as they sat quietly reading. They went into their bedroom and took their stand beside their three sleeping children. Escape by sea was impossible, even could they get to their boat—the night being stormy. Mrs Robertson turned to her husband and said, 'Do you think they could touch those sleeping lambs?' He smiled bitterly, 'What do they care for our sleeping lambs?' Yomit, a devoted Erromangan teacher, came in to them, and she turned to him saying, 'O Yomit, do you think they could have the heart to kill those little sleeping darlings?' He raised his arm and said, *'Missi, they'll have to cut this body of mine in pieces ere ever they get near them!'* He started off and collected all the available help necessary, sending secret messages overland in different directions to their friends, so that before morning the mission house was surrounded by two hundred warriors ready to give their lives in defence of their missionary. And these were the very men who murdered the Gordons—explain the change! Jesus has been amongst them!

Our visit there was all too short, as the Synod lasted only a week. We commemorated the Lord's Supper together, on the Sabbath evening before we broke up. One evening too there was an interesting Bible Society meeting, at which John was chairman; and, in response to an urgent appeal from London, Mr Copeland proposed that missionaries and seamen should all add a day's wages to their usual subscription—which was most willingly agreed to.

We tore across from Erromanga with a good wind, landing about sundown, and got a warm welcome from our dear old darkies, who had all turned out in their best garments to meet us—though it was pouring rain. John went on in the *Dayspring* to be left on Tanna for a fortnight at Kwamera, to make some small return for the Watts' great kindness to our natives while we were in Melbourne. He enjoyed his fortnight there intensely. The mission premises were like a new pin, and the Tannese longing for Mr and Mrs Watt's return with their whole hearts. Their little boys and girls at the station attended to John so faithfully, and continually followed him about, asking daily and often in a day the same question, *When will our Missis be back?* There are more than the Tannese longing for their return, and it will be a glad day when we see their dear faces again.

John has decided not to make any change for another year, if at all able to hold on. It is no use now for me to pretend I'm delicate, as appearances so tell against me! But I insist that I've got *heart* disease, and that only the sight of my bairns can cure it. Frank and I have been begging and pleading with Papa night and day to agree to a plan I've set my heart on—viz., to get all the three down by the *Dayspring* next trip, as she will only be a month on the islands before returning to Sydney, and that would not lose them much schooling. I should not care a straw if it did! It all seems so feasible; for the *Dayspring* lies a month in Sydney this time, and there would be time to prepare. I know that dear Mrs McGregor, and Mr too, would fully sympathize with me in this plan, and not set me down as daft. The bairns would go back all the better for the change, arriving in Melbourne again a little after New Year. Oh, how it would set me up to have one look at them; but I fear it's building castles in the air!

It is only a week yesterday since John returned from Kwamera, and was overwhelmed with such an ovation as he never yet got from our natives. They opened their hearts to the most unheard-of generosity, and actually parted with their precious *pigs* to show their love for him, besides a great quantity of yam. They also gave a present about half the size of ours to the captain of the *Dayspring*—pigs, yams, cocoa-nuts, and bananas. His were laid on the centre patch of grass before the house, and John's to the side in front of the study door. The pigs (13 in number!) all tied and laid out to be seen to the best advantage (they were *heard* too), so that when Captain and Mrs Braithwaite and John arrived they were greeted with—

Pigs to right of them,
Pigs to left of them,
Pigs in front of them,
Guzzling and grunting!

How they did grunt! The captain growled out his thanks in sailor's phraseology, which having translated John walked round to the side, followed by his grinning parishioners, and politely thanked them for their kind gifts to us, telling them that it was the feeling which prompted it more than the gift itself which he valued. I feel that he was telling the truth in all sincerity, for he hates the very sight of pork, and whispered aside to me, 'What on earth are we to do with all these beasts?'

We expect the *Dayspring* in about a fortnight to call for our mail, and as I have a very large one to answer it is time it were begun, for we'll be very much interrupted by the arrowroot making. The whole of the natives are busy digging it up at present, and the premises will be like a beehive in a few days when they begin to grate it. We were so pleased to be able to tell them that the last sold so very well, through the great kindness of Melbourne friends. The calico in the South Yarra boxes—worth its weight in gold—is being sewed up into sheets and bags for drying and packing it, as fast as ever we can; but we hardly expect it to be ready to go till the December trip of the vessel. They are to have *another book of the Bible* printed in the Aniwan language.

Ever with warmest love,
Your loving sister,
MAGGIE WHITECROSS PATON.

17

To Her Dear Sister-in-Law

ANIWA, NEW HEBRIDES,
JULY, 1879.

MY DEAREST LIZZIE,

I wrote a long general epistle yesterday, but have reserved the best news for you.

Your most welcome letters of August last arrived by the *Dayspring* in April, and were greedily devoured. The February packet came a month later, just as we were leaving for Erromanga; so we did not get them looked at, till we arrived there.

As soon as we got on board, Mr Laurie gave us the parcel from home, and how am I to thank you? We are just ashamed of all your kindness from time to time, and have never yet sent you a curio in return; but I'm really going to get up a box of shells, etc. There are not many very valuable specimens here, but we'll send the best we can get.

We were two days going across to Erromanga, as it was a head wind; and I was dead sick. But my curiosity and Frank's eagerness to see the knife which Fanny wrote about rose to such a pitch that the parcel had to be brought on deck, the second morning; and even their Reverences gathered round to behold and admire, as the things of delight were passed from hand to hand. John and dear Copeland, sitting on the deck and their backs against the *Companion* near me, had the first look. *The House that Jack Built* and *John Gilpin*, illustrated, were heartily laughed over. I was badly teased about the dash I was going to cut at Erromanga, in my new lace, which is very handsome, and far too kind of your dear mother to give me!

It is queer that both James and she should have been guided to the very things I most need; for, do you know, that my entire stock of good collars and handkerchiefs were ruined by the great hurricane in January. The japanned box, in which they were, was quite forgotten till some weeks later; and then, on raising the lid, I had to lift them out in bits, just to be thrown away. Thank James heartily from me for the dozen fine new handkerchiefs, as I forgot to mention that in his letter.

Minn's heart will be fairly uplifted with her beautiful brooch; which, they all said, was the prettiest in silver they had ever seen. I'm just vexed at all your kindness—and then that handsome dress for Baby, a real boy's costume! I must admit, though, that he admired the *ball* most of all, and went sprawling after it all over the deck. As for Frank's *knife*, it is like to come between him and his wits; for, boylike, it is the thing he most covets. If the bairns come to us from the Colonies, as I want them, the next trip, the brooch is to be put on Minn's plate on her birthday, December 13th, which she will in that case pass here at home.

By the way, we had quite a little stir here on her last birthday, just a few days after the *Dayspring* left us. I was waiting on John for tea, which was very late, as he was at some out-of-door work with the natives; and, Baby being restless, I strolled out to the veranda, giving a careless look towards the sea, as I moved along. What was my amazement to behold, in the dim light, a vessel in full sail, and close in to the shore! I thought I must be dreaming, and stared again to make quite sure; but there she was as large as life, a two-masted schooner, sailing slowly past, and didn't I shout *Sail ho!* John and his niggers came running to the side gate to see; and the girls tumbled out of all sorts of odd corners, trying to get up a whimper about a French invasion, though they were dancing with excitement over this new sensation.

John thought it might be one of the English *gunboats*, and sprang into his most respectable 'blacks' to rush out and receive worthily the representative of Her Majesty. He had a most picturesque train of the darkies flying at his heels; and they were all in full gallop down the 'brae' leading from our gate, when they came bump up against their visitors, emerging out of the shadows of the night. Meanwhile I had been making frantic exertions to 'put my best foot foremost' in the mission house—had got out my silver salver ('cabbaged' out of my housekeeping in the Colonies), and had arranged on it the tumblers, and my precious frosted crystal jug filled with milk; had cut fresh cake for the cake-basket, lighted up the drawing room, and placed out all my best 'tidies,' and all this barely in time to welcome two half-naked *slavers*! They made, however, ample apologies for their attire, and enjoyed without any apology the milk and cake as only sailors could. John and I could hardly drink our tea for laughing, after they left—the laughter would recur in irrepressible bursts; and the natives, who have instinctively a very keen sense of the ludicrous, yelled and shouted and jabbered till after ten o'clock at night.

Frank has had a grand laugh at my expense just now. I was praising up Baby for all the *darlings* and *Mother's pets* for creeping to me under the table, and put down my hands to protect his wee head, when, instead, Master Jim's (or Jay, as he styles himself) curly pate bobbed up! He is a sturdy specimen, with golden brown curls, and the most comical speeches. Last Sunday I was reading his little 'Peep o' Day' about Adam's fall, and explained that it had made us all naughty; but Jay had no notion of being responsible for his forefather's transgression, and said, *I'se not naughty. I didn't eat de fruit!* What theology for a missionary's son!

I think, though, that our wee Walter is going to be 'the flower of the flock.' He is desperately interesting at present; full of fun and dimples; a very pale clear complexion, and magnificent dark eyes, speaking ones. But, a few months ago, I thought they were too beautiful for this world; and I used constantly to say, if James saw them (your James), he could not choose but sit down and write a screed of poetry about them on the spot! They had no settled colour, and varied from slate colour to purple and blue, with such liquid depths. Now, don't you think I'm *daft*? Frank decidedly says I am; and one day, while chattering some outrageous nonsense to my baby, telling him I never knew what true love was till I laid eyes on him, etc., etc., Frank said gravely, *What fibs you do tell, Mamma! Did you go on like that to all your babies?* I said, 'Yes; I suppose they all got it in turns,' and the rogue replied with mock solemnity, 'Oh, what an example to set before your children! It's a wonder we didn't all grow up storytellers.'

We had a charming time at the Synod, and the Robertsons had all their arrangements made to perfection; but John insists that I shall write my *Journal Letter* as usual (I didn't mean to, having nothing sensational enough!), so I needn't tell you about it here. It was there we read your February letters—they had been stuffed into our hands as we went aboard—and how we did laugh, Lizzie, at your description of the Country Managers' and Elders' party! We could just fancy that chap's 'recitation.'

John laughed till I had to order him to be quiet, for fear of waking the baby. You'll have to order Bob or Fred home for the next 'cookie shine,' as they've both made their *début* as public performers. Fred was first, the young monkey, reciting some story at a Band of Hope meeting and Bob followed suit, next night, with a parody on 'Sir John Moore,' a laughable piece about mosquitoes!

O Lizzie, my heart's just like to break, when I think of all their little ways, and I can't be with them! It was always such a delight just to open the door for them, on their return from school, so full of spirits, and nearly always some news to tell, or some good-humoured bit of mimicry; and then, if they had got an unexpected holiday, their hurrahs were deafening. Fred used to let off his steam by lifting me clean off my feet (weak arm and all), before I knew what I was about. It's more than he could do now, for I've got so strong and fat, plumper than I have been since our marriage. I'm very thankful to be so well, and praise God for this and all our family joys.

I'll not dare read over this, else I would be ashamed to send it so far.

Ever with best love,
Your loving sister,
MAGGIE WHITECROSS PATON.

18

Days of Sunlight and Shadow

ANIWA, NEW HEBRIDES,
JULY, 1880.

EVER DEAR ONES,[1]

'The fierce light that beats upon a throne' is just nothing to the way that missionaries are watched and commented upon in public! Have seen some lovely criticisms in an old paper that came in the *Dayspring*, making John out an accomplished scoundrel, for selfishly wishing to keep the natives from the grand benefits which the slavers can offer them in civilization, and all for his own gain. Now, between those brave white men (I believe they call themselves *men*), who wax valiant against the missionary when he is too far away to see or reply to their attacks, and the natives who look up to him as a sort of demi-god, he might be tempted to wonder what sort of man he really is!

One poor over-worked skeleton, who was brought back from the sugar plantations to die lately, had such unbounded faith in the missionary, that he was perfectly willing he should negotiate matters for him in the other world. He did not know where he was going; he had never heard the name of Jesus, all the years he was in Queensland; but he trusted in the Missi that he had only known and loved for a short three weeks, because he cared for him like a human being, and

[1] To the family circle.

ministered to his dying wants. It is not the work we object to; labour is to them and to us a blessing; and I often wish the natives had less time for idling, and 'bad talk' about witchcraft and the like. Still, providence has neither made them, nor meant them, for such toils as white men; and they are quite of this mind, having the means of subsistence all easily within their reach. They have not the stamina we have, and ought not to be forced to exercise what they have not got. It only kills them. The worst of all is that, so far as facts under our observation seem to go, no man cares for their souls. They are too often treated as mere beasts of burden.

I must admit, however, that they may look rather like wild animals to the planters, if they are *heathen* natives; and their expressions won't be any the more angelic, when they know they are there simply for what can be got out of them. They feel things of that kind more than some would imagine. On our last visit to Australia, for instance, when Yawaci was with us as nurse, and treated in the kindest manner, she had many a good cry over the way that people stared at her. I did not know of this till, one day, she was called in to shake hands with a worthy friend of missions, who settled her *specs* properly to take an inquiring look from head to foot. Yawaci slipped out of the room; and, later in the evening, she sent in a note by one of the children (they *write* it, even when staying under your roof, if they have anything special or disagreeable to say), saying: 'Our Father in heaven made us all, both black and white; and why should the white children stare and stare at the black ones, as if they were wild beasts?' I flew to comfort her, and reminded her of how the Aniwans not only stared at us, when we first arrived, but even felt us all over. She rejoined: 'But I don't think you would feel it as I do. You were above us, and you knew it, and did not expect anything better from savages!'

Yawaci's perception and penetration often astonished us.

She was, indeed, civilized to a degree, and fairly *blushed* (I can tell when a native blushes, from the soft warm glow that suffuses the dark skin), when she saw the *nude* statues in the Fitzroy Gardens, asking if they were put there 'to show how darkhearted the people had been here, before they *took the worship*.' There was a smallpox scare in Melbourne at that time, which resulted in a decree going forth that all the world should be vaccinated, and she was in a perfect 'stew,' for days beforehand, at the idea of having to take her arm out of her dress in presence of the doctor! I was so very pleased at this delicate bashfulness in one who, a few years before, had come to us as an untutored savage.

While I write, we have had a prolonged earthquake, which always leaves me like a piece of animated jelly. The first time I ever experienced the sensation, shortly after landing on Aniwa, I imagined, as we were roused out of sleep, that it was the natives under the house trying to kill us; and when John said, 'Earthquake!' the sense of relief was heavenly. I never before felt so intensely the meaning of the psalmist's words, 'Let me fall into the hands of God, and not of men.'

Polygamy on Aniwa is now a thing of the past, as Waiwai, the only man who clung to it, lost both his wives last year. They were both exceptionally fine women, and he an affectionate husband, and one, moreover, who loved plenty of attention and good living. When the second one died, he came very desolate-looking for a spade to dig her grave, and said, 'Missi, there's a great void here.' But, instead of laying his hand upon his heart, which in the circumstances might have been supposed to illustrate the vacuum, he significantly clapped his stomach, saying he had no food, and, *Could we give him some tea?* No doubt, the poor fellow's heart was legitimately sore, when he thought of the *purris*, the *tamamotas*, the *takeifis*, and other dainties that would be cooked for him no more!

Not another chance of a wife for poor Waiwai, either—women of all sorts at a premium on Aniwa! How scarce they are you may better understand, when I tell you that one was married lately—without a nose! It had been lost in a conflict with her late lamented husband, and she has great moral courage to tackle another. She is, however, such a conscientious good woman, with a sweet disposition; and yet I always feel nervous about meeting her, wishing oftentimes that she would not insist on coming to the mission house, as she does most religiously.

Natives indulge very little in what you call sentiment; and when you naturally look for something of the kind, you are often met by hard matter of fact. One day, I was trying to reproduce a grand sermon I had heard in Melbourne, on the text, 'He saved others, himself he cannot save,' and explained how the Lord could not, because he would not. After entering fully into the subject, and trying to impress upon my audience the wonderful love of God in voluntarily giving himself a ransom for us, I asked, why he stood the jeers and taunts of wicked men, the agony of the cross, and didn't come down and save himself? The staggering answer came back, 'Why, Missi, because he was *nailed*!'

Waiwai gave a telling address, that day, over the open grave, urging the young men especially never to keep anything back from the Lord, as he had done in clinging to his two wives. Barring that little weakness, Waiwai has been a great help to us from the first, a truly lovable man, and one that could enter into your feelings. It was he, and the first great hurricane together, that gave us our lovely sea view. He owned the thick belt of trees that stood between our house and the shore; and when the hurricane destroyed so many on that terrible night, that we could actually see a shimmer of water between the fallen ones, next morning, from our veranda, I determined with Waiwai's assistance to complete the havoc so auspiciously begun. I had some long chats with him, and told him how insupportable life had been without a view of the sea, that no landscape was to me complete without water, and that I was born beside the sea, which perhaps explained the fascination it ever had for me, etc., etc. The result was that scores of great trees were levelled to the ground, and gradually cleared away, grass being planted in the vacant space. I paid, of course, for the trees and the labour, and would not grudge ten times the amount for the lovely view of the Pacific, which mirrors the most glorious sunsets you ever saw.

As the sun approaches and recedes from the winter solstice, it sets exactly opposite our Aniwan home, and we can see it sink into the ocean. One evening I can never forget, when John and I stepped on to the veranda, as the sun began to decline. Sea and sky gave us a new revelation of the Creator's glory. The sky was an outpour of colour, of glorified radiance and mellowed light, every shade and tint reflected back from the liquid depths of the Pacific. One could hardly breathe for delight; and John voiced our mutual thoughts when he chanted in a low and adoring tone, 'All thy works praise thee!' I forgot, for the moment, that the context is, 'And thy saints shall bless thee!' Well, we were unconsciously doing this; and, if we can't take to ourselves the appellation of 'saints,' we were, at any rate, two very appreciative sinners.

I often think John a perfect saint, indeed, in his whole-hearted consecration, and singleness of aim for God's glory in the conversion of the heathen; and yet he is delightfully *human* if you rub him up the wrong way. There are more scenes witnessed from that veranda than brilliant sunsets; and, before daylight, a few mornings later on, we saw or thought we saw what turned out to be a huge joke. I had gone out for a look round in the fresh morning air, and thought I saw an enormous fish, stranded on the reef and wriggling to get free. Muhow was sweeping the veranda; and, on calling her attention, she cried excitedly, *Taffra! Taffra!* (= Whale). John was called out; and, after one look, he set up in the still morning air what he conceived to be the *fish-cry*, to rouse the natives. They failed to recognize it as such, but sprang from their beds, thinking it was either murder, or the mission house on fire—and he met a number of men rushing to the rescue!

Hurried explanations thereon followed, and eager excitement; then the real genuine *fish-cry* rent the air; and, in less time than it takes to tell it, every man and boy within earshot, with whatever weapon had come nearest to hand—clubs, spears, muskets, sticks, bows and arrows—was flying helter-skelter at the Missi's heels, soon leaving him in the rear, clearing fences, ditches, fallen trees, everything, in the chase, with women and bairns following, hard in the train. All this we saw, from our vantage ground on the veranda; and we also saw, what in the brightening light they didn't see, that the whale turned out to be the huge leafy branch of a tree, stuck in for shade to the arrowroot workers of the previous day, with an arrowroot cloth hanging on it and flapping in the wind. In the dim haze of the dawning light, it had indeed looked 'very like a whale!'

I really thought Muhow would have gone into hysterics. She lay down, and shrieked with laughter, and had difficulty in keeping her face straight for more than a week. To this day, our cheery natives will still go off into roars, at the faintest suggestion of whales being seen about; and even Missi has had to stand no end of twitting on the subject! He admitted to having calculated, during the race, how much oil he might secure for the mission, never waiting to reflect that there was not a single appliance for extracting it!

He might have managed that, somehow; for he is a perfect 'Jack of all trades,' and tries his hand at anything. Once, when he had been urging me strongly to paint some of the beautiful scenery around, and would not take as an excuse the want of time, I brought forward the want of an easel, as mine had been left behind, and declared I couldn't paint in the open air without one. Nothing more was said, and I felt relieved; as the mother of a family, and a missionary's wife to boot, feels she must lay aside some of her accomplishments and give her time to 'the trivial round, the common task.' Not that the accomplishments have been superfluous; she gets the benefit of them every day. A knowledge of drawing makes one admire nature the more—a sunlight, a shadow, a reflection, having meaning and beauty, not likely otherwise to be perceived. To my astonishment, however, John triumphantly presented me with a properly made easel one morning, saying, 'Now, go ahead! You have no excuse.' I did not imagine that he even knew what an easel meant; and here was a perfect though rough specimen—a door hinge being used for the back support.

We had some delightful picnicking after that, as I had to go to a distance for a view of the volcano on Tanna from our shores; and then, from the same point, but in the opposite direction, I took Erromanga in the dim distance, with some canoes that happened to be on the water, to the great delight of their owners. I painted them in watercolours, and they make nice companion pictures; but oh, what gems they would be, if only I could have got the atmospheric effects reproduced—a real artist could, but they are lacking in mine! The natives are prouder of these pictures, than any others we have and I have got no end of praise from them, besides a huge turtle which they presented to me not long after—whereon we had quite an aldermanic dinner, 'with real turtle soup.' It is considered 'chiefs' food' here, and the women are not allowed to cook it, but only the men.

John has been translating another Gospel; and we have had such interest for days, hunting for the word *tempt.* He wanted to give a good rendering of that passage, where our Saviour was answering the Jews, when they asked whether it was lawful to give tribute to Caesar—'Why tempt ye me? Show me a penny. Whose image and superscription is this?' Neither of us knew a word in Aniwan for *tempt*; and John's pundit seemed to think there was none, or couldn't be got to understand what was wanted. It is so difficult in a foreign tongue to put just such questions as may elicit the word you want.

After consulting several of the most intellectual natives, to no purpose, we sent for Litsi Soré, who had been with me once in Australia. I reminded her of all the pretty things she used to gaze at in the shop windows of Melbourne, and how she often wished she could have them. 'Now, Litsi,' I continued, 'what did those people try to do to us, by exhibiting all those pretty things?' She replied, 'They were trying to make us buy them, of course!' We explained that we wanted to know if there was an Aniwan word which would express what the shopkeepers were doing, in making us wish to buy. Her answer was: 'Missi, I see what you mean; but there is no one word for it in our language, as in yours. We can only say, *they cause us to covet*.' So, with that, John felt he must be content.

We happened to sit up later than usual that evening; and, on retiring about midnight, we were surprised to see our cook come stealing into the room, in manifest excitement. He said, 'Missi, would you mind breakfast being a little late tomorrow morning?' I said, 'Certainly not. But why?' 'Oh, I've been thinking about that word the Missi wants, and I remembered that Lopu (a man in a distant village) is half Aniwan and half Erromangan (the cook himself was Erromangan), and that he knows both languages thoroughly. I will go to his house, before daybreak, with my Erromangan Gospel, and catch him before going off to his plantation. He will read the passage in Erromangan; and he will be sure to know if there is an *equal* word in Aniwan.' He did so; but Lopu only confirmed Litsi's version—to tempt is *to cause to covet.*

As I write, I hear the wild weird music of the death-wail, for an old man who was a great favourite; and they are recounting all his good deeds in a native chant. The wailing, of course, is not all sorrow; they set about it as deliberately as we would order mournings; and, in either case, the louder the howling, the deeper the crape, there is too much that is mechanical. Besides, they always count on a great feast after the burial, to reward them for all their exertions. I was struck with their cool way, when a sudden death occurred here on Sunday. At the close of service, the women asked me not to have my usual Bible class, as they had to go and wail.

I willingly consented, being glad of a rest through that hot afternoon, and was trying hard to get my husband to follow my example and stay at home, when a dear old woman flattened her smiling face against the window. I said that I was sorry not to have had the Bible class, if any of them were waiting, but she replied: 'They have all gone but me, Missi. My throat is a little sore; and, you see, I could not yell loud enough!'

The old man in question used to be called, good-humouredly, the 'Missing Link.' It is convenient to have a pet name for some of our best-known natives, that we may talk of them without arousing their suspicions. He was, in appearance, the nearest approach to an ape of any man we had ever seen, and would have delighted the heart of old Darwin. You may be sure, the Darwinian theory is not among the doctrines taught to our natives. It does seem a preposterous one, even here among the lower, if not lowest, types of humanity. It's not the absence of the *tail* that bothers me. Science may explain that away, and a dozen other points of difference; though I remember hearing an interesting lecture from Dr S., after he brought his gorillas to Britain, proving that the points even of physical difference were too great to be explained away. It's the presence of the *soul*—that is what I never can get over. There certainly is an unbridgeable gulf between the noblest animal, a sagacious dog for instance, without this soul, and the lowest specimen of human nature, say a savage cannibal, with one. One can receive the gospel; the other can't!

New Year's Day, 1881.—How little I dreamed, when penning the last entry in my journal, six months ago, what terrible suffering I was to undergo before I wrote again! God in mercy hides such scenes from our eyes. It seems truly a miracle that I live, after five months of great agony night and day with rheumatism, and unable to lift my hand to my head; then, for variation, diphtheria, and grievous bedsores. The oppression and prostration were very hard to bear; and the intolerable discomforts, for want of the alleviations of civilization, were no less so. I was struck down, just as I had planned a hurried visit to Australia, by the short trip of the *Dayspring* (she goes twice a year now, which is a great improvement), to have a week with my precious children; and, oh, it was hard to be resigned!

I have since thought that it was not an unmitigated evil, in the afflictions of poor Job, that his wife used strong language. My better-half was too good for that; and I fear I did a little 'bad talk' myself, just at the first. It seemed as if we were forsaken, both of God and man, when the *Dayspring* spread her sails, and disappeared to the Colonies, leaving us in such awful plight. It was, indeed, a very thick and black cloud into which I had entered, and which I cannot bear to look back upon even yet—why then should I inflict it upon you?

Yet there were rays of light that pierced even that darkness, and shone all the brighter as the night fell deeper; and the Lord had lessons for me to learn there, that could not be taught in the sunshine. The first thing that comforted me, when battling with the physical pain, and the heart-pain of prolonged absence from my children, was a text I had never noticed before: 'He knoweth what is in the darkness; for the light dwelleth with him.' What a glow of trust and comfort that brought me—*he knoweth*! Again, months after, when I was taking myself to task for my over-keen appreciation of the discomforts of the sickroom, instead of counting my blessings, which were many—the kindest husband in the world, and three darling children round me, etc.—Hutshi, the girl I had had most trouble with on the island, came into my room, burst into tears, and cried passionately: 'My heart is breaking for you, Missi! I can't think of you lying there, month after month with not a white woman to look after you. We can't turn ourselves into white people, or cook things to make you eat; but keep up, Missi; you don't know how much we love you, and we are all praying for you. I pray for you often in the day; and I am going home to pray for you now.'

How overwhelmingly sweet was such sympathy! I told Hutshi, that it was worth being ill to get it, and that I felt strong now to bear anything. Not a bit more brave was I, though, when a heavy footfall sent a shiver of agony through me, or my medicine was presented to me in a dirty glass. That glass was a real trial! Every kind of medicine would be put into it, without being rinsed. You will think, surely it was easy enough to get the glass washed. Nothing easier, if you look at it apart from the surrounding circumstances; or had there been anyone to perceive that it was needed, as well as the hundred-and-one little attentions that make acute illness bearable. John had always a dozen things to do at once; and I can't think how he got the time for his patient nursing of me, as he never missed a single service all the time.

It is bad taste to praise one's own, and I wouldn't indulge in it for the world; only, I must say, I have had some rare chances to die, if John had been less lovingly vigilant. Three times over, he, along with the natives who kindly took the night watching, knelt round my bed, thinking the end had come. It was, on all hands, feared I could not live to see our dear Bob, who was sent for to come in the *Dayspring*. When she appeared, on a Sunday, the excitement was intense, till we were sure that he was on board. John dared not leave me, even to go to the gate, though he often ran to the window. He was in an agony of suspense, for he knew I had not strength to bear a disappointment. At last, glimpses of the visitors were seen through the cocoa-nut grove; then the captain's figure was made out; then a tall slim young fellow by his side, towering inches above him. My heart fell at the description, for I knew my boy was not quite sixteen!

When their footsteps could actually be heard on the coral walk, by our strained ears, John left me to welcome them; and Litsi *Sisi* (= the Little), a dear faithful girl, rushed in saying, 'Rejoice, Missi, and live! It is your own child, your firstborn son!' and then she burst into a flood of happy tears. A few seconds more, and my heart had the sight it had been longing for three years and more. One of our sable elders crept in along with them, and stood sobbing like a child over the meeting of the mother and her son. From that moment, new life came to me every hour; and when Captain Braithwaite, the kindest-hearted and truest tar (sailor) that ever walked the deck, offered to leave his wife with us, John felt the load lifting from his shoulders, and praised the Lord. Dear Mrs Braithwaite is one of a thousand in kind care and gentleness; and, oh, what a comfort to have a refined woman's hand about everything!

Captain Braithwaite has told us since, that when he saw what a skeleton I was reduced to, he thought there was no hope, and left her to perform the last offices for me; instead of which, she welcomed your new nephew, the bonnie little

John Whitecross, and mothered him till the dear Watts came, who are always, next to the Lord, our mainstay in every trouble. Mrs Watt is with us now, and Mr Watt is coming over for her in his boat, when he will also baptize our baby.

We hope to rejoin our two other dear ones in Australia, some time this year. John makes such a capital missionary *beggar*, that the Victorians have commanded his services in that capacity for a season; so I emphatically beg you to understand that it is not his wife's health that is taking him away from the mission field! The 'dear wives' sometimes are trotted out as a very touching excuse, but I won't serve the purpose. On the contrary, I have kept him a year longer, for we were to have gone last year—had I been able to be moved!

February 20th, 1881.—It is said that we shall enter the kingdom *through much tribulation*; and our Lord has seen fit to make us sound the very depths in his dealings with us. Since penning the last lines, death has been in our cup. Our darling wee Walter, whom we loved as our own lives, and who brightened these lives as with an angel's ministry for two years and a half, has been taken away in the midst of health and glee. Short and sharp was the way to the Shepherd's fold, dear lamb; and the circumstances surrounding his death make the tide of anguish swell so high that I have sometimes feared it would sweep away our reason.

The whole place is teeming with associations of him; and today, when I went to church again, the first time for seven months, the little empty space, where he used to sit with his nurse, close to his father's platform ('Papa's wee shadow' he was called, for he never would keep away from him), was too much for me! It was hard to keep one's heart down, and see the tokens of sympathy all around—my poor girls and the women with bits of black sewed into their hats with white thread—and when a wee fellow, about Walter's own age, came trotting up with one of his dear familiar dresses on, and a black sash his mother had tied round him, the floodgates burst open at last, and with a vengeance.

I fear most of all for dear John. He has scarcely eaten or slept, since the dear lamb was taken, as he suspects by an accident about the medicine, though God only fully knows. All through the day, he braces himself, and neglects no duty or call; but his interest in everything else seems dead, and he paces the study floor for hours every night. The Lord sustain, and the Lord heal!

August, 1881.—Left dear old Aniwa; and I hope to God that I may never again have to go through such a parting. How our hearts were stirred to the depths, in leaving the beloved and familiar associations of so many years! I had no idea how much I truly loved our dear old darkies, nor how intensely they were attached to us, till we came to say farewell. When we had fairly quitted the mission house at last, I felt like one walking in a dream, as we passed, one after another, the shrubs and flowers we had planted, on our way to the gate. I thought the bitterness was past, when we took leave of the precious graves; but the scene at the boat harbour was such as I cannot bear to recall!

How our Aniwans walked right into my inmost heart, by their genuine sympathy, at little Walter's death! I have strongly recoiled from the formal visits of condolence, in civilization, and have often wished to smite dumb a certain type of ministers, who glory in turning a mother's heart round and round in the pulpit, and cutting into it, apparently for no higher purpose than intensifying the pathos of a sermon. It has been my wicked wish that they themselves might have, at least, as much sorrow as would make them 'keep their tongues between their teeth,' as the Scotch say. Some of us have been 'so built by God,' that, while grateful for the throb and glance of silent sympathy, and answering to it as the barometer to the pressure of the air, we quiver and suffer when people try to put it into blundering words.

With our natives, somehow, things were not so. Whether it is that they are so much like little children, and a child's touch upon your spirit is never hard or coarse, I cannot tell; but sympathy from them never pained, but always soothed me. They would come before us, sit down on the floor and cry, and bring to mind all the little sayings and doings of the dear one—just like a bairn chattering sweetly about an absent playmate. The very night before we left Aniwa, the loving Hutshi said almost in a frenzy of exultation: 'You yourselves may go away, Missi, and leave us; but you can't rob us of the little ones in the graves. These two are ours; they belong to the people of Aniwa; and they will rise with the Aniwans in the great Resurrection Day, and they will go with us to meet with Jesus in his glory!'

Ever faithfully and affectionately yours,
MAGGIE WHITECROSS PATON.

19

A Tour Round the Islands in 1889

MELBOURNE,
NOVEMBER, 1889.

DEAR SISTERS, BROTHERS, AND FRIENDS,[1]

Our six months' visit to the New Hebrides has been most joyful and refreshing. We three, John and Minn and I, set out from Melbourne on March 26th, and found our faithful friend, Captain Braithwaite, waiting for us at Sydney, with the *Dayspring* boat manned by natives to carry our luggage straight to the old familiar ship. It looked like a good-sized *canoe*, after leaving the *S.S. Adelaide*!

Two days thereafter we cleared out for the New Hebrides; but, owing to head winds, we took exactly three weeks to do what would easily have been done by steam in six or seven days. We were dreadfully sea-sick, and the *Dayspring* felt very small and stuffy. The bunks are so narrow that you have to make up your mind on which side you are going to sleep, before getting in, owing to the difficulty of turning! Yet we enjoyed the voyage and the company—all having so much in common. There were eight of us, including the young missionaries, and the Rev. Mr Bannerman and Mrs, besides Captain and Mrs Braithwaite. Mr Bannerman is convener of the Heathen Missions Committee in Otago, and we rejoiced in his and dear Mrs Bannerman's society immensely. We had

[1] To the family circle.

nice readings aloud on deck, from 'Rudder Grange' to Shakespeare's plays and Byron's *Hebrew Melodies*; and the young missionaries delighted us with their fine voices for singing.

When we had been a fortnight at sea, we passed close by Norfolk Island, the seat of Bishop Selwyn's mission. The little island adjacent, Pitt's Island, was the loveliest patch I had seen on the ocean for many a day—a magnificent rock, furrowed and dotted all over with rich crimson tints, showing exquisitely in the slight haze of the morning sun.

There was an exciting time, when we approached Aneityum. We were all on deck, by six in the morning, to see the vessel go into Anelquahat Harbour, and were in the midst of our joy at the prospect of landing, when all at once a *grate-grating* was felt and a quivering of the vessel from stem to stern. The *Dayspring* was on the reef. There we stuck for nearly four hours, with consternation on every face. I felt most of all for the captain, who had been up at duty the whole night, and is always so very cautious; but the narrow entrances between those hidden reefs are both deceptive and dangerous. He gave his orders calmly and promptly. The sailors worked as one man got out the anchors and tow ropes in their boats, and tried to draw the vessel off. Most fortunately, the tide was rising, and this gave them hope. The missionaries, having given all the help they possibly could, assembled in the cabin, and kept praying, in turn, to the Lord for our relief. Blessed was the sound to us all, when the captain shouted, in a voice *falsetto* with excitement, 'Hallelujah! She's off! She's off!' He admitted, however, that John was the very first to feel the delightful 'lifting,' and to praise the Lord for answer to his servants' prayers. It was but another illustration of how, in all God's dealings with his children, 'prayers and pains' go hand in hand to bring us the blessing.

It was now about nine o'clock, and we began to realize that we had been hungry. What a joy at the breakfast table! The captain asked such a fervent blessing, with both hands raised, and spoke so touchingly about the loving Providence watching over us, that all were visibly moved. We had, of course, put out again to sea; but we got safely into the harbour in the afternoon. The place looked so lonely without a missionary. But we got a most cordial invitation to dinner with the Martins of the Saw Mills, to which we did ample justice, enjoying it as only seasick voyagers can, when they get ashore.

To me it was most refreshing to see my own first impressions of the tropics reproduced in the Bannermans and the young missionaries. It was, also, all new to Minn—she was such a young child when she left Aniwa. I had been wondering, further, if my own vivid imagination would be borne out by this visit in maturer years. But, when we entered the bay, and set eyes again on those lovely shores that seemed to float on a sea of melted jewels, with the grand old mountains towering up behind, I felt that I had never half realized how gorgeous was the beauty of these islands. The changeful tints on the water, from the palest transparent green to the deepest purple, baffle description.

The captain had to *water* the *Dayspring* there; and, as I had brought my painting materials, I picnicked on the brow of a hill, and painted the harbour, with Dr Geddie's church in the foreground. The result was, of course, disappointing. One would want a month of close study, to secure even a faint resemblance of the lovely scene, instead of only three short sittings. But Mrs Bannerman was very pleased to have it as a memento of their visit; and she writes me since that Mr Bannerman has sent it to the Otago Exhibition. It was great fun, as they had never the option of refusing it as a work of art, for it is placed in the New Hebridean Court—among the other *curios*!

Our next stopping-place was Fotuna. But, on approaching the mission station, and eagerly looking through the glass, we found, to our dismay, that Dr Gunn's house was nowhere to be seen. It had been levelled to the ground by the hurricane, all except a room or two at the back, and there they were living. It seems hard that such able and devoted missionaries should suffer so! They were most kind and hospitable, and appeared to take joyfully the spoiling of their goods, for Christ's sake.

Our next halt was at dear old Aniwa, and we had a heart-stirring day there, after eight years of absence. We were welcomed by a crowd of our old parishioners, many of whom had grown out of my recollection (John had seen them more recently), but I did not dare to show that to them! One of my old girls understood the dilemma, and kept close beside me, whispering the names without almost moving her lips. They had all the mission premises in apple pie order—the loveliest and dearest place I have seen, since the day we left it.

The natives were charmed to see Minn again, and asked eagerly for our boys. We had taken 'the sinews of war' from the *Dayspring* for a picnic in the dear old familiar dining room, as our goods were only landed, not unpacked, till our return from the Mission Synod. It was nice to have dear friends with us ashore, and to hear the Aniwans eagerly inquiring for our children; but, just at first, if it must be confessed, I would have given the world to be left alone. The flood of memories was too overpowering. Every room, every spot of ground teemed with recollections, and my heart was like to burst, sometimes in gladness, sometimes in sorrow, as the past rose to view. We had a little service in the church, after lunch; and then, all our stores being landed safely, we, in the prospect of an early return after the Synod, bade them all a cheerful goodbye.

We called next at Kwamera, after three days of most disagreeable head winds. This visit meant a great deal, especially to John and to me, for the Watts have always been true brother and sister to us. We were greatly shocked with Mrs Watt's haggard appearance. She had been dangerously ill, and I never saw such a change in anyone—may God soon restore her! She did not know Minn, but thought she was a very young missionary's wife, and was wasting much sympathy upon her for leaving her mother so soon! Had to rush off, after a hasty repast; but with the hope of soon meeting again at the Synod.

We had a pleasant trip, next day, to Mr and Mrs Gray on the other side of Tanna, who hospitably entertained us all at lunch, which was as long as we were allowed on shore. And there I met with my dear old faithful Litsi *Soré* (= the Great), who cried so when she saw me, and would like us to come back to them. But she and her husband are usefully and happily employed, as teachers and helps to Mr and Mrs Gray.

We next spread sail for Erromanga, which we could have reached in a couple of hours by steam, but it was two days later when we cast anchor in Dillon's Bay. It was beautiful as ever, and I got a nice painting of it and the mission station from the deck; but we missed our usual warm reception from the Robertsons, who are on a short visit to Australia for much-needed rest and change. We made free use of their good servants, though, and got some laundry work done. The Sabbath services were very interesting. Morning worship for the natives in the *Martyrs' Memorial Church*—Mr Bannerman giving a good address, which Yomit translated into Erromangan.

Our next stopping-place was Erakor, Efaté, and we had a charming day with our dear friends Mr and Mrs Mackenzie. We all look on the Mackenzies as *ideal* missionaries; and the native teachers of their training are sure to prove satisfactory, wherever they go. They too have had to part from their children for the sake of the work, and have only little Alice left.

They took us in their boat up the lagoon—the loveliest sail one could imagine; we were so closely walled in on either side by the richly clad hills and tropical foliage. We crossed the isthmus, where the *Dayspring* boats were waiting us on the other side; and had another lovely sail through Fila Harbour, where the *Dayspring* went round to anchor, after we left her in the morning.

You will think we do nothing but *enthuse* over the fairy-like scenery here. Well, we can't help ourselves; and I have not properly begun yet; for, on entering Fila Harbour—*La Belle Fila*, the French call it—I felt that if there were any place more beautiful on God's earth, I would require enlarged capacity to do it justice! It was a daydream of delight, with its burst of colour, tropical foliage, and greenery down to the water's edge, reflected back in wondrous beauty; bluest mountains in the background; sunlights, hazes, and gorgeous skies; a sea of glass, clear to the very depths, and revealing the grandest aquarium in the world. Three round rocks rise abruptly from the water, with tufts of greenery on their top, standing out for all the world like huge flowerpots! The people who invented the proverb, *See Naples and die*, had never seen the beautiful Fila in these Pacific Seas.

We had a pleasant few days next at Havannah Harbour, which one could almost imagine to be a Highland loch; and there we were the guests of the Rev. D. and Mrs McDonald. It charmed us to see, not only the results of their long and devoted labours, but also their darling children. They are the most lovable, bright little pets you ever saw, and the two eldest boys in Melbourne are great chums of our Jay's. We heard there the astonishing news of the wreck of the *S.S. Fijian*, off the coast of Tanna, last Monday, the very time we left Erromanga. They must surely all have been asleep, else they never could have succeeded in performing that feat in the beautiful moonlight.

Our next resting-place was Nguna. It was a real joy to meet once more my dear friend Mrs Milne and her beloved ones; and, as we stayed over the Sunday, we had the pleasure of worshipping there in the 'cathedral,' which we call *St Peter's*, after the Reverend Peter Milne, the best architect among our missionaries. It is by far the finest church in the New Hebrides; and, what was best of all, we saw many hundreds of well-dressed people assembled therein to worship the true and living God—Mr Bannerman and John giving addresses, and Mr Milne translating. Mrs Milne conducts Sunday School in the afternoon, while Mr Milne is holding worship on an adjacent island; and she gave them an address on part of the *Pilgrim's Progress*, which she has been translating into Ngunese, and to which they listened with rapt attention. The work on Nguna has taken gigantic strides, and very much of the success is due under God to the spirit of Mrs Milne.

What sweet intercourse I had with her, when living on Aniwa! We used to write a 'monthly thought' to each other, on the first Monday of every month. It might be a text, and our thoughts about it; or it mightn't be a text at all, just any subject, and the Lord's dealings with us. It did seem as if he guided our pens what to say to each other, the 'thoughts' so frequently bore upon our own peculiar circumstances, and how often we thought alike! Those 'monthlies,' though we didn't of course receive them every month, came to me with far more freshness and power, and did me more good than any sermon; and the opening of the budget was more delightful than even cutting up the leaves of a new publication.

One of the new missionaries mended Mrs Milne's harmonium, and we had a little music. The house was immediately surrounded by eager listeners; so Mrs Milne had it taken into the church at the urgent request of the natives, and we had a rare concert! Not altogether a sacred one, I fear; rather a medley of all sorts, everyone contributing what he or she could. During intervals in the singing, I rattled off things from Stephen Heller's *Tarentelle*! It was so jolly to give such pleasure to an enthusiastically appreciative and uncritical audience. Natives generally are so fond of music; you have only to play a few bars to gather a crowd. We got lovely views at Nguna, from which fourteen islands can be seen from a hill behind the mission house. I got a good sketch of these, but had no time to paint.

At Tongoa, our next place of call, Mr and Mrs Michelsen kindly entertained us all on shore for the night, which we enjoyed exceedingly. Next day we witnessed a grand sight, when Mr Michelsen assembled his people from all parts of the island, and we had open-air worship on the grassy brow of a hill, outside the mission premises, there being assembled about six hundred natives in every colour and description of costume. All the missionaries addressed them, Mr Michelsen translating; and then, what a volume of praise ascended to heaven from that sable throng! They were too many to shake hands with; so Mr Michelsen announced at the close of the service, that the chiefs and church members alone were to come forward. Three of the chiefs happened to be church members; but instead of coming first with the other chiefs, they waited and came as members of the church, which we thought beautiful.

Next day, we arrived at Api; and the few hours we had with Mr and Mrs Fraser did us real good—they are so devoted and so bright. It was now all calm and pleasant sailing, through the northern islands. We passed Lopevi, a high mountain peak and an extinct volcano, 4,000 feet above the level of the sea. The following day, being May 24th, was remarkable for birthday celebrities—being the Queen's, and John's, and the cook's!—and we had Mrs Bannerman's shortbread in honour of the occasion.

Ambrim was reached the morning after, and most of the

mission party went ashore to encourage the native teachers; then we steered our course for Malekula. The wind died off, and we feared deadly delay; but up it came again, and off we flew, sighting three vessels in our way, and were anchored in Sasoon Bay by four o'clock. A Roman Catholic priest has the site, the ground, at the anchorage, and Mr Leggatt's station is much farther on. So we had a bit to go by boat; but we got a right hearty and cheery welcome, when we arrived at their pretty and hospitable home. We had only ten minutes to stay; but we three Patons were not allowed to return to the vessel.

Next day being Sunday, Mr Leggatt, John, and I had a charming walk to the anchorage, partly by shore, and partly through the bush, to have service at a village on the way. There were twenty-one naked darkies at the worship, Malekula having been only recently occupied; and finely carved wooden idols and drums were all around! We looked in at the priest's gate, intending to pay our respects to Monsieur le Pére; but he had gone off to a distant village, and we had only the satisfaction of seeing his little footprints on the sand. On getting opposite the *Dayspring*, Mr Leggatt signalled, and a boat was sent for us to get on board for English service, after which we were rowed to land again, and walked back to the mission house.

After dinner, there was a native service in church, and Tookaro, a devoted native teacher, was asked by Mr Leggatt to add a few words; whereupon he gave us a rather mixed address in sandalwood English, and on the story of Moses. We were all feeling so much for the Rev. A. H. McDonald, who was staying with the Mortons, as we had brought the news of his good father's death. Mr Leggatt managed to get the mail sent over early next morning, along with letters of sympathy to prepare him for the tidings. Dr McDonald was a lifelong and highly valued kind friend to us and the New Hebrides Mission, and was for many years convener of the committee at Melbourne.

Two days thereafter, we anchored at Pangkumu, where we had a very warm reception from the missionaries, and from the weather! The mission house is charming, but ought decidedly to be higher up to get into the sweep of the air currents. We enjoyed our stay there very much, but for the awful heat. Being detained several days, for lack of wind, we saw a lot of the natives.

One horrible practice on Malekula is knocking out the two upper front teeth of every girl, as she reaches womanhood. The fine white teeth of the natives being one great point of beauty, to think of the Malekulan women being so disfigured suggests to some that they had proved vicious to their husbands in former generations and so had come to be disabled. One or two girls escaped to Mr Morton's, as they were about to be operated upon; but the old women, who themselves had suffered in like manner, were the first to seize and carry them back to torture.

The Malekulans were greatly taken with Minn's abundant hair, but argued that the thick coils could not all be her own! Mrs Morton translated what they were saying, and begged her to gratify them by taking it down. She unwound it at the window, all the black faces gazing on intently, and when it showered like a cloud around her, they gesticulated and shouted with delight, declaring it was *as fine as a pig's tail*! Mr Morton assured Minn that that was their highest possible form of praise—they think so much of those interesting brutes!

We got wind enough at last to take us out of Pangkumu; but we soon represented vividly 'a painted ship upon a painted ocean.' Ample time was at our disposal to admire the scenery; and we sat watching the stars at night, especially Saturn, with his brilliant diamond flashes, the only planet that twinkles. Venus was on show at 4 a.m., but I for one was too lazy to get up and admire.

Malo was reached on the following Sunday, and the younger missionaries went ashore; but it was not fit for ladies at low tide. Captain and Mrs Braithwaite and we three went after tea; but there was such a mighty roll on the reef, we had to turn back to the *Dayspring*—waving our handkerchiefs to Mr Landells, as he rushed to the landing to meet us. He looked rather 'had,' as they say in Australia, and we felt no less so; but the evening service with the sailors on board was very pleasant, and the Landells' kind and hearty welcome was only delayed till next morning, as the captain landed us before seven o'clock, and Mrs Braithwaite followed in time for breakfast.

The view from the Landells' veranda is most exquisite; the spreading bay, the great Santo Mountains beyond, draped in blue purple hazes and sunlights, and the little islets between. We had a walk with Mr and Mrs Landells, through the Malo bush, and passed a village, where they were wailing for a man who had died that morning. There were heathen ceremonies connected with it; but the earnest labours of these devoted missionaries will bear fruit, in due time, by the blessing of the Lord.

In the afternoon, Mr Annand's boat was descried, and soon there was another meeting of friends. It was delightful to meet with our old fellow workers; and Mr Annand informed us he had strict orders from Mrs Annand to bring us right back with him that very afternoon. It was too tempting to be refused; and Mr Annand called with us on board to get a few things together; and then we had a lovely sail of two hours—enjoying a gorgeous sunset by the way, the side of the high Santo Mountain being enveloped in the radiance as if itself a part of the glory. We had a delicious welcome from dear Mrs Annand on her mountain home on Tangoa—a small island, off the mainland of Santo.

I shall never forget my earliest sight of Mrs Annand, when

she entered the mission, and *first* came ashore at Aniwa. She suggested to me a beautiful lily, with her tall slim figure, fair hair and complexion, and finely cut features; dressed in a loose double-breasted Rob-Roy jacket, and black hat with feathers. As she bowed and smiled, while still at a little distance, I just wondered if a fairer girl had ever entered a mission; and I was greatly pleased, afterwards, to learn that her mother was dead, and had been spared the pain of parting. I watched her husband very closely, to see if he were worthy of such a wife, and was speedily more than satisfied—which is the highest praise I can give him!

This is a new field to them. They laboured for years on Dr Geddie's old station on Aneityum. But when it was thought, owing to the scarcity of missionaries, that *one* ought to serve that island, they nobly volunteered to move, and tackle a new language and another people—building on no man's foundation. We had two or three delightful days with them; and, such are their illusions, Minn and I were duly admired, by some of the native women, as John's two wives!

Having reached the most northerly island and the last of the mission stations, we began to wind southwards again, picking up the missionaries by the way for their Annual Synod, till we were packed like sardines in the little *Dayspring*. It was a good thing that all the missionaries didn't come! Several, as it was, had to sleep on the floor; and there were always two relays at meals.

We had a fine view of Monument Island, passing close to it in the moonlight—great rock, full of arches and dark caves, rising sheer out of the water to a height of five hundred feet, exactly like a sugarloaf. We passed our silver wedding day, on that return voyage, very quietly, as nobody knew but we three and dear Mrs Bannerman. It seemed befitting that we should spend that day on the dear old *Dayspring*, and in the New Hebrides. There was food for many varied emotions in looking back over all the way God had led us during the five-and-twenty years of our married life. The next day, we got a huge mail on calling at Havannah Harbour; and there was eager and merry excitement, as we all rushed down to the cabin after the captain, who shouted out the names and handed the letters, being playfully answered by each in university style, *Adsum* [I am here].

On June 26th, there was a fine fair wind for Kwamera, and we joyfully did our packing, as the captain gave us hope of taking our tea on shore. But 'there's mony a slip 'tween the cup and the lip'; and we had barely finished, when black clouds came, then squalls and torrents of rain; and we were battened down below, and parboiled for the next two days. It was charming to get to Kwamera at last, in the early morning, with ravenous appetites for breakfast; and what a glorious time we had, all together, at the Mission Synod.

All Mrs Watt's arrangements were simply perfect, could not have been more so at a first-class hotel, and everything planned so as to avoid the least confusion—even cards, with our names, at our table seats, and on the bed each was to occupy. The servants and helpers had each certain duties to perform, for which they were responsible: one to attend to the *Punkahs* (fans) at meals, etc.—a new luxury, and a very desirable one, since *we* were in the mission field; one to fill and empty the baths, as they were used, etc. The appointments at table were precisely what you would use in such homes as ours in civilization; but the bedrooms showed, as well as taxed, the ingenuity of our host and hostess. Bright chintz and muslin gave a very inviting appearance to what had been general store, mangle room, or printing office, and hid some rather unpromising looking materials in the way of old boxes for beds, tables, etc. Twenty-three guests were sumptuously entertained on the fat of the land for fully a fortnight, to the praise of the management and energy of dear Mrs Watt.

Much interesting work was accomplished during the sittings of this Synod. It was the jubilee of the New Hebrides Mission, if we date it, as we well may, from the martyrdom of Williams and Harris on Erromanga. There were twelve missionaries, counting Mr Bannerman, and we nicknamed them The Twelve Apostles. They arranged for a new distinctive flag for the mission, for which Mr Watt asked me to paint the design. It is Presbyterian blue, with a white St Andrew's Cross (*The Whitecross Banner!*), and the letters N.H.P.M. in red, for New Hebrides Presbyterian Mission. We made a flag for Mr Watt, after the new pattern, which was hoisted on the flag staff amidst the cheers of the missionary party. Out of Synod hours, croquet was the order of the day—tennis being too heating for the climate; then there was walking, and music, and getting photographed, of course. There was also a Magic Lantern exhibition and a concert (I think it was sacred) for the natives. And I should not have failed to mention that, the first Sunday after our arrival, at the English service we all partook together the Holy Supper of our Lord.

The settlement of the two new missionaries was very interesting. Mr and Mrs Gillan go to Port Stanley on Malekula, and Mr Smaill to Api. They will make splendid missionaries, and John devoutly wishes we had twenty more like them. The sittings were formally closed, after ten days' work, by a very fine address from the Moderator, Mr Gray. Then we had a few bright and pleasant days of leisure, till the *Dayspring* came for us. Some of the missionaries got up for the general amusement a neat little daily newspaper on the cyclostyle, called *The Kwamera Morning Herald*, and a copy was laid on each plate at breakfast. It caused great merriment, most of the jokes, latest news, etc., being good-humouredly personal.

We left Kwamera, with the bright hope of a speedy reunion with the Watts, who are to go with us to Australia on their way to the Old Country. But it was hard to see the others setting out for their isolated homes. I do not know how it is, and can't account for such feelings, as my own mission life was decidedly happy; but it is always like to break my heart, to see any other missionary and his wife left on a lonely island.

We had a swift run across to Aniwa, only a few hours; and we three had barely time to land before dark on the Saturday evening. How thankful we were, not to have another night of sea-sickness and close packing! The missionaries on board must have been right glad of our room instead of our company; and our large airy house looked a palace after the wee overcrowded *Dayspring*. The natives had all our belongings out of the boat in a twinkling; and Litsi Sisi (Litsi the *Little*) had the lamps lit and the kettle boiling for tea when we arrived.

The two months we spent on dear old Aniwa were hallowed and busy ones. The delicious calmness and quietude of that first Sunday, I felt I could not sufficiently drink in. I had time to *live* the old associations; could go round all the familiar spots; stand in the empty rooms; remember what had happened in each; and let my heart surge up, if it wanted to! Never before had I felt, in such a degree, the charm of being *alone*—that is, so far as the outside world is concerned, for John and Minn are part of my very self, and if only our five laddies had been there too, the bliss would have been complete.

On the Monday morning, we discovered to our dismay that the box of kerosene had been left on board and we had no more oil than was in the lamps! Our Aniwans own a boat of their own, of which they are very proud, and eagerly offered to go across to Tanna, and get a supply from the Rev. Mr Gray, who was our nearest neighbour; and kind, kind friends Mrs Gray and he proved, always sending us needful things; for the boat went back two or three times, and their boat came to Aniwa. There was nothing we enjoyed more than the bottles of milk which Mrs Gray so kindly remembered.

I had no household cares, having elected four natives to attend to our daily wants. Eight of them, however, insisted on coming; and we had not the heart to put them away, poor things, so loving were they. But if I had no household duties, the natives took good care to provide plenty of other work; for, they were eager to be taught and to take all the good out of us they possibly could. The tables *were* turned! Instead of us urging them on, as we used to, it was now the other way, with a vengeance. They knew we were not to be long with them, and would come, especially the native teachers, and ask John the meaning of different passages in their Gospels. In the evenings, after native worship in the dining room, always packed to overflowing, and long Bible talks, we could hardly get them to leave us.

One day, after hard work in visiting, ministering to the wants of the sick, teaching and talking without a moment to ourselves, I got the room thoroughly aired after they had all gone, and felt fairly entitled to a good long *read*. Minn was trimming native hats. John had gone off with his pundit to the study. So I got on to the sofa with the fourth volume of Carlyle's *Cromwell*; when, to my discomfiture, Nalousi, one of our young native teachers, made his appearance and promptly announced his business. He wanted a new hymn translated, 'Who is He in Yonder Stall?' into Aniwan, as Mr Watt had done into Tannese. I told him the Missi was engaged, and didn't want to be disturbed any more tonight. He said that didn't matter a bit, as I would do it. I told him that I couldn't, but he informed me with certainty that I could! I explained that I was very tired, and wanted to rest, besides wanting to read, as the books were lent by a missionary and had to be returned. Nalousi showed a serene contempt for my reasoning, and stood waiting. I sat back, with my book up, to signify that the interview had terminated; but Nalousi coolly drew out a chair, and sat down, to signify that it had *not*! I could hardly help grinning behind my book, but soon tossed it aside, rather ashamed of myself. Before midnight, with Nalousi's help, we had the whole hymn translated.

He was triumphant; and, on rising to leave, he said, 'Now, Missi, if you will teach us to sing it tomorrow morning, we will come and take the organette into the church for you and your daughter.' I said, 'Why, how can the people know to come? They don't even know that a new hymn has been translated.' 'Leave that to me, Missi,' said the worthy fellow, not destitute of resources. And, sure enough, we heard the church bell next morning, as we were lingering over breakfast. So Minn and I hurried into church, to find quite a large congregation waiting for their singing lesson!

A few Sundays before, as we all walked to a distant village for afternoon service, I was reading a translation John had just made of 'Take the Name of Jesus with You,' and humming the tune under breath to see how the words would fit, when the native lads pricked up their ears and asked what it was. They became enthusiastic, and would have us teach them there and then; so we went singing along the road; and, by the time of our return home, they knew both the air and the words. Later on, they learned the bass, and they can sing the hymn very nicely in parts.

The Aniwans are exceedingly fond of Mr and Mrs Watt, as well they may be for they have superintended the mission on Aniwa, ever since we were withdrawn, and done everything for them that we could have done. By their yearly visits, they have kept everything in vigorous action, at a great self-sacrifice on their part, and we never can feel too deeply grateful to them. It might reasonably have been supposed, that things would have gone back a bit in the absence of their missionary; without exactly taking Mrs Poyser's view in reference to converts, that 'they could no more be expected, when left, to keep on in their religious ways, than a dog would continue to stand on his hind legs *with nobody to look at him*!' With them it was far otherwise.

It did us great good to be with our darkies once again. I understood them better than before, and had more real sympathy with them in many respects. A conversation I had with a dear old woman deeply touched me. Her daughter is married to one of our old mission boys, and both are off to Tanna as native teachers. She cries for her daughter; and she says she now knows what my heart suffered, when our children had to be sent away. She said: 'Missi, you did not think we felt like you. You never told us your troubles. You used to smile, when you spoke of your children in the far-off land, when we knew your heart was crying out for them. *We knew the language of your heart, Missi*, though you tried to hide it from us; and we mothers often cried about you!'

They were all very proud of Minn, and of her efforts to learn their language. They told her a hundred times a day that she was a *real woman of Aniwa*—thinking her worthy even of such an honour. She took special care of all the invalids; and two dear old men, lying at the gate like Lazarus, and as poor, wept bitterly when we left, saying she had never missed taking tea to them night and morning, and 'that her bright young face did them good.'

The loveliest child by far on this island is a little *John Paton*, whom his venerable namesake would dearly like to bring up with his own family, and educate as a missionary. But don't you think we have enough of our own, with a blessing?

Ever affectionately yours,
Maggie Whitecross Paton.

20

To Her Husband[1]

ANIWA,
JUNE, 1894.

Before leaving Sydney for the New Hebrides, I had a nice visit to the 'South Sea Island Home' with Mrs Macdonald, who gives so much of her time to the welfare of the 'boys' (as the men are called) who frequent it. The home is self-supporting. It might also be termed a Black Men's Christian Club. No assistance of white people is given, except in the way of teaching those who can attend in the evenings, having Bible talks with them, and helping them to keep their weekly accounts, etc. Each 'boy' pays a small sum weekly for the privilege of becoming a member, and when any are in need of rest, or out of work, they are boarded cheaply. One of the most capable and Christian of their number is the caretaker.

They have got the home decently furnished bit by bit, the latest additions being a bookcase and small mirror over the sitting-room mantelpiece. They flocked with great interest to see their new possessions, and Charlie (the caretaker), who was standing beside the mirror with a twinkle in his black eyes, called out, 'All you black fellow, look in here, and you see plenty monkey!' It is so pretty to hear them talking to

[1] Her husband was at this time on deputation work in Britain. This material has been taken from A. K. Langridge and Frank H. L. Paton, *John G. Paton: Later Years and Farewell* (London: Hodder and Stoughton, 1912).

each other in broken English, as they rarely understand each other's languages, coming as they do from so many different islands. One of those black apostles was earnestly trying to show his brethren how Christ could transform their whole lives, and said: 'Oh, do give your black hearts to Jesus, and he make you new. He make you such good-looking fellows.'

I so missed dear Robbins (Mrs Macdonald's black servant) this time. He died some months ago, testifying for his Saviour to the very last. He was a native of Malo, New Hebrides, and rejoiced greatly over the translation into his native tongue of the Gospel of Mark. He was speaking of it to Mrs Macdonald one day, and in his earnestness sat up in bed, his thin, dying face and large eyes lit up with eagerness as he said: 'Oh, Missi Macdonal', I pray Jesus to make it one very lighthouse to show all people Malo the road to him.'

Nothing could have been better planned for us than the Mission Synod being held on Aneityum—our first place of call. The whole mission to me, and all my interest in it, for the time being, was rolled into its youngest member, and my great concern was lest I might not be able to keep perfectly calm when I met my laddie. Our excitement was intense—mine almost unbearable when we got in full view of the mission house, and eagerly passed the glass to each other, scanning the beach to see which of the missionaries would come off in the boat to welcome such a valuable contingent! I was sure Fred would be the first, but not a solitary figure appeared, and we were left to possess our souls in patience as best we might. Captain Reid of the *Croydon* came on board, and I was assured of Fred's welfare. Strange, I did not think anything could happen to the others! It is what is most precious that we always think most in danger.

At last we descried the missionaries rushing to the beach, and Captain C. had his boat ready to send us ashore. We had all stepped into our boat, when they said the mission boat was fast approaching. I flew back on board again, just as it rounded the stern. Two or three missionaries were in it, but I only saw Fred, heard his old familiar salutation. In three bounds he was at my side, and my heart was at rest. He was extremely pale, from excitement. He had not received our last letters, and was not sure of my coming, but otherwise he looked splendidly well, and not a bit altered. I thought a year of solitary mission life and fever might possibly have sobered him a little, but he has not lost an iota of his fun and energy. He is as full of life and merriment as ever, was the life of the mission party going south, and such a favourite from his kindness to the seasick ones.

As we were being rowed ashore the news was broken to me of the sudden death of dear Mrs Watt, of Tanna, only four days previously. We learned some of the details of her last days. She seemed perfectly well on the morning of Thursday, April 26th, but when she got up complained of giddiness. Mr Watt thought she breathed peculiarly and sprang to her side, to find she had fainted. When she was brought round she said to him, 'Oh, I am so thankful you woke me just now, or I should have died. I have never been so near death.' She looked weak, and Mr Watt persuaded her to lie down for a little, and helped her back to bed. She got sick, but revived again, then suddenly said she thought death was coming on. Mr Watt had no apprehension, and tried to cheer her, but got a fright on feeling her hands were cold, though she was in a profuse perspiration. He felt her feet, which were also cold. She wished for hot water to warm them, and he was going to give the order when she quietly died, without a struggle, before 7 o'clock. All within one short hour!

Mr Grey, of Weasisi, got round to Port Resolution (it was there she died) by midday, and was a great comfort to Mr Watt, helping with the burial. They laid her close by the beautiful little church which she and Mr Watt collected the money for during their last visit to Scotland. Oh, how she had longed, and prayed, and laboured unceasingly for twenty-five years for the conversion of Tanna; and though a rich harvest was not vouchsafed, yet, like Moses, she was allowed a glimpse of the promised land before she was called to her reward.

Mr Watt bears up wonderfully, and went through all his Synod work and his duties as host in the kindest manner. I was placed next him at table, and he told me a lot about her, but I noticed he often spoke of her in the present tense, as if he could not realize that she had really gone.

The missionaries were in the midst of their business when we arrived, on the third morning of their sitting, and you may imagine their speeches were pretty much to the point when they were so limited to time! There was a tremendous hurry-scurry next morning (we had only one clear day on Aneityum). At morning prayers, ere we parted, we sang the 63rd Paraphrase, and as the rich voices blended, it was almost too thrilling for me. Such praise must be very precious in God's sight, and I sometimes wish I could be in heaven just to hear the different ring of this praise sent up from men and women who have counted not their lives dear unto them, compared with paid singers in a fashionable choir in civilization! The most notable business of Synod was the new training institution for teachers. The idea is to have all the training for teachers placed in the hands of one missionary set apart for that special work. The 'material' for the manufacture of teachers is to be gathered form all the different islands. The students will be made to learn English, which will be an easier task for them when taken away from their own language. That they will be capable of instructing their fellow-islanders in English when they return as graduates nobody expects, but they will have received a thorough training, and as much benefit as possible from a foreign language, and that under the most advantageous circumstances. And they will be able to roll out the message of the gospel in their own mother tongue with all the greater sweetness and freedom after experiencing the difficulties and constraint of a foreign one.

We had a pleasant passage to the northern islands. The missionaries had mostly provided themselves with canvas stretchers, standing a foot high, so that in shipping seas the water can roll about below, but woe to those who had their mattresses on the deck! We had some experience of this the first night after leaving Aneityum. I had undressed below, and came on deck arrayed, like the other ladies, in dressing-gown and bath slippers, rejoicing in the prospect of sleeping in the pure air. Everybody was being made snug for the night, when down came the rain in torrents—a regular tropical downpour, which continued the whole night. The awning above and round the sides kept it off for a bit, but soon the rain flooded the deck. I was all right underneath, Mr Annand having made me take his stretcher for the whole voyage, but Fred and others lay drenched the whole night.

We had to wait a few hours at a trading station on Tanna next morning, Captain Reid having some business to do for the company to whom the *Croydon* belongs; then we skirted along its shores, passing dear old Kwamera, with its white walls gleaming in the greenery, and calling up many bright, hallowed associations.

We reached Port Resolution before noon, and though the *Croydon* had only a few minutes to wait, we had time to get up to the house and see Mrs Watt's grave. Everything about the house was in perfect order, just as she had left it, and when we entered we could feel her hand in all the arrangements. Things had not begun to be displaced. Only nine days before she had been going about in her wonted health! The ground was in perfect order, and laid out so that it could be easily kept—mostly grass, with a few ferns. In a little centre plot in front there is a magnificent tree-fern, giving shade to a variety of exquisite small ferns planted underneath.

Our next place of call that day was Weasisi, on the east of Tanna, where we picked up Mr and Mrs Grey, who were packed and ready for their annual missionary visit to Aniwa; and we managed to pay a flying visit—a very flying one—to our own island the same evening. It was dark when we stepped into the lantern-lit boats, eagerly excited to see our dear old home. There were great fires on shore, and torch-lights to guide us between the reefs to the boat-landing.

The landing was crowded with eager natives, and I could distinguish familiar forms standing between the red glare and the boat. Our faithful teacher Masitaia was nearest, and I shouted *'Alofa'* to him as the rowers pulled in their oars, and the boat slowed in. They knew my voice and what a buzz there was! *'Ta Missi-finé! Ta Missi-finé!'* was excitedly passed from lip to lip, and I had hardly regained my equilibrium, after scrambling on to the rocks, when someone, with a baby tied to her back, flung her arms tightly round me, her face on my shoulder, and sobbed like to break her heart. I tried to lift her face to see who it was, but it was no use. She had to have her cry out before I found it was my good faithful Litsi Sisi. I never knew her to give way so in her whole life. She was always too energetic to indulge in sentiment, but the natives had no notion I was coming, and the sudden appearance was too much for her. What a shaking of hands there was! Fred received his *full* share of welcome! They could not believe that the great, tall, moustached fellow laughing down at them was the wee 'Freddy' of long ago, and sorely do they begrudge him as missionary to the Malekulans! They said: 'He belongs to *us*. He was born on our soil—our first white chief—and here he should stay as our missionary. The Malekulans can't love him as we do,' etc.

We had to make speed to cover the distance between the boat-landing and the mission house, as we were only allowed a few minutes on shore while Mr Grey's things were being landed. Fred was trying hard to recognize landmarks by the light of the lantern as we went along. Litsi Sisi, after her tears, was completely herself again, commander-in-chief of the procession, and laying about with her tongue in all directions—pitching into the man carrying the lantern for not holding it properly, to the natives guiding us for letting our feet get into ruts, and consequently into water owing to the late rains, to some lads for walking with us when they ought to be helping with Mr Grey's goods, issuing commands for one to rush on and light the house lamps, and to another to have the front gate opened, and so forth. They knew better than to disobey her. Between times she gave me, *sotto voce*, all the news and behaviour, good, bad, and indifferent, of the population, introduced the bonny babe on her back as her own latest arrival, and told me I was its grandmother! So altogether I felt pretty well posted up in the current history of Aniwa before leaving its shores.

They all asked why the *Missi-tané* was not with us, and I explained he was in Britain still. Fred exclaimed with delight as we entered the gate. There was the large rockery up which they used to climb as children and pull the ferns when I didn't see them! The house looks about as well as ever outside, only it may tumble into ruins any day with the white ants.

The Aniwans are working hard making copra to pay for the erecting of a new church—the frame to be bought in Australia. The foundation for it has already been laid, under Mr Grey's supervision. It is closer to the mission house than the old one, and stands between it and our sacred little burying-plot. I felt so glad we had Mr and Mrs Grey to leave with our poor 'darkies,' for it was a *hard* tug to get away that night. We were there and gone almost before they could realize they had seen us. My great disappointment was not seeing Litsi Soré, my best beloved friend on Aniwa, and it would be a woeful disappointment to her. She had been at the mission house that day and returned to her home at the other end of the island before the steamer was announced.

We had a fine view of the grand old volcano on Tanna, and I had intense pleasure in comparing Yasur with Vesuvius, very much to the disparagement of the latter! Of course, what sleepy old Vesuvius can do upon occasion, Pompeii and Herculaneum remain to testify, and of all the intensely interesting sights we saw on the Continent, Pompeii is the most *intensest* (a double superlative is here quite allowable!) its history suddenly arrested, so that one can see exactly what were the habits and surroundings of its people away back to the time of our Saviour. But I must arrest my own digressive propensities, and stick to the New Hebrides.

Next morning we breakfasted on Erromanga with Mr Robertson, and had two hours on shore. I had the finest view of Venus before daybreak that morning that I ever remember. It was dazzlingly bright, like an electric light, and shed a pathway of radiance on the water. We anchored at night in Villa Harbour, and so enjoyed the prayer meeting with Mr McKenzie and Miss Jessie McKenzie. Next morning we anchored in Havannah Harbour and went ashore. Then we sailed through the short passage for Nguna, and got there in time for a royal tea and welcome from Mr and Mrs Milne. I had been looking forward with keen delight to meeting Mrs Milne again, but it was very sad to have to tell her of Mrs Watt's death, which distressed her greatly.

I felt inclined to hurrah for joy that our next stopping-place was Malekula. We got there early next morning, and Aulua, Mr Leggatt's station, which Fred has had charge of in Mr Leggat's absence, came first in order. He and I went off in the first boat before breakfast, and found everything well kept by the natives, who, however, seemed greatly disappointed at not seeing Mr and Mrs Leggatt. Fred explained why they were staying on Tanna, and that they would arrive in about four weeks. They wanted to get us breakfast, but we were expected on board. However, as one or two of the others joined us from the ship, we thought we would indulge in a cup of coffee while waiting the landing of the goods. It was delicious, with nice fresh milk, and they gave it us in the best china on a snowy tablecloth. They offered to open a tin of biscuits, but I would not allow this.

In three hours more we were all in my laddie's bachelor home. Little did I think when we visited Mr Morton's station, five years ago, that it was to become invested with such interest for us! The knowledge would not have elated us, for Pangkumu is pre-eminently the fever-hole of the New Hebrides. Mr and Mrs Morton's short stay and broken health prove that. The house itself is perfectly healthy. Mr Morton knew how to build a good substantial house, and spared no pains to make it commodious, airy, and convenient. It is on a high foundation and has six rooms, three larger and three smaller ones, including a fine pantry (which Fred has meanwhile converted into a dispensary), besides the cookhouse and other outhouses, which are strong and in good order. The objections are not to the house, but to its situation and locality; it ought to have been perched on a hill with plenty of cleared ground round it.

On leaving for Synod, Fred had given strict orders to Tom, the native who acts as his cook, to prepare dinner as soon as he heard the *Croydon*'s whistle, so we had not long to wait before getting our hunger appeased, and then the steamer continued her voyage north, and Fred and I were left alone at last.

Being Saturday afternoon, I only unpacked and made a leisurely inspection of the rooms and premises, making mental notes of where a woman's hand was needed (that was pretty much everywhere), and waited rather impatiently for Monday morning to begin the work of reformation.

We had a quiet Sunday—to Fred a busy one, as he goes off at dawn to hold services at some of his out-stations and gets home to nine o'clock breakfast. A chief's wife, who had begun to attend school, died during worship, and there was great excitement. The heathen said her death was caused by the worship, and worshippers retorted that it was because she had attended a *manki* (heathen dance) while their missionary was at Synod. We had a service here in the afternoon, with an attendance of about fifty—women in the majority. They come freely about, and are so bright and confiding, only among the heathen, judging from their faces alone, I hardly know them from the men until they smile. It is when they smile, poor things, that the want of the two upper front teeth proclaim them to be the weaker vessels—slaves to a horrid custom, which still prevails, and I suppose will prevail till Christianity has got a firm hold on Malekula. A dear little girl got hers knocked out last week by the usual dentist while Fred was out of the way. He was so vexed as he had hoped to save her.

On Monday morning, when I got up like a giant refreshed, eager to begin household reform, I found I had 'reckoned without my host' considerably. I began with the dining room, and was clearing the sideboard of old papers, etc., to put it to its legitimate use, telling Fred that the papers would have to be taken to the study. But he thereupon expressed himself in decided terms of opposition—'Not if I know it,' etc. His study, he declared, was full enough. Everything was just right. He could lay his hands upon anything in the dark—nothing required altering. As you may imagine, everything was altered before the day was far advanced, but always under protest. The heterogeneous collection of dishes which Booka Tom (Fred's factotum) had piled up in odd places—dinner and tea sets, glassware, etc., all mixed up in picturesque confusion and thrown together with unstudied carelessness were separated and put in order and Tom shown where he would find things in future. I had far less trouble with Tom than with his master. He looked on, and helped with smiling approval when his domain was invaded.

One thing Fred entered heartily into was the rehanging of all his pictures. He has a very good taste himself (inherited, of course), but only got his pictures here by degrees, I bringing the last of them with me. So I had them all together to select and group and arrange them to the best advantage, getting them hung as much as possible in a position to be viewed from the point of sight at which they were taken. It was delightful getting up window-curtains, etc., upholstering, and giving the house an air of comfort and brightness. But all along I had to exercise some generalship in tackling the different rooms, and did most of the clearings when Fred was out of sight. The study I did not dare attempt, Fred guarding that as the dragon did the Hesperides, till one day he had to visit sick natives at a distance, when I promptly seized the opportunity to give it a good 'ridding up.'

I have had nothing to do in the culinary department, as Tom makes a good cook, and is quite 'up' in his duties. He comes solemnly in to lay the cloth at the appointed times, and as solemnly removes the dishes when we have finished. He is not the cook who, on Fred telling him the eggs were too hard, got up next morning before daylight and boiled them *two hours*, thinking to have them nice and soft for his Missi!

It has been very pleasant, this visit to dear Fred; but for all that, one would not by any means choose this life. One requires a specific reason—a divine command—to live in heathenism.

There have been three murders since I came here. The first two victims were such opponents of Christianity (though friendly to Fred personally) that one cannot be so sorry as one would like to be at their sudden exit. The last murder I can't get over. The victim was a poor native woman who had been a long time sick. Her husband got tired of the bother of keeping her, so they buried her alive! Weak though she was, she fought hard to keep above ground, till the chief gave her a blow on the head to kill her before her face was smothered—'because he was sorry for her.' How terribly true it is that the tender mercies of the heathen are horrid cruelty! Mr Gillan was telling us that, on Malekula, for trying to run away from her husband, the awful practice is to put a red-hot stone under a woman's knee and tie back the leg to keep it there till the stone grows cold. No running away after that—the woman is lamed for life!

Since penning the above an hour ago, I have had a delightful opportunity of witnessing what natives may become under the power of the gospel. A number of Fred's teachers and two or three Malekulans gathered today in the dining room for the usual Wednesday evening meeting. As the teachers come from different islands, the Bible talk is carried on in broken English.

You must not confound Thomas with Booka Tom, the cook. There is an epidemic of 'Toms' on Malekula. Both are as nice as they can be, but Thomas, whose name before baptism was Merib Navus, is one of the best trained Malekulans, and is one of Fred's best helpers. He is a splendid, vigorous Christian, with a hearty laugh, and shrewd in his dealings with his fellow islanders.

There is a delicious story of Thomas. Some months ago Fred and Thomas were going to a distant village to try and stop the war that was raging. To the consternation of his Missi, Thomas appeared with a loaded musket!

'Perhaps you had better leave that behind; we want peace,' Fred said.

'Yes, Missi, we want peace,' answered Thomas, 'and suppose man Malekula see my gun, he want peace too!'

They were joined on the way by two other teachers—one with a persuasive-looking stick, equal to an Irish blackthorn, and the other with an axe! Fred usually carries a malacca cane when walking, so altogether their appearance commanded respect from the Malekulans, who listened humbly to their exhortations and promised amendment.

They have all been very curious to see their missionary's mother, so I have been 'on show' more or less ever since arrival here. They are very particular always to ask Fred if I am his *real* mother, the word having such a wide meaning here. They have come from afar to see me, and get quite excited when their curiosity is gratified. How often I wish for one of the missionaries' cameras to take a 'snapshot' while they are gesticulating.

I had a nice sail with Fred to Aulua, as he wanted to look after some sick natives. We spent the night there the distance being too great to return the same day. One teacher was suffering acutely from rheumatism, and Fred brought him and his family back with us. The patient was carried into the boat on a ladder, and out of it the same way. Fred and I got out at a point from where we could walk home, a walking distance of two miles, but very much farther by sea round the reef. Though we got drenched in the long grass, it was preferable to being baked under the broiling sun. Malekula is the hottest place I have been in. The southern islands of the group are much cooler, though they only vary about six degrees in latitude from the northern.

The natives of Malekula are very lovable—at least, those I have seen—and, like our other islanders, capable of taking on a true polish, not veneer, when they are Christianized. Gentle—almost courtly—manners seem to come naturally to them, after they are delivered from their savagery, and have mixed in civilized life. Tom always thanks me when I give an order. It is often, 'Tank you very much,' for the trouble I am giving him!

The other night Fred had a bad attack of fever, and one of his teachers (Thomas, I think) was sitting in the room giving a report of a distant village he had been sent to visit. I jumped up about every minute to change the vinegar cloths on Fred's forehead, and often between times I kept standing. On these occasions I began to notice that Thomas was on his feet likewise, and as he did not leave as I expected, but sat when I did, his innate gentlemanliness dawned upon and amazed me. He could not sit while a woman stood! I think I have seen white men who could! Candour compels me to add, however, that I would not care to vouch for Thomas behaving in like manner to his black sisters!

We were awakened the other midnight by the loud bang of a musket-shot not far away. The teachers rushed off to ascertain the cause, and found that two men had been creeping round the next village, and when called upon to give their names did not answer. It is a native law here that if a man is challenged at night, he must answer at once or take his chance of being killed.

The shot did no damage, the prowlers got away, and the people met to consider whether they could have been ghosts! Fred does not know what fear means, and sleeps with his doors and windows wide open all night. I take the precaution of securing mine before I go to sleep!

Charlie Lean (they nickname him 'Charlie Fat,' he is so stout), who had charge of the South Sea Island Home that I mentioned in the beginning of this epistle, has just arrived to be a teacher to his fellow countrymen, after fourteen years' absence. He was kidnapped as a little boy and taken to Queensland.

He tells his own story very touchingly: 'White man tell me, "Come look at big ship," and he give me things. Then when I want jump back in my canoe, he push it away and hold me firm—get up anchor, and go away. Oh, I cry, cry, cry *plenty*, but he tell me dry up or he would *shot* me. I cry, for I not want him to shot me, but my heart break for my mother all the time, and I no can help myself—he got me there!' His home is two miles distant from Pangkumu.

Fred hopes to get great help from Charlie, who is a true Christian, and intends to make him one of his teachers. He has a fine staff at present; the other day one of them took the entire service here when Fred had to be at another village. He was very eloquent. I should like to have understood what he said, but I could only admire the earnest tones and generous gestures of the teacher, who stood close to where I sat. It gets a bit tiresome listening to a strange language, and one does appreciate the rare luxury of an English service in foreign lands.

This is my fifth week at Pangkumu and we expect the *Croydon* to call for me ten days hence. How I am to leave Fred in all his noble loneliness I dare not think. It is nothing comparatively to give one's self to the mission. It *is* something to give one's children, and I begin to have some conception of what it was for our Father in heaven to give up his own Son unto the death.

21

The Passing of Margaret Whitecross Paton[1]

Mrs Paton's health was gradually failing. Her family noticed that she was getting thinner, and more frail, but none of them dreamed that the calm strong face was veiling such a growing intensity of pain. It was only when she became so weak and ill that even her strong will could no longer hide the facts, that they realized there was cause for alarm. They pleaded with her to see a specialist, and at last she agreed. Her son-in-law, the Rev. John Gillan, of the New Hebrides, went with her into Melbourne to consult Dr Maudsley.

After a careful examination, the doctor took Mr Gillan aside and intimated that Mrs Paton's condition was very critical. It was his intention not to tell Mrs Paton the grave nature of her case, but a few direct, incisive questions from her brought everything to light.

'Then that means death?' she said, with disconcerting bluntness. And the only answer the doctor could give was a quiet 'Yes.' The only outward sign of the shock was the fact that she dropped her fan and did not notice it. Mr Gillan led her back into the cab. The whole world was changed for her now, but none could so judge from her calm and resolute face.

[1] The following account is taken from *John G. Paton: Later Years and Farewell.*

'That is pretty decisive,' was her first remark, and then she added quickly, 'Mind, this must be kept from Minn' (her only daughter).

Nor would she allow Dr Paton to be told. He was just on the eve of a three weeks' tour of meetings, and she would not have the arrangements upset.

A trained nurse was immediately summoned, and the doctor tried a special treatment in the faint hope that his diagnosis might be wrong. It was then decided to call in another specialist in consultation with the family doctor. Her eldest son, the Rev. Robert Paton, had just arrived from Nagambie. To him she herself broke the news, and sketched in rapid outline the short stages of the crisis. She told how the first intimation of her hopeless condition had created a great hunger for the sympathy of her children, and how, in their absence, she had been driven to God and her Saviour. That thus she had passed through her Gethsemane alone, and that now all was over; and intensely as she had loved life, God had completely taken away all that desire, and in its place had planted a great longing for the home beyond. That prospect to her now brought perfect peace and heavenly joy.

An hour later the three doctors arrived. After the examination, they retired to hold their consultation, and then called in Mr Robert Paton and Mr Gillan. Mr Paton writes of that trying scene:

'We were called in to hear the decision. In calm tones we were told that there was no hope of recovery, but that the suffering to be faced could and would be palliated with drugs, to give relief and quietness. These men stood for human skill, but the power of death was there, and they were beaten and helpless. After this interview that had chilled our hearts with its note of doom, the doctors accompanied us into Mother's room. She was still bright and joyful. Nothing could alter her confidence and quietness of soul. When the doctors had broken as gently as possible the news that the consultation left no room for hope, she said quietly:

'"Well I want to tell you, doctors, that there is a Power above all your power, and it is the Power of my God. He can raise me even from this bed if it be his will, and it is in his everlasting love and mercy that I am trusting. Long ago I committed my life to my Saviour, and now all is peace and joy."

'Her face was lit up with the foreglow of victory. On that sick bed lay the conqueror, and these strong men could only stand and wonder at the triumph of it. "The secret of the Lord is with them that fear him."'

The diagnosis was that the disease must have been at work for at least twelve months, and one doctor asked her in surprise:

'How is it, Mrs Paton, that you were able to keep this to yourself for so long?'

'By sheer determination of will, doctor,' was her characteristic reply.

At first it was thought that life might be prolonged for some months, but the disease made rapid progress, and on Sunday, 29 April, she became suddenly worse. It was now decided that her daughter Mrs Gillan must be told, and in the anguish of grief, following that dread news, little baby Gillan was born. The doctor kindly arranged for a motor to go up country and recall Dr Paton.

It broke down, however, and instead telegrams were sent. Meanwhile, Mrs Paton's brother-in-law, the Rev. James Lyall, of Adelaide, arrived, and his moving ministrations were very comforting and helpful in that hour of pain and weakness. The following day the missionary arrived with his two sons and their wives. It was an intense relief to Mr Gillan to see them, and to share with them the responsibility and anxiety of watching. The family can never forget all that they owe to him in those sadly happy, solemn days.

Contrary to expectations, Mrs Paton rallied a little, although the suffering was intense. She bore it all patiently, and every now and then flashes of humour played like summer lightning across the dark background of pain; and on her face there was always that look of heavenly peace. One day she was telling the doctor that she wished to slip away quietly, without any fuss of farewell messages. 'But your whole life has been a message to your children,' he said. 'Ah, no,' she replied wistfully, 'not a message, but a pure white-heat of love.'

Speaking to her son one day about the same thing, she said, 'My whole heart is beating with love for you all—every vein of it. What can paltry words express at such a time? I have made it right with my Saviour. I love him, and he has forgiven all my sins as a thick cloud. Isn't it wonderful that he does so? Wonderful! We must look at things not from our sinful point of view, but from God's, and in his pure, pure light. I see that now, and would like to do many things over again in that light. But we don't get that opportunity. And may be if we did, we would not do very differently after all. Life here is an apprenticeship for eternity, and we'll do better there. I'll see the King in his beauty. And the wonderful thing is that we will become like him. It takes wonderful love to do that.'

There was an intensely touching scene when her daughter's little baby girl was placed in Mrs Paton's arms. Her whole face lit up with joy as she wound her long gold chain about the baby's neck and laid her watch upon its little breast. The child was called Margaret Whitecross, that she might bear her grandmother's name after she was gone. At her special request little Margaret was baptized in her room, and those present will never forget the moving pathos of that touching service. Mrs Gillan could not rise to see her baby baptized, but her door was left ajar that she might hear. The family gathered in the hall between, and, at the bedside of his dying wife, Dr Paton took the little babe into his arms and baptized her into the Triune Name.

That mother and daughter, who had been such close companions, were thus separated in these last precious days was a bitter drop in their cup of sorrow. But they bore it bravely as part of the Father's plan of love. 'What I do thou knowest not now, but thou shalt know hereafter.'

As the days passed her mother-heart yearned to see her medical son—then away in England, and her missionary son in the New Hebrides—bearing his own dread sorrow, as we afterwards learned. But she was thankful to have her husband and the rest of her children about her. She felt more and more vividly that death was only an interval of life. 'Won't I be watching for you all, each one!' she said, with eager face.

For six weary weeks the pain grew fiercer. All that human skill and tender sympathy could do to relieve the suffering was done by Dr Cowen and Nurse Hunter, to both of whom the family owe an unpayable debt of gratitude. Her two sons, Robert and Frank, and Mr Gillan, took their turns with the nurse in watching by the sickbed. It was a priceless privilege, and the inspiration of those quiet hours in that heroic presence will never leave their hearts.

It was Mrs Paton's wish that she should pass away in sleep, and God gave her the desire of her heart. On the evening of 16 May 1905, she gently fell asleep, and those who stood round could imagine the joy of the homecoming after the long and weary journey.

It was a fitting close to a brave and unselfish life. Long ago the cultured girl had given up home and country to go with the man she loved, and face the loneliness and the unspeakable horrors of savage lands. Something of the joy and sorrow, the humour and the pathos of that life, is vividly revealed in her book *Letters and Sketches from the New Hebrides*. But the darker side is left untold. That long agony of pain was so bravely hid that even her children saw only a mother's smiling face. It would have been altogether unsuspected, even by then, had they not sometimes, when she thought them asleep, listened with awe to her strong crying and tears as she pleaded with the Father to take away the agony which was greater than she could bear. Yet in the morning the face was brave and calm again, and because they could not speak of that which they had overheard, the memory of it was burned the deeper into their souls, and their reverence for their mother became a part of their very being.

Later on, when the time came to face that supreme trial of missionary life—the handing over of the little children to another's love and care—she so conquered the storm of passionate grief that raged within her own heart, that she was able to comfort her weeping children and smile bravely upon them at the parting. It was only when the night closed in, and there was none but the Father's loving eye to see, that she gave way to the sobs that shook her body, and the flood of tears that drenched her pillow.

Still later, when the call of duty came to her husband, and he had to make long journeys round the world, she bravely faced the loneliness which that separation brought, and bore alone the greater part of the responsibility of home and children.

Her influence over her children was deep and permanent. There was in her nature a rare combination of saintliness and humanness, that made the Christian life very real and winsome to all with whom she came into touch. Beneath all the naturalness and the sparkling humour there was an intense devotion to Christ, and a heroism that nothing could daunt. And with it all, her life was, in her own words, 'a pure white-heat of love for her children.' No wonder they loved her passionately, and with deep reverence sought to follow in her steps.

And now she was gone, and life was infinitely lonelier. They laid her to rest on the beautiful slopes of the Boroondara cemetery, 'Until the day break and the shadows flee away' (Song of Sol. 2:17).

Key to Principal Missionaries Named

The publishers are grateful to the Rev. Peter Barnes of Sydney for checking some of the details given.

ANNAND, Rev. Joseph and Mrs, Fila (Aneityum), and Tangoa, 1873–1913.

ELLA, Rev. Samuel and Mrs Ella, Aneityum, Wea, from 1864.

GEDDIE, Rev. Dr John and Mrs, Aneityum, 1848–72.

GOODWILL, Rev. John and Mrs, S.W. Santo, 1870–74.

GORDON, Rev. George and Mrs Ellen, New Hebrides from 1857, martyred on Erromanga, 1861.

GORDON, Rev. James D., Erromanga and N.W. Santo, from 1864, martyred Erromanga, 1872.

INGLIS, Rev. John and Mrs, Anamé (Tanna) and Aneityum, 1852–79.

LANDELLS, Rev. J. D. and Mrs, Malo, 1887–1901.

MCCULLAUGH, Rev. William and Mrs, Anelgauhat (Aneityum), 1864–66.

MACNAIR, Rev. James and Mrs, Erromanga, 1866–70, where he died.

MILNE, Rev. Peter and Mrs, Nguna, 1869–1924.

MURRAY, Rev. J. D. and Mrs, Aneityum, 1872–76.

MORRISON, Rev. Donald and Mrs, Efaté, 1864–69 (he died in New Zealand, 1869).

NEILSON, Rev. Thomas and Mrs, Port Resolution (Tanna), 1866–82.

NIVEN, Rev. J. and Mrs, New Hebrides, 1865, and soon after resigned.

ROBERTSON, Rev. Dr H. A. and Mrs, Erromanga, 1872–1914.
WATT, Rev. William and Mrs, Kwamera (Tanna), 1869–1910 (Mrs Watt died on Tanna, 1894).

Index

Because references to Dr John G. Paton, Mrs Margaret Paton, the New Hebrides (Vanuatu) and Aniwa are so frequent in this volume, these terms are not used as entries in this index.

Adelaide 89, 105, 136, 150, 156–157, 192
Ambrim 14–15, 280
Anamé (Aneityum) 10, 138, 140
Aneityum 6, 8–10, 17, 22–23, 79, 92, 98, 111, 133, 136, 158, 160, 172, 227, 245, 274, 292
Anelqauhat 136, 274
Annand, Rev. J. and Mrs 147, 150, 228, 283
Arrowroot 230
Australia 1, 49, 76, 84, 87–90, 150, 151, 159, 193, 207, 257
Autobiography
  why undertaken vii
Baptisms 10, 65, 92, 166, 269, 310
Cannibalism 49, 184
'Carpenter' 197
Church-building work 37–39, 169–170
Clock, Aniwans' view of 48
Communion services 66, 226, 246
Darwinism 265
Dayspring, The 2, 8–9, 10, 15, 20–21, 22, 26, 27, 34, 41, 45, 51, 55, 64, 69, 72, 75–80, 88, 90, 92–93, 101
  The new *Dayspring* 151–152, 154, 158, 163, 183, 184, 189, 223, 227, 245–248, 273–285
  wreck of 105, 108, 111, 133
Dress 29–30, 96–98, 102, 142, 158, 167, 183, 226
Earthquakes 112, 163, 178–182, 209, 259
Efaté 13, 15, 21, 71, 140, 239
Ella, Rev. Samuel and Mrs 6, 11–12, 14
Erromanga 16, 18, 76, 91, 93, 244–246, 251, 277
Family life, preserving 94–95
Flood, tradition about the 101
Fotuna 21–22, 55, 141, 275
Fraser, Captain and Mrs 6, 13–14, 18, 20, 53, 70, 72, 80, 88, 92
Geddie, Rev. John and Mrs 26, 28, 88, 98, 182, 275
Gillan, Rev. John 307–308
Goodwill, Rev. John and Mrs 139–140
Gordon, Rev. J. D. 16–17, 20, 93–94, 245

Heathen dance 32–33
Hurricanes 108–109, 138, 167–169, 208, 235–236
Hutshi 141, 144–145, 157–159, 172–178, 267
Infant salvation 129
Inglis, Rev. John and Mrs 9–12, 14, 17, 19, 26, 28, 43, 51–52, 56, 60, 92, 112, 137–140, 149, 160, 172, 211, 228
John Williams (ship) 67
'Joiner' 197, 241–243
Kafoi 242
Kagaru 31, 35
Kahi 63
Kalangi 108, 146
Kamani 62
Kanathie 26–27, 34, 44
Kawiwi 241–243
Kwamera 98–99, 132, 141, 209, 247, 276, 285–286, 295
Landells, Rev. J. D. and Mrs 283
Language study and translation 52–53, 61, 83, 86, 153–154, 263–264
Lifu 11, 14, 72, 79
Litsi 53, 66, 89–91, 106–108, 157, 193–219, 240, 277
Litsi 'the Little' 113, 143, 146, 154, 268, 287, 296
Mackenzie, Rev. and Mrs 277
Malekula 281–283, 298–304
Maré, Loyalty Islands 5, 11, 15
Marriages 51, 63, 87, 144–145, 157, 194, 203, 240–243
McCullaugh, Rev. William 8
McNair, Rev. James and Mrs 34, 66, 76, 88, 246
Melbourne 5, 26, 55, 150, 163, 183, 187, 189, 191, 201, 230, 249, 273, 307
Milne, Rev. Peter and Mrs 69, 98, 146–147, 161, 227, 239, 279
Moody and Sankey 148, 183
Morrison, Rev. Donald and Mrs. 15, 17, 21
Mungaw 67, 189–218
Murray, Rev. J. D. and Mrs 137, 155
Music 16, 44, 59, 106, 147, 279
Nagitshi 159
Nalihi 179–181
Namakei 43–44, 57–58, 66, 81, 91, 99
Native teachers 26–27, 34–36, 43, 50, 60, 115, 118, 153, 165, 172, 198, 288–289
Neilson, Rev. T. and Mrs 132, 157, 164–166
Nelwang 144–145, 158
New Caledonia 53
Nguna 279
Nisei 183–186
Niven, Rev. J. and Mrs 6, 14, 18
Nowar 19, 41–42, 166, 184
Paragon (ship; later the new *Dayspring*) 111, 132–133
Patesa 170–171
Paton, Frank 71–72, 103, 113, 137, 155, 180, 183, 184, 190, 251, 253
Paton, Frederick 35, 53–54, 105, 117, 159–160, 186–187, 192, 233, 254, 296, 298–304
Paton, Lena (the 'Angel-Child') 113–118, 143
Paton, Margaret ('Minnie') 80–82, 137–138, 155, 183, 184, 233, 252, 273, 282, 290,

308–309
Paton, Robert 28, 32, 46, 105, 107, 114–115, 117, 130, 159–160, 186, 192, 233, 254, 268, 308, 311
Paton, Walter Watt 231, 236, 254, 269–270
Pavingin 40–41
Polygamy 259–260
Port Resolution, Tanna 16–19, 41, 99, 165, 229, 295
Printing 45, 61, 162, 168, 181, 183
Qualifications for mission work 84
Rangi 83, 175–177
Rhu 21–22
Robertson, Rev. H.A. and Mrs 53, 100, 142, 225–226, 245
Ropu 63
Sandalwood English 7, 238, 281
Santo 69, 283
Sciatica 112, 114
Sea view 110–111, 260
Sewing class 44, 59–61, 97, 114, 130, 152, 198, 214
Sewing machine 47
Singing 10, 14, 16, 18, 28, 44, 97, 274
Slavers 196, 198, 233–235, 238–240, 253, 257
Smoking 90–91
South Sea Island Home 291
Steele, Dr 135–137, 139–140, 142–143, 147, 149–150, 152, 156
Sydney 1–7, 14, 135, 150
Taia 57–58, 102, 179–181
Tanna 13, 17–20, 41–43, 56, 98–99, 130–132, 140, 164–166, 208, 220, 227, 247
Telmonoutha 108
Tidal wave 182
Traill, Robert 148–149, 161
Tupaia 130
Vasi 65
Village schools 152, 190, 198
Volcano (Yasur, on Tanna) 20, 98, 156, 298
Watt, Rev. William and Mrs 69, 98–100, 106, 132, 141, 147, 155, 185, 208, 227–228, 231, 269, 285–286, 293
Wea 6, 11, 14
Whitecross, Elizabeth 1–3, 25, 71–73
Williams, John 17, 245, 286
Williang 116
Writing class 107, 153–154, 198–199
Yawaci 142, 176, 186–187, 190, 195, 210–212, 258
Yomit 246, 277

ALSO PUBLISHED BY THE TRUST

John G. Paton
The Autobiography of the Pioneer Missionary to the New Hebrides (Vanuatu)

ISBN: 978 1 80040 450 2
552 pp. clothbound

The autobiography of John G. Paton contains everything necessary to make it a missionary classic. Born into a Christian family near Dumfries in 1824, Paton's early years were marked by a struggle against poverty. He was self-educated, and the training ground for his life's work was the slums of Glasgow where he laboured with success as a city missionary. With 'the wail of the perishing heathen in the South Seas' continually sounding in his ears, he prepared himself to serve overseas and was ordained as a missionary to the New Hebrides in 1858. This group of thirty mountainous islands, so named by Captain Cook, with its unhealthy climate, was then inhabited by savages and cannibals. The first attempt to introduce Christianity to them resulted in John Williams and James Harris being clubbed to death within a few minutes of landing in 1839. The difficulties that confronted Paton were accentuated by the sudden death of his wife and child within months of their arrival. Against the savagery and the superstition, despite the trials and the tragedies, Paton persevered and witnessed the triumph of the gospel in two of these South Sea islands. His life is almost without parallel in missionary annals and his account of it is moving and gripping.

John G. Paton
Missionary to the Cannibals of the South Seas

Paul Schlehlein

ISBN: 978 1 84871 765 7
208pp. paperback

'I am grateful to Paul Schlehlein for providing a new look at the life and ministry of John G. Paton. Early in my life I was enduringly impacted by Paton's autobiography edited by his brother, James. The story was a stunning account of dedication, desperation, sacrifice at the most extreme level, and selfless love to Christ. I was marked for life by the amazing missionary adventure and the far reaching and lasting gospel impact of that one man empowered and protected by the Holy Spirit. In this age when giving a trophy to everyone is standard, and when minimal Christian dedication is celebrated, all believers need to go back to the past to see what true devotion to Christ and the gospel really looks like. You will see it in John Paton.' — JOHN MACARTHUR

'Few books are more inspiring to the Christian reader than a compelling missionary biography. This book is no exception. Paul Schlehlein has given us a heart-moving, soul-stirring survey of the life and labours of the famed missionary to the flesh-eating cannibals of the South Sea Islands, John G. Paton. Paton's zeal for reaching this remote people group with the good news of the gospel will both encourage and motivate you in your own Christian walk. These pages will challenge your commitment to Jesus Christ and intensify your zeal to live for the glory of God. You simply must read this book and, by God's grace, learn the lessons Paton's extraordinary life sets forth.' — STEVEN J. LAWSON

Five Pioneer Missionaries

Various Authors

ISBN: 978 1 80040 317 8
408pp. paperback

There are few more thrilling periods of church history than the great missionary movement which stretched from the eighteenth into the nineteenth century. Recognizing that Jesus Christ was the missionary sent by the Father, and that the Bible is the Magna Carta of missions, men like John Eliot, David Brainerd, Henry Martyn, William Chalmers Burns, and John G. Paton left home, family, and love for the sake of Christ and to spread his good news. The narratives of their monumental labours and sufferings, and their strong longings to see Christ glorified in the salvation of the nations make awe-inspiring and God-honouring reading. *Five Pioneer Missionaries* tells the story of each of these servants of God. In doing so it not only outlines some of the great biblical principles of missions, but also challenges Christians today to live lives completely dedicated to serving Jesus Christ wherever he calls us to go.

The Banner of Truth Trust originated in 1957 in London. The founders believed that much of the best literature of historic Christianity had been allowed to fall into oblivion and that, under God, its recovery could well lead not only to a strengthening of the church, but to true revival.

Interdenominational in vision, this publishing work is now international, and our lists include a number of contemporary authors, together with classics from the past. The translation of these books into many languages is encouraged.

A monthly magazine, *The Banner of Truth*, is also published, and further information about this, and all our other publications, may be found on our website, banneroftruth.org, or by contacting the offices below:

Head Office:
3 Murrayfield Road
Edinburgh
EH12 6EL
United Kingdom

Email: info@banneroftruth.co.uk

North America Office:
610 Alexander Spring Road
Carlisle, PA 17015
United States of America

Email: info@banneroftruth.org